Classical Literature in Rinehart Editions

EDITED AND TRANSLATED BY KEVIN GUINAGH

Vergil, *The Aeneid*

EDITED BY PHILIP WHALEY HARSH

An Anthology of Roman Drama (The Twin Menaechmi, The Rope,
The Phormio, The Brothers, The Medea, The Phædra,
The Thyestes)

EDITED BY C. A. ROBINSON, JR.

An Anthology of Greek Drama: First Series (Agamemnon, Oedipus
the King, Antigone, Medea, Hippolytus, Lysistrata)

An Anthology of Greek Drama: Second Series (Prometheus Bound,
Choëphoroe, Eumenides, Philoctetes, Oedipus at Colonus,
The Trojan Women, The Bacchae, The Clouds, The Frogs)

Selections from Greek and Roman Historians (Herodotus,
Thucydides, Xenophon, Polybius, Livy,
Sallust, Suetonius, Tacitus)

AN ANTHOLOGY OF

ROMAN DRAMA

AN ANTHOLOGY OF
ROMAN DRAMA

EDITED WITH AN INTRODUCTION BY

PHILIP WHALEY HARSH

HOLT, RINEHART AND WINSTON, INC.

NEW YORK • CHICAGO • SAN FRANCISCO • ATLANTA • DALLAS
MONTREAL • TORONTO • LONDON • SYDNEY

The Twin Menaechmi by Plautus

Translated by Edward C. Weist and Richard W. Hyde, in *The Complete Roman Drama* edited by George E. Duckworth. Copyright 1942 by Random House, Inc. This translation is not a reprinting of the 1930 version, published by the Harvard Press, but a new translation. Acts Two and Five were translated by Weist, Acts One, Three, and Four by Hyde. The prologue, which in the original version was translated by Spencer Brown, contained many insertions and omissions and has been revised by Professor Duckworth. Reprinted, with occasional minor changes, by permission of Random House, Inc.

The Phormio and *The Brothers* by Terence

Translated by William Abbott Oldfather, in *Latin Literature in Translation* edited by Kevin Guinagh and Alfred P. Dorjahn. Copyright 1942 by Longmans, Green and Co., Inc. Reprinted, with occasional minor changes, by permission of Longmans, Green and Co., Inc.

The editor has made occasional minor changes in the other translations in this volume.

FOR VIRGINIA, PHIL,

AND MARJORIE

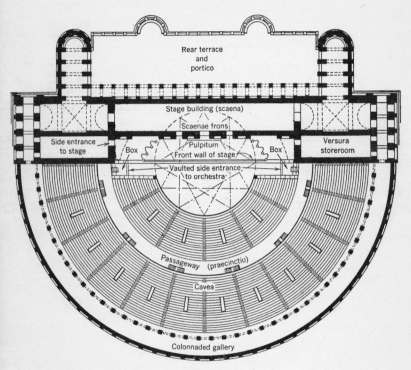

The Theater of Marcellus at Rome (Reconstructed Plan, taken by
permission from Margarete Bieber, *The History of the Greek and
Roman Theater*, Princeton University Press, 1939, Fig. 453).

CONTENTS

˥˩˥˩

INTRODUCTION

⌐⌐⌐

THE ROMANS inherited classical Greek culture and assimilated it more thoroughly than did any other people of the ancient Mediterranean world, including the later Greeks themselves. The Romans passed this culture on to the medieval and modern world. In some fields, such as epic poetry or law and government, they added important contributions of their own. But when a legacy is as rich as that of the Greeks, originality is limited and can succeed only within the framework of the tradition.

In the field of drama the Romans made certain technical and formal changes of great importance, but their main service was in passing on to the Renaissance some of the great accomplishments of the Greeks. Occasionally original plays on Roman subjects were attempted, but never with much success. Adaptations of Greek plays were first presented at Rome in 240 B.C. The earliest preserved, however, are twenty comedies of Plautus dating from about 210 to 184 B.C. No Greek original of any of these is extant, but from the same period we do have very extensive Greek fragments and two comedies complete or almost so.* This type of Greek drama is called New Comedy (*ca.* 336–250 B.C.).

Old Comedy, now represented by eleven plays of Aristophanes, was very different. Its favorite subjects were political and social satire, with some literary travesty and burlesque. Marked by wit, fantasy, and unlimited exuberance, it was an amazing, careless conglomerate of bitter personal abuse and other indecencies, low comedy, serious theses eloquently set forth, and beautiful poetry. It had a unique formulaic structure. In the first half of the comedy a "happy idea" was presented and debated. The chorus of twenty-four members were closely associated with this debate, and after giving their decision on it, they made a direct appeal to the audi-

---

* *The Dyskolos* of Menander, practically complete, is a recent sensational discovery. See Bibliographical Note, page xxix.

ence. The second part of the play was normally a series of episodes, often not connected with one another, portraying the happy results of the idea in action. Old Comedy was directed toward the day and the hour and the Athenians, probably with no dream of reproduction or preservation.

New Comedy is in part the child of the romantic "melodramas" of Euripides. The plot of his *Ion*, for instance, concerns the violation of a maiden, concealed childbirth, and recognition. If such a play is reduced from the heroic to the life of every day, and its attempted murders played down to mere family quarrels, then we have essentially the plot of one of the most famous comedies of the most famous playwright, *The Arbitration of Menander* (discovered almost complete in 1905). New Comedy is interested in character and human relations. It is generalized before a timeless and, compared with Old Comedy, somewhat colorless cosmopolitan background. The structure is that of Greek tragedy (exposition, complication, climax, and solution), but the chorus has become a dispensable interlude. The Greek proper names, which are retained in the Latin versions, are indicative of social status and sometimes of character. Often, of course, this is true also in Renaissance or modern comedy, as Molière's Harpagon ("snatcher") or Orgon ("rager").

The plots of New Comedy varied greatly, but for most of them Error is the patron divinity. They were often mere farces (the term is derived from the Latin word for "stuffing"), such as *The Twin Menaechmi;* often plays of intrigue, especially the devices of the clever slave to rob a pimp of a girl or to trick an old master out of money for the girl friend of a young master; often, too, intricate plots concerning the violation of maidens, separation of lovers, concealed identities, and final recognition and happy reunion. Here are the ancient romances. Courtship of the modern type did not exist in Athenian society. In plots involving concealed identities, an omniscient prologue is regularly employed so that the audience may appreciate the elaborate ironies of the play, as in *The Rope.* All is pervaded by humor, and nothing is too implausible to be supported by the long arm of coincidence.

Plautus (*ca.* 254–184 B.C.), born at Sarsina in Umbria, is said to have come to Rome and made some money in theatrical work, then to have lost it in a trading venture. After he returned to Rome and was earning his living by servile work in a baker's mill, he is said to have written certain plays. If these details are invented, they are well invented, for Plautus was as obviously a man of the practical theater as Seneca was a man of the study. Plautus chose his originals from a considerable number of Greek authors, including the leading writers of New Comedy, Menander, Philemon, and Diphilus. His plays show astonishing variety in many respects: in length from 729 lines to 1,437; in subject from farce (*The Twin Menaechmi*) and mythological travesty (*Amphitryon*) and trenchant satire (*Truculentus*) to studies of character (*Aulularia*) and romantic comedy (*The Rope*). Some of these are soberly presented almost wholly in simple iambic and trochaic verse; others are filled with elaborate *cantica* suggestive of modern comic opera. This variation in meter seems to be due to Plautus. He apparently began his career by using simple meters like those of the Greek originals, but he quickly developed elaborate lyric measures. Change of tone within a play is often emphasized by change of meter. Such variation is especially effective in a melodramatic play like *The Rope*.

All these comedies, however, have certain characteristics in common, especially vigorous and rapid dialogue and racy, exuberant wit. This exuberance may be in part Italian, since there were spirited native dramatic forms, and since Plautus obviously handles his originals with great freedom, occasionally, it seems, omitting a scene or adding one from another play. His style abounds in alliteration, redundancy, puns, and wordplays. He has certainly done a good job of translating the Greek, much better than most moderns do in translating his own Latin. To retain in English all his wit and humor and ironies is very difficult. Normally Plautus adapts Athenian references to Roman. Occasionally he apologizes for portraying the licenses of the Greeks: when a slave is impudent to his master or cleverer than he or carouses like a gentleman. Plautus, as Aristophanes before him, is fond of low comedy, such as the scene of pummeling in *The Twin Menaechmi* or Labrax' vomiting in *The Rope*. The chorus has practically disappeared, though the fishermen in *The Rope* may be a vestige. There are no acts and no intermissions.*

---

* See the "Note on Divisions into Acts and Scenes," p. xxxi.

The Twin Menaechmi is a gay and spirited farce, a type well adapted to the elaborately lyrical treatment which Plautus gives it. Confusion of twins, of course, has always been a favorite subject for the comedy of errors. We hear of some eight Greek comedies entitled "The Twins" (none extant), and this motif is used in various other plays of Plautus. In plots of this type the omniscient prologue renders its most valuable service in giving the audience the secret of the identities. Characterization, as we should expect in such a farce, is very slight. The two brothers here do resemble each other as much in their dishonesty as in their appearance, but the most noteworthy characterizations are those of minor figures, who are elaborated for mere comic effect, especially the practical old father-in-law and the physician. The quack, one of the oldest comic characters, is here portrayed with his inevitable traits: technical jargon, impertinent questions, extravagant claims, incorrect diagnosis, and of course the most expensive treatment. The parasite, too, is colorfully presented but is used primarily, and somewhat implausibly, to facilitate the plot by becoming the link between the double lives which the Epidamnian Menaechmus is living.

The precise date of the play (possibly about 190 B.C.) and the author of the Greek original are unknown. Together with *The Amphitryon, The Aulularia,* and *The Miles Gloriosus, The Twin Menaechmi* has been one of the most influential of Plautus' comedies. There are many adaptations, but Shakespeare's *The Comedy of Errors* is by far the most famous. He compounds the improbabilities by introducing the motif of twin slaves (from Plautus' *Amphitryon*), develops melodramatic suspense, vacillates between the comic and the tragic—both sentimentalized—adds an abundance of romance and emotional appeal, and finishes with the happy reunion of Aegeon and Aemelia and a grand finale, which are both taken from a source different from comedy, that of ancient prose fiction. (Greek and Roman plays were presented with a limited cast, and there are very rarely more than three speaking characters on stage at a given time.) This colorful "glad" ending of Shakespeare contrasts strongly with the classical cold cynicism of the ending in Plautus, where the wife, far from being reconciled, is offered at auction with a suggestion, *caveat emptor.*

The Rope (Rudens) is a romantic comedy of shipwreck,

maidens—and a lover—in distress, and final restoration of a long-lost daughter and marriage. Even the villainous slave dealer is in the end forgiven and invited to dinner. The action is elaborate and vivacious though the plot remains simple. Most of the play is high comedy: the winsome humor of the fishermen, for example, or the delightful irony of Gripus' extravagant dreaming of fame and fortune at the very moment when his spying adversary, seen by the audience but not by Gripus, is following his every move. But low comedy punctuates these scenes: the vomiting of the seasick men and the pummeling of the slave dealer. The emotional range is amusingly varied in the scene between the two slaves, Sceparnio and Ampelisca: Sceparnio catches fire at sight of the pretty girl and conceives high hopes of an easy conquest, which are quickly extinguished at the disappearance of the girl. Indeed, the rapid vacillation from one type of comedy to another within the play and the "pulsation" of emotions from one scene to the next, emphasized by appropriate metrical variation, constitute a distinctive virtue of the play. Other melodramatic features are found in the picturesque setting and the manner in which events dominate the characters. The plaintive entrance monody of Palaestra (lost before the house of her father!) is mock-tragic, and the scene in which the girls flee in terror to the altar may well be a parody of a specific Greek tragedy. The high emotional pitch of the scenes with Trachalio and the happy Daemones or the ecstatic Plesidippus is accompanied by amusingly elaborate wordplay.

The Greek original was written by Diphilus. Numerous adaptations have been made, including *The Captives* of Thomas Heywood.

Terence (*ca.* 195–159 B.C.) was born at Carthage, perhaps of North African stock, and came to Rome as a slave. He was properly educated and soon freed because of his beauty and his genius. When he offered the first of his comedies to the officials in charge of games and theatrical performances, he was directed to read the work to an older established writer. He arrived as dinner was being served, and, poorly dressed, he was directed to a humble bench. But when he had read a few verses he was invited to dine with the master, after which he read all the play, to the great admiration of the older dramatist. In the early period at Rome many of

the literary figures were of low birth. But the times were changing:
Terence was admired and fostered by some Romans of the highest
station. Neither he nor they made any effort to stifle reports that
they aided him in his literary productions. He was never as
popular as Plautus and had difficulties producing some of his
plays. Cliques were now rampant, and establishment was difficult, especially for one of low birth and superior ability. After
writing the six plays which are extant, Terence met with some
mischance on a journey to Greece. According to one version, he
died from grief and worry over the loss of his baggage containing
new plays!

All of Terence's plays were originally produced by the same
actor-manager, and the music for all of them was composed by
the same slave. All are adapted from Greek plays of the famous
Menander or a follower, one Apollodorus. They are all of about
the same length, and the meters of all are simple compared with
the meters of Plautus. Terence avoids Roman allusions, and he
prefers high comedy. His winsome humor and thoughtful character studies, even though they have undeniably lost some of the
delicate sensitivity and charm of Menander, are very congenial to
Molière. The style of Terence is modeled after the beautifully
chaste style of Menander—very different from the lusty exuberance of Plautus. Indeed, having only two writers of Latin comedy
extant, we are most fortunate in having two that are so different.

Terence made various technical innovations, perhaps more than
any other writer of New Comedy. He regularly employs a minor
plot. In *The Woman of Andros*, we are told by an ancient commentator, this minor plot is his own addition. It concerns a young
man who desires to marry a girl of good family—girls had more
freedom in Roman society than in Greek society. The plots of
New Comedy were all too often pitifully thin, and a romantic sub-
plot is precisely the type of complication which Renaissance or
modern dramatists add in adapting classical plays: the romance of
Luciana and Antipholus of Syracuse in *The Comedy of Errors,*
Mariane and Cléante in *L'Avare* of Molière, Phillis and Tom in
Steele's *The Conscious Lovers*. In the four other plays having
minor plots, Terence may have taken these from the Greek, but if
so, he probably had to choose them deliberately. The important
point here is that Terence knew the proper use of the minor plot.

Sometimes (as in *The Miles Gloriosus* of Plautus) a minor plot is merely juxtaposed or suspended within the major. Terence employs it not only to make a universally happy ending but to complicate the major plot. The solution of the minor may be maneuvered to heighten the climax of the major. The minor plot also facilitates the portrayal of character by contrast.

Another important innovation is the elimination of the omniscient prologue and its divinities. Terence uses the prologue (often omitted in translations) as a literary defense against certain adversaries and not to discuss the plot. At times he thereby loses some ironies, but suspense and surprise are thus at last given their opportunity. Terence substituted dramatic dialogue for some of the monologues in the Greek originals, or action for narration. The scene of abduction in *The Brothers* is his addition. He sometimes begins a scene in the middle of a line (Plautus had abandoned this), and he eliminates direct address to the audience (frequent in Menander). All the changes effected by Terence show a good sense of theater and make ancient plays much more readily adaptable to modern drama.

Delightful comedy and extremely deft construction unite in *The Phormio* to make it one of the most successful Roman comedies. The various strands of the double plot are most intimately interwoven. The difficulties concerning Antipho's marriage are arrested at their point of greatest tension by the development of Phaedria's need for money to have his sweetheart, and the securing of this money complicates the marriage situation. Later, the clarification of this situation causes the marital troubles of Chremes to worsen. Thus the false pessimism so characteristic of high comedy (in contrast to the false optimism of tragedy) is maintained throughout the play. Portrayal of character, also, is skillfully handled. The determination of Demipho, though shaken by conflicting advocates, brings out the vacillation of Chremes, who now is so cautious about appearances and reputation, although in the past, when his blood was less frigid, he was so careless. Deliberate marital infidelity on the part of the wife is beyond the pale of Greek New Comedy, and an unfaithful husband such as Chremes is held up to ridicule.

It is recorded that *The Phormio* was first presented at the annual "Roman" Games in 161 B.C. The original Greek play, by Apollodorus of Carystus, probably had an omniscient prologue in which the secret marriage of Chremes was told. The technique of Terence's play is distinctly more modern; indeed, no ancient comedy exploits suspense and surprise more effectively. This play has always been popular. Its most famous modern adaptation is that of Molière, *Les Fourberies de Scapin*.

The Brothers is a brilliant exposition of one of life's most perplexing problems. "Every father is a fool," says a fragment of Menander, and a German proverb runs: *Vater werden ist nicht schwer, Vater sein aber sehr.** The urbane and spineless Micio at the opening of the play is a firm believer in modern education with no fear and no discipline; love and trust are sufficient. The boorish Demea is equally convinced of the need of old-fashioned severity and suppression. These ideas are dramatically illustrated by their results: the resourceful young Aeschinus, who loves Micio but is deplorably inconsiderate of him and of others, and the profligate Ctesipho, whose feelings for Demea are hardly more than respectful hatred, born of fear and frustration. Portrayal of character by contrast is extended even to the slaves: the clever Syrian and the plodding Nordic (Geta). Here, especially, character is elaborated for its own appeal and beyond the requirements of the plot. But throughout, not the external action—though the two plots are skillfully maneuvered—but the characters are the main concern. This is high comedy at its best. Incidentally, this play gives a charming view of the cultured sophistication of Athens.

True soliloquies are repeatedly used to expand the portrayal of the main characters. From these and from Micio's overconfidence and Demea's futile busyness it is clear that both fathers have blundered and must in the end abandon their prejudices and compromise. Demea is the first to recognize his error, and he changes with a vengeance—a vengeance on Micio, who cannot say "no" to anything, even marriage in old age.

The Brothers was produced in 160 B.C. It was adapted from a play of Menander of the same title, though the scene of abduction was taken by Terence from a comedy of Diphilus to add action and to improve the dramatic characterization of the two boys. This

---

* "To become a father is no weighty task, but to be one is—very."

play inspired Molière's *L'École des Maris* and Fielding's *The Fathers.*

"No author," writes T. S. Eliot,* "exercised a wider or deeper influence upon the Elizabethan mind or upon the Elizabethan form of tragedy than did Seneca." On the whole this influence was desirable. The Elizabethans had in abundance what Seneca lacked: sensitivity and inspiration. Seneca had what the Elizabethans needed and knew that they needed: a mastery of the rhetorical use of language and a dramatic form inherently at least of great effectiveness. The Greeks were very distant from the Elizabethans in many ways, but Seneca was an easily recognizable ancestor. His intellectual outlook, like his language, was part of the Elizabethans' cultural heritage. Foreign to them were the Greek gods, whose symbolism dominates Greek tragedy. Foreign, also, was the intimate engagement of the Greek chorus with the action and interpretation of the play. Even the crudity of Seneca and his skeptical pessimism had strong appeal.

Lucius Annaeus Seneca was born of Roman family in Corduba, Spain, about 4 B.C. Long before his birth letters had become fashionable in the highest circles at Rome, as with Julius Caesar, and they remained so. Seneca's father had a passion for rhetoric and doubtless found his most apt "pupil" in this son, who early came to Rome and distinguished himself not only in rhetoric and oratory but in philosophy as well. Unfortunately, he distinguished himself also with the imperial family, especially its women. One of these in A.D. 41 secured his banishment to Corsica for alleged adultery with another. Some scholars conjecture that it was in this bitter period of his life that Seneca wrote his tragedies. Others place them later. This was not the only bitter period of his life. He tells us that in his youth he had contemplated suicide because of poor health but refrained out of consideration for his father (like Hercules at the end of *The Mad Hercules*).

In A.D. 49 Seneca was recalled through the influence of the new empress Agrippina to be made tutor for her own son Nero, whom she was grooming to replace the son of the emperor Claudius as heir. Nero succeeded at the age of seventeen, in 54, when the death of the emperor was perhaps induced by Agrippina.

---

* T. S. Eliot, *Selected Essays, 1917–1932* (New York: Harcourt, Brace & Company, Inc., 1932), p. 51.

Seneca and the prefect Burrus now became practical regents of the Roman empire and for five years gave it excellent government. In 59, however, Nero asserted his majority with the murder of his politically minded mother. Seneca fell into disfavor and in 65 was forced to commit suicide. This he did with Stoic nobility.

Seneca's philosophical essays and letters, though read today mainly by the courageous or the rash, were widely admired in the medieval period and the Renaissance. He was close to Christianity in his profound pessimism and in his preoccupation with suffering and death. Not infrequent in his prose works and in his tragedies is the theme of the "twilight of the gods" and the end of the world. Indeed, from Seneca alone it is easy to see why Christianity found such a fertile seminary in this very period. Though Seneca in his prose works often quotes Epicurus with admiration, he was by nature a Stoic, indeed one of the chief exponents of Roman Stoicism.

The only Roman tragedies that have survived are the ten traditionally attributed to Seneca. Modern scholars usually accept this attribution except for *The Octavia,* a play concerning the tragic end of Nero's wife and having Seneca as an important character. The plots of the other nine plays are versions of Greek originals which are all extant except *The Thyestes.* Comparison with these originals, mostly by Euripides, suggests that Seneca was not trying to imitate the Greek poets, for if he is judged by their standards, he is much inferior. Some of his favorite "vices," however, were inherited from later Greek tragedy, as is revealed by *The Orestes* and *The Rhesus;* in others he resembles earlier Roman tragedy, as we may observe from its fragments. But Seneca was attempting something very different from classical Greek tragedy. Professionally he was not a man of the theater but a statesman, an orator, and an essayist with a broad interest in philosophy. It is often assumed that his plays were never produced and were not written for production.

The most obvious interest of their author is his inherited passion for rhetorical expression. Eliot remarks: "In the plays of Seneca, the drama is all in the word, and the word has no further reality behind it. His characters all seem to speak with the same voice, and at the top of it; they recite in turn." *

---

* T. S. Eliot, *op. cit.,* p. 54

The proper amount of artistry in the use of language is that amount which will most greatly impress the audience. If artistry becomes patent, that is, if it is recognized as artificiality, then it defeats its purpose. But the proper amount, obviously subject to the whims of taste, varies greatly from age to age. In our own, the limit is low; but it was high in the age of Euripides and much higher in the age of Seneca. His reader or audience was impressed with epigrammatic sentences. Thus Hippolytus' one consolation for the death of his mother is that now he·may hate all women. The appearance of great learning, also, was much admired in Seneca's day. Such is his reference to the antipodes and his prediction of the discovery of a new world in *The Medea* (375– 379).* Often his lines are overloaded with recondite references to Greek legend which constitute their point. Again, the description of the monster from the sea that frightens the horses of Hippolytus is done in Euripides in two or three lines; Seneca (*The Phædra*) takes more than twenty lines. The purpose of such descriptions is not to enlighten the plot. It is rather the purpose of the plot to furnish opportunities for such displays.

But language cannot greatly impress unless it is freighted with thought. Stoicism obtrudes everywhere in Seneca. Following Plato, the Stoics viewed man's rationality as an element of divinity and the one source of solution for the problems of life. Man's passions and his ignorance are the plagues of life. In all the plays of Seneca the dominant theme is the tragedy of passion overwhelming reason. With this philosophical theme goes Seneca's conspicuous interest in the psychology of passion. He cultivates tours de force in creating moods and in the study of extreme emotional states. At times, however, he reveals great subtlety of observation. Thus Phædra protests at the haughty name of mother, and she sees in Hippolytus a fairer pattern of his father. Besides Seneca's philosophical and psychological interests, his political pronouncements should not be overlooked. The few facts of his life mentioned above are sufficient to suggest that he may in his plays be preaching to Nero or to the world in protest against the crimes of this

---

* It is said that Ferdinand Columbus (Colón) in his copy of Seneca's tragedies wrote (in Latin) opposite these words, "This prophecy was fulfilled by my father, Admiral Christopher Colón, in the year 1492."

imperial house. No royal family ever needed Stoic sermons more or heeded them less.

Finally, in our consideration of Seneca's interests we must not overlook the dramatic. Crude indeed but undeniably spectacular is the closing scene of *The Medea* where Medea, high above the helpless Jason, flings down the bodies of their children. Even a reader can hardly fail to hear the thud of the bodies. Again, no scene in Greek tragedy is more dramatic than Phædra's appeal to Hippolytus, and Phædra's final confession of her guilt satisfies our sense of theater more than the scene with Artemis in Euripides. In brief, it is a mistake to find in Seneca's tragedies only rhetorical exercises or philosophical essays: his plays mirror the cosmic breadth of his interests. The Greeks were simple; Seneca is confusedly complex.

These plays are all concerned with catastrophe and death. There are no sweetness and light as in various melodramatic and romantic "tragedies" of Euripides or Sophocles. There is no trace here of the firm belief of Aeschylus in the justice of Heaven and in the sure enlightenment and progress of man. Seneca's pessimism is profound. It is not only elaborately set forth in the choral songs. It is seen also in his portrayal of character—and most importantly so. Here for the first time the true villain appears upon the stage. In later Greek tragedy Menelaus and Odysseus are sometimes depicted as base (Aristotle protests against this tendency), but normally in Greek literature virtues and vices are very humanly compounded. Compare the character of the Phædra of Euripides with that of the Phædra of Seneca. And Atreus in *The Thyestes* reminds us of the Moor in *Titus Andronicus* or of Iago.

Seneca's dramatic form, also, is new to us. In Greek tragedies the number of choral songs is adapted to the structure of the particular play. In Seneca, however, there are regularly four songs dividing the play into five acts. The first act is devoted to exposition, especially emotional exposition. The amount of information revealed is usually slight. It is assumed that the audience knows all the details of the action. Indeed, at times it seems as if the characters themselves know their future as definitely as they do their past. This is an important aspect of these dramas. We are not concerned with what will happen and little concerned

with how it will happen. Interest is centered in the thought and
the word. Suspense and surprise are limited to the verbal. The
second act of a Senecan tragedy is often a long scene in which
a subaltern attempts to deter the main character from crime.
Since this attempt never succeeds, it serves primarily to bring
out the evil determination of the main character. The third act
may be taken up with the execution of the crime; the fourth
with a description or exhibition of the crime; the fifth with the
effects. The whole tends to be a concatenation of sensational
or spectacular scenes rather than a skillfully articulated drama.

Like Euripides' famous masterpiece, *The Medea* of Seneca is
a tragedy of revenge. Euripides, however, made every effort to
convert the formidable heroine of legend into a thoroughly under-
standable human being. Seneca does his best to exaggerate the
monstrous crimes of a barbarous witch. In this regard, the *Medea*
of Robinson Jeffers is closer to the Roman than to the Greek. From
the first lines, Seneca's Medea screams for vengeance. (The
children are not here displayed on stage, as they are so effectively
in Euripides.) She recites a catalogue of her past atrocities and
casts about for a crime worthy of her maturity. That this will
involve her children is plain from her words, but later in the
play she seems to discover her plan when Jason expresses his
great love for his sons. Here dramatic consistency is given up for
rhetorical effect. Medea's later speeches are composed in the same
key, and throughout the play she views herself as already a
legend:

NURSE: Colchis is far away, thy husband lost;
Of all thy riches nothing now remains.
MEDEA: Medea now remains!

Jason in Euripides lusts for property and power, and he has no
qualms at sacrificing Medea to his ambition. His sophistic defense
of his action adds to his baseness. In Seneca, Jason is being forced
by Creon into a marriage of political convenience, and he submits
out of concern for the safety of his children—a nice point. His
kindly portrayal emphasizes the heartlessness of Medea.

A noteworthy technical innovation of the play is the omission
of the conventional long messenger's speech. Medea's clairvoyant

prayer has made further description quite unnecessary, and the brief scene with the messenger is effectively dramatic.

Seneca achieves a harrowing and spectacular finale with a final line that is at once a denunciation of Medea and a despairing cry of man that in this evil world there are no gods.

The Phædra is often considered Seneca's best play, although some scholars attribute much of the brilliant scene where Phædra throws herself upon Hippolytus to Euripides' earlier (lost) version of this legend. Comparison of Seneca's version with the later (extant) *Hippolytus* is very enlightening. Euripides eminently succeeds in making his heroine a character that appeals to our sympathies; he uses Aphrodite to symbolize the irresistible power against which Phædra struggles nobly; the Nurse seduces Phædra rather than, as in Seneca, Phædra the Nurse; Phædra will not approach Hippolytus directly; and she prefers her own death to disgrace, although by writing the letter of indictment she does encompass the death of the innocent Hippolytus. In Seneca, all this is changed. "Reason pandars will," and will is enslaved by passion. The craftiness of Phædra's faints and the subtlety of her attack and the sophistry of her appeals to be slain and the deliberateness of her indictment all add blackness to her character. Fascinating also is the comparison of these plays with Racine's *Phèdre* and with *The Cretan Woman* of Robinson Jeffers. The French poet has combined the best of Euripides with the best of Seneca and introduced a love affair for Hippolytus. The American poet, somewhat like the Roman, but more from the aesthetic than the moral point of view, has used the legend to expose the crudity of his own age.

In the Renaissance, *The Thyestes* was a model play of revenge. This subject, crude as it would seem inevitably to be, was a favorite with Greek poets, used by Sophocles, Euripides, and six or seven others. Some scholars assume that Seneca was influenced by Euripides in this play. Among Roman writers of tragedy this was perhaps the most popular of all subjects. Quintilian (*Education of the Orator,* 10.1.98), no mean critic, considered *The Thyestes* by the Roman poet Various comparable to any Greek tragedy.

In some versions (none extant) Thyestes returned from exile of his own accord. Thus the suspicions of Atreus seemed more plausible. Seneca has Atreus invite his brother to return. This deliberateness is obviously designed to make the crime more monstrous. So is the sympathetic portrayal of Thyestes, who is here presented as something of a Stoic wise man, quite inconsistently with his reported crimes, but in effective contrast to the mad passion of Atreus. Truly Elizabethan is Atreus' exuberance in his villainy. All nature is revolted by the deed—all nature except Atreus, who in his denial of right reason is himself contrary to nature.

In this play the choral songs become longer and longer as the play progresses. This reverses the tendency of Greek tragedy (and of *The Phædra*). These extemporizations of the chorus seem to concern the author more than does the progression of the action.

The palace and the customs described are not those of Mycenae but those of the Palatine in Rome (the palace of the emperors). At the end of the play, Thyestes' assurance that the gods will punish Atreus may look forward to Seneca's *Agamemnon,* which opens with the ghost of Thyestes.

The theater at Rome as at Athens was a state institution. Productions in Rome took place at the funeral games of great men, at celebrations of victories, or at the various games of annual holidays. During the time of Plautus and Terence, only temporary stages were erected. The stage was long and shallow (some asides are not unnatural on it). The scene normally represented a city street with two or three houses at the back. Very unusual is the scene of *The Rope*: a wild coast with a cottage and a shrine of Venus. The plays were presented in Greek dress by male actors, perhaps without masks. There were no handbills: characters had to be introduced to the audience by one device or another. At some games in the huge city various amusements were presented simultaneously, and theatrical productions had difficulty in holding their audiences from the attractions of tightrope walkers and other such artists.

Although permanent theaters were common in southern Italy, conservative Roman prejudice against the allurements of Greek culture and the licenses of Greek free speech obstructed permanent theaters at Rome until 55 B.C., when Pompey by a clever strategem—the only one recorded in his long public career—so devised a theater that its auditorium served as steps to a lofty and comparatively small temple of Venus. Soon after, Augustus built the great theater of Marcellus, extensive remains of which impress everyone who visits Rome today. The Romans combined the auditorium and the stage building into one structural unity: the auditorium is normally mounted by a colonnaded gallery; the background of the stage (*scenae frons*) is tiered up to the level of this gallery, adorned by a profusion of marble statues, and topped with a roof slanting sharply out toward the audience to serve as a sounding board for the actors' voices. The whole is built on level ground with massive concrete substructures and impressive perfection of engineering detail. Before Seneca, therefore, Roman theaters, though lacking the simple and exquisite beauty of the Greek, were among the most magnificent that the world has seen. Roman audiences, as we gather from the remarks of the poet Horace, were among the worst. This, of course, was the fundamental reason for the inferiority of Roman drama, as it is for the inferiority of contemporary American drama.

In the houses or villas of the rich, intimate private theaters were frequent. Here troupes might perform mimes or dramas, or a single professional might dance or recite, or the owner or his friends might read their own masterpieces. These private audiences were very different from the public. But too often they came for social reasons or because they knew that if they did not attend and applaud—loudly—no one would come to their own readings!

P. W. H.

Stanford, California
September, 1959

ACKNOWLEDGMENTS

For helpful suggestions I am grateful to many, especially Professors Charles Babcock, Pennsylvania; S. Palmer Bovie, Indiana; Mason Hammond, Harvard; Gilbert Highet, Columbia; E. N. O'Neil, U.S.C.; Harry Rogers, Ohio State; L. V. Ryan and G. J. Sullwold, Stanford; A. H. Travis, U.C.L.A.

BIBLIOGRAPHICAL NOTE

பாய

Translations of all Greek and Roman plays may be found under the names of the original poets in the various volumes of the series, Loeb Classical Library (Cambridge, Mass.: Harvard University Press); also in W. J. Oates and E. O'Neill, Jr., *The Complete Greek Drama* (New York: Random House, Inc., 1938), and in G. E. Duckworth, *The Complete Roman Drama* (New York: Random House, Inc., 1942). A convenient collection of translations of Greek plays is that of C. A. Robinson, Jr., in the Rinehart Editions, *An Anthology of Greek Drama*: First Series, *Agamemnon, Oedipus the King, Antigone, Medea, Hippolytus, Lysistrata* (New York: Rinehart & Company, Inc., 1949); Second Series, *Prometheus Bound, Choephoroe, Eumenides, Philoctetes, Oedipus at Colonus, The Trojan Women, The Bacchae, The Clouds, The Frogs* (New York: Rinehart & Company, Inc., 1954). An English translation of *The Dyskolos* is included in the original edition: Ménandre, *Le Dyscolos*, publié par V. Martin (Cologny-Genève: Bibliotheca Bodmeriana, 1958), Papyrus Bodmer IV. A more literary English translation of this work is that of Gilbert Highet which appeared in *Horizon* (July, 1959).

Recent works on Roman drama include the following: W. Beare, *The Roman Stage*, 2nd ed. (London: Methuen & Co., Ltd., 1955); G. E. Duckworth, *The Nature of Roman Comedy*: *A Study in Popular Entertainment* (Princeton, N. J.: Princeton University Press, 1952); P. W. Harsh, *A Handbook of Classical Drama* (Stanford, Calif.: Stanford University Press, 1944). Bibliographies may be compiled from these volumes. For Seneca, however, see the elaborate critical review of Michael Coffey, "Seneca, Tragedies . . . Report for the years 1922–1955," in *Lustrum: Internationale Forschungsberichte aus dem Bereich des klassischen Altertums* (Göttingen: Vandenhoeck & Ruprecht, 1958), pp. 113–186.

NOTE ON DIVISIONS
INTO ACTS AND SCENES

In ancient and medieval manuscripts of Plautus, Terence, and Seneca, the characters of each section of the play are listed and sometimes identified in scene headings (e.g., Chremes, old man; Geta, slave; Phædra, Nurse, etc.), but the scenes are not numbered and there is no indication of acts. Division of the plays into five acts dates from the Renaissance editors,* although basis for act divisions in Terence is found in the ancient commentaries. (For Plautus and Seneca no such commentaries have been preserved.) In the present anthology, the conventional act divisions for Plautus and Terence are given to facilitate reference, but these are placed in brackets since Plautus and Terence seem not to have composed their plays with any regard for such division. The Roman poet Horace (65–8 B.C.), in his work *The Art of Poetry*, line 189) declared: "Let your play not fall short of the fifth act nor exceed it." Seneca seems deliberately to have composed in accordance with this rule, and therefore the obvious act divisions are retained in the text in this anthology.

---

* The editor of this volume possesses a copy of Seneca's tragedies produced in Venice by the printer Capcasa in 1493; this has the acts indicated in the text. Since Seneca employs a chorus, act division is easily determined. In the comedies, however, there is no chorus, act divisions are difficult, and often the conventional ones are unsatisfactory.

PLAUTUS

THE TWIN MENAECHMI

TRANSLATED BY RICHARD W. HYDE AND EDWARD C. WEIST

CHARACTERS IN THE PLAY

PROLOGUE SPEAKER
SPONGE * (PENICULUS), *a parasite, "Little Tail"*
MENAECHMUS I, *a young man of Epidamnus*
EROTIUM, *a courtesan, "Loveling"*
CYLINDRUS, *cook of Erotium, "Roller"*
MENAECHMUS II (SOSICLES), *a young man of Syracuse*
MESSENIO, *slave of Menaechmus II*
MAID *of Erotium*
WIFE *of Menaechmus I*
FATHER *of wife of Menaechmus I*
DOCTOR
SLAVES

ACROSTIC ARGUMENT

A Sicilian merchant had twin sons and died when one was stolen from him. His paternal grandfather gave the boy at home the name of the stolen twin and called him Menaechmus instead of Sosicles. When this boy grew up, he began to search for his brother in every land. At last he comes to Epidamnus; it was here that his stolen brother had been reared. Everyone thinks that the stranger is Menaechmus, their own fellow-citizen, and his brother's mistress, wife, and father-in-law so address him. Finally the two brothers recognise each other.

---

* By the kind permission of Random House, Inc., the present editor uses the name "Sponge" for the parasite (instead of "Brush"), and accordingly slightly modifies the few sentences in which the name occurs. In the Greek writer Alciphron a parasite is named "Pinakospongisos" ("Plate-sponger"). Sponges were widely used in ancient times: to wash tables, clean shoes, bathe oneself. In the days before the invention of paper, sponges were also put to certain other practical uses, and the word *peniculus* is obviously somewhat obscene. These facts will help the modern reader appreciate the jokes on this name which follow.—*Editor P. W. H.*

THE TWIN MENAECHMI

(SCENE: *A street in Epidamnus in front of the houses of*
MENAECHMUS I *and* EROTIUM.)

PROLOGUE

Now first and above all, spectators, I'm bringing a few
Of the best of good wishes to me—and then also to you;
I'm bringing you Plautus—by mouth, of course, not in person,
And therefore I pray you receive him with kindliest ears.
To the argument gird up your minds, as I babble my verse,
And I shall explain it—in briefest of terms, have no fears.
  And this is the thing that poets do in their plays:
The action has all taken place in Athens, they say,
That the setting will seem to be Greek to you all the more.
But from me you'll hear the truth—where it actually happened.
The plot of the play, to be sure, is Greek, but not
Of the Attic variety; Sicilian, rather.
I've given you now of the argument merely the preface;
And next the plot I'll generously pour out
Not merely by peck or bushel, but by the whole barn,
So kindly a nature I have for telling the plot.
  Now, an old merchant was living in Syracuse city,
And he by some chance had a couple of twin sons—yes, two of
    'em—
And they looked so alike that the nurse couldn't tell (more's the
    pity)
Which one she gave suck to; no more could their mother, for
    whom
The nurse was called in, no, not even their mother who'd borne
    'em.

3

Much later, the boys being now about seven years old,
Their father filled up a big ship with a lot of his goods
And, putting one twin in safekeeping with them in the hold,
Betook himself off to Tarentum to market, to turn 'em
To cash; and the other twin stayed at home with his mother.
When they got there, Tarentum was holding some games, as it
          happened,
And people were flocking to town, as they do for the games.
The little boy strayed from his father among all the crowds;
The lost was soon found by a rich Epidamnian merchant
Who seized him and took him off home. But the father
Was sadly dejected at heart at the loss of the boy,
And only a little while later he died of despair.
Syracuse at last heard the bad news that the father was dead
And that someone had stolen the twin who had wandered away.
So the grandfather changed the remaining twin's name then and
          there,
Since the other had been so beloved—the one stolen away.
The other one's name he bestowed on the twin safe at home,
And called him Menaechmus, the same as the one I have said.
The grandfather's name was Menaechmus too, it so happened,
And with ease I remember the name, as they called it aloud.
And lest you get muddled, both twins now have the same name.

   But now on the poet's rude feet I must seek Epidamnus,
To speed on my tale. Should anyone wish to have business
Transacted there, let him be bold and speak forth and give me
The money with which I may carry out all his commands.
But unless the money's forthcoming, he's wasting his time,
And he's wasting his time even more, should the money be given.
And while standing still I've returned to my point of departure.

   The old merchant I told you about, who kidnapped the boy,
Had no children whatever, unless you should count all his
          money.[1]
He adopted the stolen young twin as his son, and to him
Gave a wife and a dowry, and made him his heir when he died.
For, wandering into the country not far from the town, the
Epidamnian stepped in a freshet, where torrents of rain

---

[1] There was apparently a jest here in the Greek original. The Greek
word τόκος means both "children" and "interest on money."

Had been falling; the current caught quickly the kidnapper's feet
And carried him off to the place where he'll get his deserts.
So from him the young man inherits a plentiful fortune,
And this is the house where the rich kidnapped twin is now
        dwelling.
    The other twin, living in Syracuse, comes with his slave
To find his own twin brother here, for whom he's been searching.
While the play's being acted, the town's Epidamnus, you see;
When another play comes, 'twill turn into some other town.
And then the families in the houses will change;
The inhabitant is now a pander, and now a youth,
Or a pauper, a beggar, a parasite, or a prophet.

[ACT ONE: SCENE I]

(*Enter* SPONGE, *who addresses audience.*)

SPONGE: My nickname's Sponge, because when I eat I wipe
the table clean.

People who keep prisoners in chains and put shackles on run-
away slaves do a very foolish thing, if you ask me. You see, if
you add insult to injury, a poor fellow will want all the more
to escape and go wrong. He'll get out of his chains somehow,
you can be sure—file away a link, or knock out a nail with a
stone. That way's no good.

If you really want to keep somebody so he won't get away,
you'd better tie him with food and drink: hitch his beak to a
full dinnerpail. Give him all he wants to eat and drink every day,
and he'll never try to run away, not even if he's committed
murder. The bonds of food and drink are very elastic, you know:
the more you stretch them, the tighter they hold you.

(*Going towards the house of* MENAECHMUS I) Now take me—
I'm on my way over to Menaechmus', where I've been doing a
long stretch; I'm giving myself up to let him bind me. He doesn't
only feed you, you see: he builds you up and makes a new man
of you. There's no better doctor alive. Just to show you what sort
of fellow he is—he has wonderful meals, regular Thanksgiving
dinners: he builds up such skyscrapers of dishes you have to
stand on your couch if you want to get anything off the top.

But it's quite a few days since I've been over there. I've been kept at home with my dear ones—I don't eat or buy anything but what it's very dear. But now my army of dear ones is deserting, and so I'm going to see him. (*He approaches the door.*) But the door's opening. There's Menaechmus—he's coming out. (*Withdraws.*)

[ACT ONE: SCENE 2]

(*Enter* MENAECHMUS I *from his house, wearing a dress of his wife's under his own cloak. He calls back to his wife inside.*)

MENAECHMUS I: If you were not
                          Stubborn, bad,
                      Stupid, and a
                          Little mad,
                 What your husband hates, you'd see
                 And behave accordingly.
                 Act the way you have today
                 And back you go to dad to stay.
                 If I say I'm going out,
                 You're on hand to ask about
                 Where I'm going,
                      What to do,
                 What's my business,
                      What's for you.
                 I can't get out anywhere
                 But you want me to declare
                 All I've done and all I do.
                 Customs officer—that's you!
                 I've handled you with too much care:
                 Listen what I'm going to do:
                 Food I give you,
                      Maids, indeed,
                 Money, dresses—
                      All you need;
                 Now you'll keep your spying eyes
                 Off your husband, if you're wise.

And furthermore I'll see that you don't have your watching for nothing: I'm going to get even with you and take a woman out to dinner somewhere.

SPONGE (*aside*): The fellow pretends he's cursing his wife, but he's really cursing me. It's me he hurts if he eats out, not his wife.

MENAECHMUS I: Gosh! At last I've scolded my wife away from the door. (*To the audience*) Where are all you philandering husbands? What are you waiting for? Come on up and congratulate me and reward me for the good fight I've put up—I've just stolen this dress from my wife in there and I'm taking it to my mistress. This is a fine way to cheat this clever guardian of mine. An excellent job, an honest job, an elegant job, a workmanlike job! I risked my life and robbed my wife, and the thing's going to be a total loss. But I got the spoils from the enemy and didn't lose a man.

SPONGE (*accosting him*): Hey, young fellow, is any of that stuff for me?

MENAECHMUS I: It's all over. I've fallen into a trap.

SPONGE: Oh no, sir, just into protective custody. Don't be alarmed.

MENAECHMUS I: Who are you?

SPONGE: Myself.

MENAECHMUS I (*turning*): Why, you sight for sore eyes, you chance that comes once in a lifetime! Good morning.

SPONGE: Good morning.

MENAECHMUS I: What are you doing?

SPONGE: I'm shaking hands with my best friend.

MENAECHMUS I: You couldn't have come at a better time than this.

SPONGE: That's just like me: I'm quite an expert on opportune moments.

MENAECHMUS I: Want to see something gorgeous?

SPONGE: What cook cooked it? I'll know if he slipped up when I see what's left.

MENAECHMUS I: Say, did you ever see the painting on the temple wall where the eagle steals Ganymede, or where Venus gets away with Adonis?

SPONGE: Plenty of times. But what have those pictures got to do with me?

MENAECHMUS I (*revealing the dress*): Take a look at me. Do I look like them at all?

SPONGE: What's that outfit you're wearing?

MENAECHMUS I: Say I'm a clever fellow.

SPONGE: When do we eat?

MENAECHMUS I: You just say what I tell you.

SPONGE: All right. "Clever fellow."

MENAECHMUS I: Can't you add anything of your own?

SPONGE: Well—life of the party.

MENAECHMUS I: Go on, go on.

SPONGE: I certainly will not go on unless I know what I'm going to get out of it. You've had a quarrel with your wife and I'm staying on the safe side.

MENAECHMUS I: What do you say we find a place away from my wife where we can have a funeral—and then we burn up the day?

SPONGE (*enthusiastically*): Wonderful! Let's get going. How soon do I light the pyre? The day's already dead up to the waist.

MENAECHMUS I: You'll wait if you interrupt me.

SPONGE: Knock my eye out, Menaechmus, if I say a word except when you tell me.

MENAECHMUS I: Come over here away from the door.

SPONGE: Sure.

MENAECHMUS I: Farther still.

SPONGE: All right.

MENAECHMUS I: Now come boldly away from the lion's den.

SPONGE: Say there, I've got an idea you'd make a good racing driver.

MENAECHMUS I: How come?

SPONGE: Well, you're always looking back to see that your wife isn't following you.

MENAECHMUS I: But what do you say—

SPONGE: What do I say? Why, anything you want, my friend.

MENAECHMUS I: I wonder if you could make a guess from the odour of a thing if you smelt it.

SPONGE: . . .[2] if you got the whole staff.

MENAECHMUS I: Well, take a sniff of this dress I've got. How does it smell? Don't hang back.

---

[2] There is a short lacuna in the text here.

SPONGE: You ought to smell the top of a woman's dress; the smell down there is awful.

MENAECHMUS I: Then smell here, Sponge. How dainty you are!

SPONGE: This is better.

MENAECHMUS I: How about it? What does it smell like? Tell me.

SPONGE: A moocher, a mistress, and a meal! . . .[2]

MENAECHMUS I: Now I'll take this to my lady Erotium here, and I'll order dinner for all three of us.

SPONGE: Swell!

MENAECHMUS I: After that we'll drink right through till daylight tomorrow.

SPONGE: Swell! You've said a mouthful. Do I knock now?

MENAECHMUS I: Go ahead. Or wait a minute.

SPONGE: Oh, you're holding up our drinking a mile.

MENAECHMUS I: Knock softly.

SPONGE: I suppose you're afraid the door is made of Samian ware.

MENAECHMUS I: Wait, for heaven's sake, wait! Look. She's coming out herself. Do you see how dim the sun is compared to the splendour of her beauty?

[ACT ONE: SCENE 3]

(*Enter* EROTIUM *from her house.*)

EROTIUM: Good morning, Menaechmus, my sweet.

SPONGE: How about me?

EROTIUM: You don't count with me.

SPONGE: That's what usually happens to the reserves in an army.

MENAECHMUS I: I'd like you to do something for him and me over at your house—get ready a battle.

EROTIUM: It shall be done.

MENAECHMUS I: And we'll both drink in this battle, and which is the better battler will be found by the bottle. You're head of the army, and you'll decide which of us—you'll spend the night with. O my heart's delight, how I detest my wife when I set my eyes on you!

EROTIUM (*noticing the dress*): Still, you can't keep from wearing her clothes. What's this?

MENAECHMUS I: Your dress and my wife's *un*dress, rosebud.

EROTIUM: You're an easy winner over all the others who possess me.

SPONGE (*aside*): The woman flatters him as long as she sees what he's stolen. (*To* EROTIUM) Now, if you really loved him, you'd have bitten his nose off with kisses.

MENAECHMUS I: Hold this, Sponge. (*Handing him his cloak*) I want to make the offering I have vowed.

SPONGE: Let's have it. But please, dance with that dress on like that.

MENAECHMUS I: Me dance? You're as crazy as they come.

SPONGE: Maybe you're the crazy one. But if you won't dance, take the thing off.

MENAECHMUS I (*removing dress*): I took a big chance stealing this—bigger than Hercules did, I guess, when he stole Hippolyta's girdle. (*Handing the dress to* EROTIUM) Here, my dear. You're the only one who really understands me.

EROTIUM: That's how true lovers should feel.

SPONGE (*aside*): At least ones who are on their way to the poorhouse.

MENAECHMUS I: That cost me four minae last year when I bought it for my wife.

SPONGE (*aside*): Four minae gone to the devil, when you add up your accounts.

MENAECHMUS I: Do you know what I want you to do?

EROTIUM: Tell me; I'll do anything you wish.

MENAECHMUS I: Then have a dinner for the three of us at your house. And get some fine food at the market—
> The son of a glandule of pork,
>   The son of a fattened ham,
> Or the jowl of a hog—
>   Some food of that sort
> Which set on the table
> Will tickle my palate
> And give me the gorge of a kite.

And hurry up.

EROTIUM: Very well.

MENAECHMUS I: We'll go on downtown, but we'll be back soon. While the dinner's being cooked, we'll pass the time drinking.

EROTIUM: Come whenever you wish; everything will be ready.

MENAECHMUS I: Hurry now. (*To* SPONGE) You follow me.

SPONGE: I'll watch you and follow you, all right. I wouldn't lose you for all the wealth of heaven. (MENAECHMUS *and* SPONGE *depart.*)

EROTIUM (*to those inside*): You in there, call out my cook Cylindrus at once.

[ACT ONE: SCENE 4]

(*Enter* CYLINDRUS.)

EROTIUM: Take a basket and some money. Here are three nummi.

CYLINDRUS: Yes, ma'am.

EROTIUM: Go and get some provisions. See that there's enough for three, not too little and not too much.

CYLINDRUS: What kind of people will they be?

EROTIUM: Menaechmus and his parasite and I.

CYLINDRUS: That makes ten, then, because a parasite does as well as eight ordinary men.

EROTIUM: I've told you the guests; take care of the rest.

CYLINDRUS: All right. Everything's done. Tell them dinner is served.

EROTIUM: Hurry back. (*She goes into her house.*)

CYLINDRUS: I'm practically back now. (CYLINDRUS *departs.*)

[ACT TWO: SCENE I]

(*Enter* MENAECHMUS II, *and his slave* MESSENIO *carrying a bag, followed by sailors with luggage.*)

MENAECHMUS II: I think, Messenio, that there is no greater joy for sea travellers than sighting land.

MESSENIO: Yes, but it's still better if it's your own land. Why,

I ask you, have we come here—why Epidamnus? We might as well be the ocean: we never miss a single island.

MENAECHMUS II (*sadly*): We are searching for my twin brother.

MESSENIO: Is this search ever going to end? It's six years now that we've spent on it. We've seen 'em all—Istrians, Iberians, the people of Marseilles, Illyrians, the whole Adriatic, all of Magna Graecia, the whole Italian seacoast. If you'd been hunting for a needle you'd have found it long ago, if there had been one. We're looking for a dead man among the living; if he were alive you'd have found him long ago.

MENAECHMUS II: If I can find somebody who can prove that, who can say he knows for certain that my brother is dead, then I shall seek no further. But otherwise I shall go on as long as I live; I know how dear he is to my heart.

MESSENIO: You might as well try to find a knot in a bulrush. Let's clear out of here and go home. Or are we going to write a book—"Our Trip around the World"?

MENAECHMUS II: You do what you're told, take what's given you, and keep out of trouble. Don't annoy me. I'm running this, not you.

MESSENIO (*aside*): Hm-m, that puts me in my place all right. Neat, complete; it can't be beat. But just the same, here I go again. (*Aloud*) Look at our purse, Menaechmus; our money is feeling the heat: it's getting as thin as a summer shirt. If you don't go home, you'll be hunting for that blessed brother of yours without a cent to bless *yourself* with. That's what Epidamnus is like, full of rakes and tremendous drinkers; a lot of swindlers and spongers live here, and everybody knows their women are the most seductive in the whole world. That's why the place is called Epidamnus; scarcely anybody can come here without getting damned.

MENAECHMUS II: I'll take care of that: just hand the purse over to me.

MESSENIO: What for?

MENAECHMUS II: What you say makes me worried—about you.

MESSENIO: Makes you worried?

MENAECHMUS II: That you may get yourself damned in Epidamnus. You are very fond of the ladies, Messenio, and I have a bad temper and lose it very easily. So if I have the money, you get double protection: your foot doesn't slip, and my temper doesn't either.

MESSENIO (*handing it over*): Take it, keep it; it's all right with me.

[ACT TWO: SCENE 2]

(*Enter* CYLINDRUS *the cook, with his market-basket.*)

CYLINDRUS (*to himself*): I've done a good job of marketing—just what I like myself. I'll give the company a fine dinner.—Glory, there's Menaechmus! Now I'm in for it! Here are the guests at the door before I'm back from the market. I'll go up and speak to him. (*To* MENAECHMUS II) Good day, Menaechmus.

MENAECHMUS II: Why, thank you. (*To* MESSENIO) He seems to know my name. Who is he? [3]

MESSENIO: I don't know.

CYLINDRUS: Where are the other guests?

MENAECHMUS II: What guests?

CYLINDRUS (*grinning*): Your parasite.

MENAECHMUS II (*to* MESSENIO): My parasite? The man's crazy.

MESSENIO: Didn't I tell you there were a lot of swindlers here? . . . [4]

MENAECHMUS II (*to* CYLINDRUS): What do you mean "my parasite," young man?

CYLINDRUS: Why, "Sponge."

MESSENIO (*peering into the bag*): Nonsense, I have your sponge safe right here in the bag.

CYLINDRUS: You are a little early for dinner, Menaechmus; I'm just back from the market.

MENAECHMUS II: Tell me, young man: how much do pigs cost here? Grade A pigs, for sacrifice.

---

[3] The text is corrupt at this point.
[4] Lindsay indicates a lacuna after this speech.

CYLINDRUS: A drachma. ·

MENAECHMUS II: Well, here's a drachma; go get yourself cured at my expense. Because you certainly must be crazy, what's-your-name, to be bothering a perfect stranger like me.

CYLINDRUS: "What's-your-name"! Don't you remember me? I'm Cylindrus.

MENAECHMUS II: The devil take you, whether your name is Cylinder or Colander. I don't know you, and I don't want to.

CYLINDRUS (*persisting*): Your name is Menaechmus.

MENAECHMUS II: You're in your right mind when you call me by name, anyway. But where did you ever see me before?

CYLINDRUS: Where did I ever see you before—when my mistress, Erotium, is your mistress?

MENAECHMUS II: Confound it, she's not my mistress, and I don't know you, either.

CYLINDRUS: All the drinks I've poured for you in the house here, and you don't know me?

MESSENIO: I wish I had something to break his head with.

MENAECHMUS II: You pour my drinks for me, do you? When I've never set foot in Epidamnus before today and never even seen the place?

CYLINDRUS: You deny it?

MENAECHMUS II: Of course I deny it.

CYLINDRUS: Don't you live in that house over there?

MENAECHMUS II: The devil take the people that do!

CYLINDRUS (*aside*): If he curses himself like this, *he's* crazy. (*Aloud*) Menaechmus!

MENAECHMUS II: Well?

CYLINDRUS: If you ask me, you ought to take that drachma you—promised me a minute ago and order *yourself* a pig, because your head isn't on straight either, you know, if you curse your own self.

MENAECHMUS II: Confound your cheek, you chatterbox! (*Turns away.*)

CYLINDRUS (*aside*): He likes to joke with me like this. Always full of laughs—when his wife's not there! (*To* MENAECHMUS II) Well, sir— (*No response*) Well, sir— (MENAECHMUS II *turns.*) Is this enough for the three of you—you, the parasite, and the lady—or shall I get some more?

MENAECHMUS II: What "ladies"? What "parasites"?

MESSENIO (*to* CYLINDRUS): Here, what's the matter with you? Why are you pestering the gentleman?

CYLINDRUS: Who are you, and what's it to you? I'm talking to *him*; he's a friend of mine.

MESSENIO: You're cracked, that's certain.

CYLINDRUS (*to* MENAECHMUS II): I'll get these things into the pot right away, so don't wander off too far from the house. Anything else I can do for you?

MENAECHMUS II: Yes. Go to the devil.

CYLINDRUS: Oh, better that you should—go inside and make yourself comfortable on your couch, while Vulcan is getting violent with the food. I'll go in and tell Erotium that you're here. I know she'd rather take you in than make you wait outside. (*He goes into the house of* EROTIUM.)

MENAECHMUS II: Is he gone? Good. Whew! I see there was a lot in what you said.

MESSENIO: Yes, but look out. I think one of those fancy women lives here, just as that crackpot said.

MENAECHMUS II: All the same, I wonder how he knew my name.

MESSENIO: Nothing strange in that; it's just the way these women have. They send their maids and slave-boys to the harbour; and if a foreign ship comes in, they find out the name of the owner and where he's from, and then, bingo! they fasten onto him and stick to him like glue. If he falls for it, they send him home a ruined man. (*Pointing to house of* EROTIUM) Now in that harbour rides a pirate craft, of which we must beware.

MENAECHMUS II: That's good advice.

MESSENIO: Yes, but it's no good unless you take it. (*The door starts to open.*)

MENAECHMUS II: Quiet a minute; I hear the door opening. Let's see who comes out.

MESSENIO (*putting down the bag*): I'll set this down then. You sailors, keep an eye on the luggage.

[ACT TWO: SCENE 3]

(*Enter* EROTIUM *from her house.*)

EROTIUM (*to slaves within*):
>   Go in, and do not close the door,
>   I want it left just so.
>   See what there is to do inside
>   And do it all—now go.
>   The couches must be spread, and perfumes burned:
>   Neatness entices lovers, I have learned.
>   Splendour to lovers' loss, to our gain is turned.
(*Coming forward*)
>   But where is the man they said was before my door?
>   Ah, there he is; he's been of use before;
>   Yet is, as he deserves, my governor.
>   I'll go and speak to him myself.—My dear,
>   I am amazed to see you standing here;
>   My home is always yours when you appear.
>   Now all you ordered is prepared,
>   The doors are opened wide,
>   Your dinner's cooked, and when you like
>   Come take your place inside.

MENAECHMUS II (*to* MESSENIO): Who's this woman talking to?

EROTIUM: To you!

MENAECHMUS II: But why? We've never—

EROTIUM: Because it is the will of Venus that I exalt you above all others; and so I should, because you're the one who keeps me blooming with your loving favours.

MENAECHMUS II (*to* MESSENIO): This woman is either insane or drunk, Messenio. Such language, to a perfect stranger!

MESSENIO (to MENAECHMUS II): Didn't I tell you that was the way here? Why, these are just falling leaves; stay here a couple of days, and there'll be *trees* falling on you. These women look like pick-ups, but they're not; they're just stick-ups.—Let me talk to her. (*To* EROTIUM) Listen, lady—

EROTIUM: What?

MESSENIO: Where did you get so familiar with the gentleman?

EROTIUM: In the same place where he got so familiar with me—here, in Epidamnus.

MESSENIO: In Epidamnus? He never set so much as his foot in the place until today.

EROTIUM: Oh, what a ravishing sense of humour! (*To* MENAECHMUS II) Menaechmus dear, won't you come in? We can straighten this out so much better inside.

MENAECHMUS II (*to* MESSENIO): And now she calls me by name too. What's going on here?

MESSENIO (*to* MENAECHMUS II): She's got a whiff of that purse of yours.

MENAECHMUS II (*to* MESSENIO): You're probably right. Here, take it. (*Hands him the purse.*) Now I'll see which she loves, me or the money.

EROTIUM: Let's go in to dinner.

MENAECHMUS II. You are very kind, but (*backing away*) no thank you.

EROTIUM: But you just told me to fix a dinner for you.

MENAECHMUS II: I told you to?

EROTIUM: Why, yes, for you and your parasite.

MENAECHMUS II: What parasite, confound it? (*To* MESSENIO) She's crazy.

EROTIUM: Sponge.

MENAECHMUS II: What is this sponge you all keep talking about? You mean my shoe-sponge?

EROTIUM: No, of course I mean the Sponge who came with you when you brought me the dress you had stolen from your wife.

MENAECHMUS II: What? I gave you a dress that I had stolen from my wife? You're out of your mind! (*To* MESSENIO) Why, this woman dreams standing up, like a horse.

EROTIUM: Why do you make fun of me, and deny what you did?

MENAECHMUS II: Well, what *did* I do?

EROTIUM: You gave me a dress of your wife's, today.

MENAECHMUS II: I still deny it. I haven't got a wife and I never had one, and I never set foot in this house before. I had dinner on the boat, came ashore, walked by here, and ran into you.

EROTIUM (*frightened*): Oh, my goodness, what boat?

MENAECHMUS II: A wooden boat—oft sprung, oft plugged, oft
                        struck with maul,
                    And peg lies close by peg, as in a furrier's
                        frame.

EROTIUM: Oh, please stop joking and come in.

MENAECHMUS II: But madam, you are looking for somebody
else, not me.

EROTIUM: Do you think I don't know Menaechmus, son of
Moschus, born at Syracuse in Sicily where Agathocles was king,
and then Phintia, and then Liparo, who left it to Hiero, who is
king now? [5]

MENAECHMUS II: That's all correct.

MESSENIO (to MENAECHMUS II): Good lord, the woman can't
be from there herself, can she? She certainly has you down pat.

MENAECHMUS II (weakening): You know, I don't see how I
can refuse. (He starts towards the door.)

MESSENIO: Don't! If you go in there, you're done for!

MENAECHMUS II: Be quiet. Things are going nicely. Whatever
she says, I'll agree to it, and see if I can pick up some entertainment! (To EROTIUM) I've had a reason for contradicting you all
this time: I was afraid this man would tell my wife about the
dress and the dinner. But now let's go in, anytime you want.

EROTIUM: Are you going to wait for the parasite any longer?

MENAECHMUS II: No! I don't give a rap for him, and if he
comes I don't want him let in.

EROTIUM: That's quite all right with me. But there's something
I wish you'd do for me, will you?

MENAECHMUS II: Anything; command me.

EROTIUM: That dress you just gave me—take it to the place
where they do that lovely gold embroidery and get them to fix it
up and put on some new trimming.

MENAECHMUS II: Splendid idea! And that'll keep my wife from
recognising it, if she sees it on the street.

EROTIUM: You can take it with you when you go.

---

[5] This list of Syracusan rulers is incomplete and inaccurate. Agathocles
ruled from 317 to 289 B.C., Hiero from 265 to 215. Between them were
two princes, Hicetas and Pyrrhus. Phintia and Liparo are not known and
are doubtless inventions. [In short, Erotium is as much confused on
Sicilian history as she is on the Menaechmi.—Editor P. W. H.]

MENAECHMUS II: I certainly will!

EROTIUM: Let's go in.

MENAECHMUS II: I'll be right with you. I just want to speak to this man a minute. (EROTIUM *goes into her house.*) Hi there, Messenio, come here.

MESSENIO: What's going on here? Come to your senses! [6]

MENAECHMUS II: What for?

MESSENIO: Because—

MENAECHMUS II: Oh, I know, don't say it.

MESSENIO: So much the worse.

MENAECHMUS II: The booty is as good as in my hands right now; the siege has just begun! (*Pointing to the sailors*) Come on now, hustle these men off to an inn somewhere, and then come back for me here before sunset.

MESSENIO: Master, you don't know what these women are!

MENAECHMUS II: None of that! If I do anything foolish, it's my loss, not yours. This woman is a silly fool. The way things look so far, there's booty to be had! (*He goes into the house of* EROTIUM.)

MESSENIO: God help me! (*Calling after* MENAECHMUS II) Sir! (*To himself*) God help him, too! The pirate ship has got the pinnace steered straight on the rocks! But I'm a fool to expect to control my master. He bought me to obey him, not to give him orders. (*To the sailors*) Come along you, so I can come back and pick him up in time. Orders is orders! (*They depart.*)

[ACT THREE. SCENE I]

(*Enter* SPONGE *from the forum.*)

SPONGE (*to himself*): Here I am over thirty years old, but I never got into a worse mess than I did today. I pushed into the middle of the assembly, like a darn fool, and while I was watching things, Menaechmus sneaked away from me. He probably went off to his mistress and didn't want to take me.— Damn the man who first got the idea of holding assemblies and taking up the time of busy men! Why couldn't they pick people

---

[6] The text is corrupt at this point.

who aren't tied up for this sort of thing, and then if they didn't show up when the roll was called, they could pay a fine right off?[7] . . . There are plenty of men who only eat once a day and never get asked out to dinner or ask anyone else in. They're the ones who ought to have the job of sitting in assemblies and law courts. If things were run that way, I wouldn't have lost my dinner today. As sure as I'm alive, he would have given it to me. —I'll go on, anyway. Maybe there'll be something left, and just the idea makes my mouth water.

(*Enter* MENAECHMUS II *from* EROTIUM's *house, carrying the dress, very drunk.*)

But what's this? There's Menaechmus coming out with a wreath on. The dinner's over, and I've come just in time to take him home. I'll see what he's up to, and then go and speak to him. (*He withdraws.*)

[ACT THREE: SCENE 2]

MENAECHMUS II (*to* EROTIUM *within*): Oh, can't you keep quiet? I'll have it nicely fixed for you, all right, and I'll bring it back on time. I bet you won't recognise it, it'll be so different.

SPONGE (*aside*): He's taking the dress to the embroiderer's. He's finished his dinner, drunk his wine, and shut his parasite outside. I'll get even for this trick, all right, or my name's not Sponge! Just watch what's coming to him!

MENAECHMUS II (*to himself*): Gods above, did you ever give more luck in a single day to a man who didn't expect it? I wined and dined with the woman,* and got away with this thing (*indicating the dress*), and she won't ever see it again.

SPONGE: I can't hear what he's saying from over here. Is he full of food and talking about me and my dinner?

MENAECHMUS II: She said I stole this from my wife and gave it

---

[7] Lindsay indicates a lacuna after this speech.

* The full Latin text here should be translated "I dined and wined and laid the wench. . . ." The point is noteworthy since Shakespeare, too, cleans up the play a bit at this point: his dinner is quite respectable. —*Editor P. W. H.*

to her. The moment I saw she was wrong, I began to agree with her, as if we'd had some sort of deal. Whatever the woman said, I said too. Why waste words? I never had a better time at less expense.

SPONGE: I'm going up to the fellow. I'm itching to smack him one.

MENAECHMUS II: Who's this coming towards me?

SPONGE: What are you talking about, you feather-weight, you scum, you crook, you disgrace to humanity, you sneak, you bum? What did I ever do to you that you should wipe me out? So you sneaked away from me downtown a while ago, did you? And you had the funeral of the dinner when I wasn't there? How did you have the nerve, when it was mine as much as it was yours?

MENAECHMUS II: See here, young fellow, what's the idea of going around and insulting a perfect stranger like me? Are you an idiot? Or do you want to get beaten up for your words?

SPONGE: Huh! After the beating you've already given me!

MENAECHMUS II: Tell me, young fellow, what's your name?

SPONGE: Are you making fun of me too, as if you didn't know my name?

MENAECHMUS II: Well, as far as I know, I never saw you or knew of you before today. But let me tell you, whoever you are, if you want to do the right thing, don't make a nuisance of yourself.

SPONGE: Menaechmus, wake up!

MENAECHMUS II: Damn it, I am awake as far as I know.

SPONGE: You don't know me?

MENAECHMUS II: I wouldn't deny it if I did.

SPONGE: You don't know your own parasite?

MENAECHMUS II: I think you're not all there, young fellow.

SPONGE: Answer me this: did you steal that dress from your wife today and give it to Erotium?

MENAECHMUS II: Damn it, I haven't got any wife, and I didn't give any dress to Erotium or steal one.

SPONGE: Are *you* all there? (*Aside*) This thing's done for! (*To* MENAECHMUS II) Didn't I see you come out of there with a dress on?

MENAECHMUS II: Go to the devil! Do you think everybody is

a rotter just because you are? Do you mean to say that I had a dress on?

SPONGE: I do, all right.

MENAECHMUS II: Why don't you go where you belong, or else get yourself purified, you imbecile?

SPONGE (*furious*): By God, no one will ever stop me from telling your wife the whole business, just the way it happened. All your insults will come back on you. I'll see to it that you don't get away with eating that dinner. (*He goes into house of* ME-NAECHMUS I.)

MENAECHMUS II: What's the matter? Why is it that everyone I meet makes fun of me? But I hear the door opening.

[ACT THREE: SCENE 3]

(*Enter* MAID *from house of* EROTIUM *with a bracelet in her hand.*)

MAID: Menaechmus, Erotium says she would like to have you take this bracelet along to the jeweler's. She wants you to have an ounce of gold added to it and have it done over.

MENAECHMUS II: Tell her I'll tend to it and anything else she wants tended to, anything at all. (*He takes the bracelet.*)

MAID: Do you know what bracelet this is?

MENAECHMUS II: Only that it's a gold one.

MAID: It's the one you said once you stole from your wife's jewel-box.

MENAECHMUS II: I never did.

MAID: Come on, don't you remember? Give the bracelet back if you don't remember.

MENAECHMUS II: Wait a minute. Why, of course I remember. It must be the one I gave her. That's it. Where are the armlets I gave her with it?

MAID: You never gave her any.

MENAECHMUS II: Right you are; this was all I gave her.

MAID: I'll say you'll tend to it, then?

MENAECHMUS II: Yes, it'll be tended to. I'll see that the dress and the bracelet are brought back together.

MAID (*coaxingly*): Please, Menaechmus dear, give me some earrings. Have them made to weigh two nummi. Then I'll be glad to see you when you come to see us.

MENAECHMUS II: Surely. Give me the gold and I'll pay for the work.

MAID: Oh, please, *you* give the gold, and I'll pay you back later.

MENAECHMUS II: No, you give it. Later I'll pay you back double.

MAID: I haven't got any.

MENAECHMUS II: Well, when you get some, give it to me then.

MAID: Anything else, sir?

MENAECHMUS II: Tell her I'll tend to the things (*to himself, as the* MAID *goes inside*) and sell 'em for all they'll bring. Has she gone in? Yes: the door's shut. The gods are certainly supporting and supplying and sustaining me. But what am I waiting for when I've got a good chance to get away from this woman's place? Hurry up, Menaechmus. Forward, march! I'll take off this wreath and throw it away towards the left; then if they follow me, they'll think I've gone that way. I'll go and find my slave, if I can, and tell him myself about the luck the gods are giving me. (*He departs in the direction of the harbour.*)

[ACT FOUR: SCENE I]

(*Enter* WIFE *and* SPONGE *from house of* MENAECHMUS I.)

WIFE: How can I put up with married life any longer? My husband sneaks off with anything there is in the house and carries it off to his mistress.

SPONGE: Oh, keep quiet. I'll show you how to catch him with the goods. He had on a wreath, he was reeling drunk, and he was taking the dress he stole from you today to the embroiderer's. But look, there's the wreath. Now will you believe me? See, this is the way he went, if you want to track him down. (*Looking down the street*) Well, for heaven's sake, there he is now, coming back. But he hasn't got the dress.

wife: What'll I do to him now?

sponge: The same as usual—treat him rough. That's my advice. Let's get over here and hide from him. (*They step aside.*)

[ACT FOUR: SCENE 2]

(*Enter* MENAECHMUS I *from the forum.*)

menaechmus: It's a very silly fashion and an awful nuisance, too,
That all of us obey, especially the well-to-do.
We want a lot of hangers-on, who may be good or bad:
Reputation doesn't matter when there's money to be had.
You may be poor and honest—as a fool you're sent away.
But if you're rich and wicked, you're a worthy protégé.
The lawless man, who when he's trusted with a thing will swear
He never saw it—that's the man for whom we patrons care:
The contentious man, the trickster, who by means of perjury
Or bribes supports a life of lawsuits, greed, and luxury.
But the patron has no holiday when law-days are decreed;
He must defend the guilty man and see that he is freed.
In just this way was I detained today by one poor sinner,
And now I've missed my mistress, to say nothing of my dinner.
I spoke before the aediles to allay their just suspicions,
And proposed a set of intricate and tortuous conditions
Which, if we could have proved 'em, would have surely won the
          case.
But then this brainless boob brought in a bondsman to the place!
I'm sure I never saw a man more clearly caught than he:
Three witnesses were there who swore to all his deviltry.
May heaven destroy the man who's made a ruin so complete
Of all my day—and me, who in the law-courts set my feet!
As soon as it was possible, I came directly here.
I've ordered dinner, and she's waiting for me; yet I fear
          She's mad at me now.
             But the dress ought to move her
          That I stole from my wife
             And took to my lover.

SPONGE (*aside to* WIFE): What have you got to say now?

WIFE: I'm blessed with a bad marriage and a bad husband.

SPONGE: Do you hear what he's saying all right?

WIFE: I should say so.

MENAECHMUS I: Now the best thing for me to do is to go in here where I can have a good time. (*He starts towards* EROTIUM'S *door, but* SPONGE *stops him.*)

SPONGE: Just a minute. You'll have a bad time first.

WIFE: You'll pay interest on what you stole, I promise you.

SPONGE: Now he's getting it.

WIFE: So you thought you could get away with all that crooked business, did you?

MENAECHMUS I: What's the matter, dear?

WIFE: That's a fine thing to ask *me!*

MENAECHMUS I: Do you want me to ask *him,* then? (*He attempts to fondle* WIFE.)

WIFE: Cut out the pawing!

SPONGE: Keep after him, ma'am!

MENAECHMUS I: Why are you angry at me?

WIFE: You ought to know.

SPONGE: He does, the scum, but he's making out he doesn't.

MENAECHMUS I: What's the matter?

WIFE: A dress.

MENAECHMUS I: A dress?

WIFE: A dress that someone—

SPONGE: What are you shaking about?

MENAECHMUS I: I'm not shaking about anything.

SPONGE: Only this: the dress does impress!—You would sneak away from me and eat dinner! (*To* WIFE) Keep after the fellow!

MENAECHMUS I: Won't you shut up?

SPONGE: No, by George, I will not shut up. (*To* WIFE) He's shaking his head at me to shut up.

MENAECHMUS I: I am not, or winking either.

WIFE: Oh dear, I am an unhappy woman!

MENAECHMUS I: Why unhappy? Tell me about it.

SPONGE: What a nerve! Why, he won't admit a thing is so when you can see it is.

MENAECHMUS I: By Jupiter and all the gods (is that enough for you, dear?) I swear I didn't shake my head at him.

SPONGE: She'll believe you about that. Now get back to business.

MENAECHMUS I: What business?

SPONGE: Oh, maybe the embroiderer's. And give back the dress.

MENAECHMUS I: What dress are you talking about?

SPONGE: Oh, I give up! He can't even remember his own affairs.

MENAECHMUS I (to WIFE): Has one of the slaves been cutting up? Are the maids or the menservants answering back? Tell me. They won't get away with it.

WIFE: Nonsense!

MENAECHMUS I: She's really mad. I don't like this much—

WIFE: Nonsense!

MENAECHMUS I: You must be angry with one of the servants.

WIFE: Nonsense!

MENAECHMUS I: Well, are you angry with me, then?

WIFE: Now that's not nonsense.

MENAECHMUS I: What the devil! I haven't done anything.

WIFE: More nonsense again!

MENAECHMUS I: Tell me, my dear, what's upsetting you?

SPONGE: Apple-sauce!

MENAECHMUS I: Can't you quit bothering me? Do you think I'm talking to you? (He goes to WIFE.)

WIFE: Take away your hand.

SPONGE: Now you're getting it. Go and eat dinner without me, will you? Then come out drunk, with a wreath on your head, and make fun of me in front of the house, will you?

MENAECHMUS I: What the devil! I haven't had dinner or set foot in that house today.

SPONGE: Do you mean to say that?

MENAECHMUS I: I certainly do.

SPONGE: This fellow's the worst yet. Didn't I just see you standing here in front of the house with a wreath on? You said I wasn't all there and you didn't know me and you were a foreigner.

MENAECHMUS I: See here, since I left you, I haven't been home until just now.

SPONGE: Oh, I know you. You didn't think I had any way of getting even with you. All right for you—I've told everything to your wife.

MENAECHMUS I: What did you tell her?

SPONGE: I don't know; ask her yourself.

MENAECHMUS I (*to* WIFE): What's the matter, dear? What stories has he been telling you? What is it? Why don't you **say** something? Why don't you tell me what's the matter?

WIFE: As if you didn't know! A dress has been stolen from **me** out of the house.

MENAECHMUS I: A dress has been stolen from you?

WIFE: Are you asking me?

MENAECHMUS I: Well, I certainly wouldn't be asking you if I knew.

SPONGE: Look at the man! What a snake in the grass! You can't hide anything; she knows the whole story. I spilled everything, all right.

MENAECHMUS I (*to* WIFE): What's the matter?

WIFE: Well, since you're not ashamed and won't own up yourself, listen and learn. I'll explain what I'm angry about and what he told me. A dress has been stolen from me out of the house.

MENAECHMUS I: A dress has been stolen from me?

SPONGE (*to* WIFE): See how the fellow's trying to catch you. (*To* MENAECHMUS I) It was stolen from her, not from you. Now if it had really been stolen from you—it wouldn't be all right.

MENAECHMUS I: I'm not dealing with you. (*To* WIFE) What have you got to say, madam?

WIFE: A dress, I tell you, is gone from the house.

MENAECHMUS I: Who stole it?

WIFE: I expect the person who stole it knows that.

MENAECHMUS I: Who is this person?

WIFE: Somebody named Menaechmus.

MENAECHMUS I: It's a dirty trick. But who is this Menaechmus?

WIFE: You, I tell you.

MENAECHMUS I: Me?

WIFE: Yes, you.

MENAECHMUS I: Who says so?

WIFE: I do.

SPONGE: So do I. And you took the thing over to your friend Erotium.

MENAECHMUS I: What? I gave it to her?

WIFE: Yes, you, you, I say.

SPONGE: Do you want us to get an owl to keep on saying, "You, you!" to you? We're getting tired, you see.

MENAECHMUS I: By Jupiter and all the gods (is that enough for you my dear?) I swear I didn't give—

SPONGE: All right, and we swear we're not lying.

MENAECHMUS I: But I didn't give it to her; I only lent it.

WIFE: Maybe you did, but I certainly never lend your dress suit or your overcoat to anybody. It's the wife's business to lend her clothes, and the husband's to lend his. Now go and bring that dress back home.

MENAECHMUS I: I'll get it back.

WIFE: Well, you'd better. You won't get into this house again unless you bring my dress with you. I'm going home.

SPONGE: What do I get for going to so much trouble for you?

WIFE: You'll be repaid when something is stolen from your house. (*She goes inside.*)

SPONGE: That'll never happen; I haven't got anything at home to lose. Damn the husband and the wife, too! I'll go along downtown. I can see I'm done with this family. (*He departs.*)

MENAECHMUS I (*to himself*): My wife thinks she's punished me by shutting me out—as if I didn't have a better place to go where they'd let me in. If you don't like me, that's your hard luck; Erotium here likes me. She won't shut me out from her; she'll shut me in *with* her. Now I'll go and ask her to give back that dress I gave her this morning. I'll buy her a better one. (*Knocking at* EROTIUM's *door*) Hey, there, where's the doorman? Open the door, somebody, and call Erotium outside.

[ACT FOUR: SCENE 3]

(*Enter* EROTIUM *from her house.*)

EROTIUM: Who is asking for me?

MENAECHMUS I: More of an enemy to himself than to your tender years.

EROTIUM: Menaechmus, my love, why are you standing out there? Come on in.

MENAECHMUS I: In just a minute. Do you know what I've come to see you for?

EROTIUM: Why, of course: to enjoy yourself with me.

MENAECHMUS I: No; it's that dress I gave you this morning. Be a good girl and give it back to me. I'll buy you any dress you want, twice as expensive.

EROTIUM: Why, I just gave it to you to take to the embroiderer's. I gave you the bracelet, you know, too, to take to the jeweler's to be done over.

MENAECHMUS I: How could you have given me the dress and the bracelet? I gave you the dress just a little while ago and went downtown, and this is the first time I've come back and seen you since then.

EROTIUM: Oh, I see your game. You're trying to cheat me out of what I let you take.

MENAECHMUS I: No, no, I'm not asking for the dress to cheat you. I tell you, my wife's found out about it.

EROTIUM (*angrily*): And I didn't ask you to give it to me in the first place. You brought it to me yourself, and you gave it to me for a present. And now you want it back. All right. Have the old thing. Take it. Wear it yourself, or let your wife wear it, or lock it up in a trunk if you want to. After today you won't set foot inside this house again—don't fool yourself. You trifler with the affections of an innocent woman! Unless you bring me money, you haven't got a chance to see me again. Now go and find some other poor girl you can deceive. (*She goes into her house.*)

MENAECHMUS I: Say, she's really mad this time. (*Rushing to her door*) Hey there, wait a minute, I tell you. Come back. Won't you stay? Won't you please come back for my sake? (*To himself*) She's gone in and closed the door. Now I am the most shut out of men! They won't believe anything I say at home or at my mistress's. I'll go and see what my friends think I'd better do about this. (*He departs in the direction of the forum.*)

[ACT FIVE: SCENE I]

(*Enter* MENAECHMUS II *along the street; he still has the dress.*)

MENAECHMUS II (*to himself*): That was a fool thing I did a while ago, giving Messenio the purse with all my money in it. He's landed himself in a clip-joint somewhere, for sure.

(*Enter* WIFE *from her house.*)

WIFE (*to herself*): I'll just have a look outside; that husband of mine should be back soon. Ah ha, there he is. And he's bringing back the dress. That's just fine.

MENAECHMUS II (*to himself*): I wonder where Messenio can be headed now.

WIFE (*to herself*): I'll step up and give him the welcome he deserves. (*Aloud*) You scoundrel, how dare you come into my sight with that dress?

MENAECHMUS II: Huh? What's the matter, lady, seen a ghost?

WIFE: Impudence, how dare you utter one single syllable? How dare you speak to me?

MENAECHMUS II: Here, what have *I* done? Why shouldn't I?

WIFE: You ask me! The cheek, the impudence of the man!

MENAECHMUS II: I suppose you know why the Greeks used to call Hecuba the bitch?

WIFE: *No!*

MENAECHMUS II: Because she acted just like you: she showered abuse on everybody in sight. That's how she got to be called the bitch—and she deserved it, too.

WIFE: This is outrageous! I won't stand for it! No husband is worth it. It's outrageous!

MENAECHMUS II: What's it to me? You can't stand marriage, you're going to leave your husband—what is it, the custom of the country to babble this kind of nonsense to perfect strangers?

WIFE: Babble? I won't stand for this a minute longer. I'll get a divorce.

MENAECHMUS II: *Get* a divorce. As far as I care, you can stay single till hell freezes over.

WIFE (*pointing to the dress*): And a minute ago you denied you stole this from me, and now you dangle it under my very nose. Haven't you any shame?

MENAECHMUS II: My God, woman, you certainly have an awful nerve. I didn't steal this dress from you. Another woman gave it to me; she wanted me to get it made over for her.

WIFE: That settles it! I'm going to send for my father and tell him how outrageously you behave. (*Calls into the house to a slave.*) Decio! Go find my father and bring him here to me. Tell him it's important! (*To* MENAECHMUS II) I'll tell him how outrageous you are.

MENAECHMUS II: Are you insane? What do you mean, outrageous?

WIFE: You steal dresses and jewelry from your wife and take them to your mistress! And that's not babbling, either!

MENAECHMUS II: I wish you'd tell me some good medicine for me to take against that tongue of yours! I don't know who you think I am, but I don't know you from Hercules' wife's grandfather.

WIFE (*pointing down the street*): You may make fun of me, but not of *him*—my father! Here he comes. Look at him. Do you know *him*?

MENAECHMUS II: Oh yes, I remember meeting the two of you the same day I met Methuselah.

WIFE: You deny you know me? And my father too?

MENAECHMUS II: And your grandfather too, if you want to drag him in.

WIFE: You're impossible and always were.

[ACT FIVE: SCENE 2]

(*Enter* FATHER.)

FATHER: As fast as my age will permit and this business requires, I'm getting along,
But if some of you think that it's easy for me, very briefly I'll prove that you're wrong.
My body's a burden, my nimbleness gone, and of strength I've a notable lack,

I'm quite overgrown with my years—oh, confounded old age is
     a curse on the back!
Why, if I were to tell all the terrible evils that age, when it
     comes, brings along,
I'm certain as certain can be that past suitable limits I'd lengthen
     this song.
However, my mind is a little disturbed at this thing, for it seems
     a bit queer
That my daughter should suddenly send to my house with direc-
     tions for me to come here.
And how this affair is related to me, she has not let me know up
     to now;
But I'm a good guesser, and I'm pretty sure that her husband
     and she've had a row.
That's what usually happens when men are enslaved by their
     wives and must come when they call;
And then it's the wives who are mostly to blame, while the
     husbands aren't guilty at all.
And yet there are bounds, which we all must observe, to the
     things that a wife can endure,
And a woman won't call in her father unless the offence of her
     husband is sure.
But I think very soon the suspense will be over, and then I'll
     know what is the matter—
But look, there's my daughter in front of the door, and her hus-
     band; he's not looking at her.
               It's just as I suspected.
I'll start with her.
     WIFE (*to herself*): I'll go to meet him. (*To* FATHER) How do
you do, father.
     FATHER: How d'ye do, how d'ye do. Now what's this how
d'ye do? Why did you send for me? What are you so sad about?
Why is he standing off from you angry? The two of you have
had a fight. Tell me, which of you is in the wrong? But be brief
about it: no long speeches.
     WIFE: I haven't done anything, not a thing, believe me. But
I can't live here, I just can't stand it. Take me away!
     FATHER: Eh, what's this?
     WIFE: He makes a laughingstock of me.

FATHER: Who does?

WIFE: The man you entrusted me to—my husband!

FATHER: Tch, tch, tch! A squabble! How many times have I told you not to come to me with your complaints, either of you?

WIFE: How can I help it, father?

FATHER: You ask me that!

WIFE (*timidly*): Yes.

FATHER: I've told you often enough—humour your husband, don't always have your eye on what he's doing, where he's going, what he's up to.

WIFE: But he has a mistress, right next door!

FATHER: Sensible man. And the more you make of it, the more he'll love her. No doubt of it.

WIFE: And he drinks there too.

FATHER: Suppose it's there, suppose it's somewhere else: can you stop him? Confound your impudence! Why not forbid him to go out to dinner, or to have his friends in for a meal? Do you want husbands to be slaves? You might as well give him piece work, and make him sit with the maids and card wool.

WIFE: Father, I brought you here to be *my* lawyer, not his, but now you're arguing on his side instead of mine.

FATHER: If he's been at fault in any way, I'll be much harder on him than I was on you. But he keeps you in clothes and jewelry, and gives you proper food and service, and so you oughtn't to be so fussy about things, my girl.

WIFE: But he steals my jewelry and dresses right out of the house! He takes all my nice things and sneaks them off to his mistress!

FATHER: If he's up to that, he's up to no good; if he's not up to that, *you*'re up to no good; that would be slander.

WIFE: But, father, he has the dress this very minute, and the bracelet he took her, too; he's bringing them back because I found out.

FATHER: I must have his account of it now. I'll speak to him. (*To* MENAECHMUS II) Tell me, Menaechmus, what are you two quarreling for? What are you so sad about? Why is she standing off from you angry?

MENAECHMUS II (*in legal style*): Old man, whoever you may be, by highest Jupiter and the gods I swear—

FATHER: Well sworn. But what?

MENAECHMUS II: —firstly, that I have done no wrong to this your daughter who accuses me of stealing and purloining from her house this dress—

WIFE: Perjury!

MENAECHMUS II: —and secondly, if I have ever set my foot within the house in which she lives, I pray that I may be the most miserable of miserable men.

FATHER: That's a fool's prayer, if you deny you ever set foot in the house you live in, you utter madman.

MENAECHMUS II: Old man, do you say I live in that house?

FATHER: Do you deny it?

MENAECHMUS II: I deny it and that's the truth.

FATHER: No, no, you deny it and it's *not* the truth. Unless, of course, you've moved since yesterday. (*To* WIFE) Come here, daughter. Tell me, you haven't moved, have you?

WIFE: For goodness sake, what for, and where to?

FATHER: I don't know.

WIFE: He's playing games with you. Don't you see?

FATHER: Menaechmus, that's enough joking. Now get down to business.

MENAECHMUS II (*hotly*): What business have we got to get down to? Who are you, anyway? You haven't got anything on me, and neither has that daughter of yours; and besides, she's a first class pest.

WIFE (*frightened, to* FATHER): Look at the green in his eyes! He's getting green in the face! See how his eyes glitter!

MENAECHMUS II (*aside*): Fine! They say I'm crazy: I'll pretend I *am*, and scare them away! (*He starts a mad-scene.*)

WIFE: See how he stretches and gapes! What shall I do, father?

FATHER: Come over here, child; keep as far away from him as you can.

MENAECHMUS II: Hola hola, Bromius! You call me to the forest, to the hunt? I hear; but I cannot leave this place: I am beset upon the left by this rabid bitch-woman, and behind her is that stinking goat who ruins innocent citizens with perjury.

FATHER: Woe to your head!

MENAECHMUS II: Lo! Apollo from his oracle bids me burn her eyes out with flaming torches!

WIFE: Help, father! He's threatening to burn my eyes out!

MENAECHMUS II (*aside*): Ha, they think I'm crazy, but they're the crazy ones.

FATHER: Psst! Daughter!

WIFE: What?

FATHER: What shall we do? Suppose I get some slaves. Yes, they can grab him and chain him up in the house before he raises any more commotion.

MENAECHMUS II (*aside*): Caught! If I don't work fast, they'll have me carried into the house with them. (*Aloud*) Yes, Apollo? I must punch her face in with my fists unless she gets the hell out of my sight? I'll do your orders!

FATHER: Run home as fast as you can, or he'll smack you.

WIFE (*retreating to her house*): Please, father, watch him, don't let him get away! That I should live to hear such language! Poor me! (*She goes into her house.*)

MENAECHMUS II (*aside*): I fixed her all right! Now for the other one. (*Aloud*) Now this dirty wretch, this bearded tremulous Tithonus, this son of Cycnus;[8] you want me to take that staff he has and beat him to pieces, joint from joint and bone from bone and limb from limb?

FATHER (*retreating*): If you touch me or come a step closer, there'll be trouble.

MENAECHMUS II: I'll do your orders: I'll take a double axe and hack this old fellow's guts to mincemeat, down to the very bone.

FATHER: Then I must beware and take care of myself. The way he threatens me, I'm afraid he will do me harm.

MENAECHMUS II: New commands, Apollo! Now I am to yoke my wild ungovernable horses and mount my chariot, to trample down this stinking old toothless lion! Now I stand in the chariot; now I have the reins; now the goad is in my hand. Forward, my steeds! Ring out the clatter of your hoofs! Fleet feet, speed swift with tireless tumult!

FATHER: Threaten me with a chariot!

MENAECHMUS II: Another charge at him, Apollo, to the death?

---

[8] Lindsay reads *Titanum* here with the Mss. Most editors prefer *Tithonum;* Tithonus was granted immortality but not eternal youth, and his name became proverbial for age and infirmity. He was the son of Laomedon; the mistake was probably intentional on the part of Plautus.

(*Pretending to have a change of fit*) But who is this who drags me from the chariot by the hair? O edict of Apollo, thy command is maimed! (*He falls and is still.*)

FATHER (*to himself*): A violent and severe disease! [9] . . . The gods preserve us from the like. See now, how strong he was a moment since, and now is mad with sudden access of disease. I'll go and get a doctor, as fast as I can. (*He departs.*)[10]

MENAECHMUS II (*rising*): Are they out of sight, I wonder, these people that make me pretend I'm crazy? I'd better get back to the ship while the going is good. (*To the audience*) Please, all of you, if the old man comes back, don't tell him which way I went. (*He departs. Considerable time is supposed to elapse before the next scene.*)

[ACT FIVE: SCENE 3]

(*Enter* FATHER.)

FATHER: I've got pains in my back and pains in my eyes, waiting and watching for the doctor to be free. He didn't want to leave his patients; I had a hard time persuading him to come. He says he set a broken leg for Aesculapius and a broken arm for Apollo.[11] Have I got a doctor, I wonder, or a joiner? Here he comes now. Get along, you ant!

[ACT FIVE: SCENE 4]

(*Enter the* DOCTOR.)

DOCTOR: Tell me, sir, what did you say was his disease? Has he hallucinations, or madness? Pray inform me. Has he the lethargy, or the subcutaneous humours?

FATHER: That's what I brought you here for: to tell me what's wrong with him, and cure him.

---

[9] There is a short lacuna in the text here.

[10] Lindsay begins Act Five, Scene 3 at this point.

[11] This is all the more amusing, since both Aesculapius and Apollo were gods of healing.

DOCTOR: Ah, that is quite simple. He shall be cured, I promise you.

FATHER: I want a careful treatment for him; spare no pains.

DOCTOR: No pains shall be spared; why, I will spend at least six hundred sighs a day on it.

FATHER (*seeing* MENAECHMUS I *approaching*): Here he comes himself. Let's watch him.

[ACT FIVE: SCENE 5]

(*Enter* MENAECHMUS I, *not seeing the others.*)

MENAECHMUS I (*to himself*): What a day! Everything going wrong, and getting me in wrong! I thought I was getting away with something; but that parasite of mine has let it all out and made a quaking criminal of me—the smart alec, biting the hand that feeds him. Sure as I live, it'll cost him his life. I'm a fool to call it *his* life though; it's mine: he lives on me and what I feed him. Well then, I'll cut his greedy throat. My mistress was just as bad; these girls are all alike. When I asked for the dress so I could take it back to my wife, she pretended she'd given it to me already. Ugh! I certainly lead a miserable life!

FATHER (*to* DOCTOR): Can you hear what he's saying?

DOCTOR: He says he is miserable.

FATHER: Go on up to him.

DOCTOR (*complying*): Good afternoon, Menaechmus. Tch tch, why do you leave your arm uncovered like that? Don't you know how bad that is for a man in your condition?

MENAECHMUS I: Go hang yourself! (*The* DOCTOR *retreats.*)

FATHER: Notice anything?

DOCTOR: Notice anything! This case will take an *acre* of hellebore, at least! [12] (*Returning to* MENAECHMUS I) Now, Menaechmus—

MENAECHMUS I: Well?

DOCTOR: Just a few questions, please. Do you drink red wine or white wine?

MENAECHMUS I: Why not ask about the bread I eat, if it's

---

[12] Hellebore was used by the ancients as a remedy for insanity.

purple, pink, or scarlet? Or whether I eat scaly birds and feathered fish?

FATHER: My goodness, hear the way he raves! Hurry up and give him some medicine before he goes completely crazy.

DOCTOR: Just a minute; I want to finish my questions.

FATHER: You talk a man to death.

DOCTOR (*to* MENAECHMUS I): Tell me, are you ever troubled with a hardening of the eyes?

MENAECHMUS I: What, you idiot! Do you take me for a lobster?

DOCTOR: Tell me this: are you subject to rumbling of the bowels—as far as you know?

MENAECHMUS I: After a good meal, no; but if I'm hungry, then they do.

DOCTOR (*aside*): Nothing crazy in that answer. (*To* MENAECHMUS I) Do you sleep soundly all night? Do you fall asleep readily on retiring?

MENAECHMUS I: I sleep like a log—if I've paid my bills! (*Losing his temper*) Oh, the devil take you and all your questions!

DOCTOR (*to* FATHER): The madness is beginning. You hear the way he talks; be careful.

FATHER: Why he's talking like a perfect Nestor now, compared to the way he was a little while ago. Just a few minutes ago he called his wife a rabid bitch.

MENAECHMUS I: I said *what?*

FATHER: You were raving, I say.

MENAECHMUS I: *I* was raving?

FATHER: Yes, *you*. And you threatened to run over me with a chariot. I saw you; I accuse you.

MENAECHMUS I (*furious*): And you stole a wreath out of the temple of Jupiter, I know, and you were thrown into jail for it, I know, and after you were let out of there you were strung up and whipped, I know, and you murdered your father and sold your mother into slavery, I know. Right back at you with your dirty insults! I'm sane enough for that, all right.

FATHER: For God's sake, doctor, hurry! Whatever you're going to do, do it. Don't you see the man is raving?

DOCTOR: The best thing for you to do is to have him taken to my house.

FATHER: You think so?

DOCTOR: Definitely. Then I'll have a free hand with his treatment.

FATHER: Just as you like.

DOCTOR (*gloatingly, to* MENAECHMUS I): I'll have you drinking hellebore for something like three weeks!

MENAECHMUS I (*savagely*): And I'll have you strung up and jabbed with ox-goads for a month!

DOCTOR (*to* FATHER): Get some men to bring him there.

FATHER: How many?

DOCTOR: Judging by the extent of his madness, four; no less.

FATHER: They'll be right here. (*Starts to go.*) Watch him, doctor.

DOCTOR (*hurriedly*): No no; I must go back and get things ready. Tell the slaves to bring him to me.

FATHER: I'll have him there right away.

DOCTOR: I'm on my way. (*The* DOCTOR *hurries down the street.*)

FATHER: Good bye. (*The* FATHER *departs.*)

MENAECHMUS I (*to himself*): Father-in-law gone, doctor gone; now I'm alone. Good God, why do these people say I'm crazy? All my life I've never had a day's illness; I don't lose my head and pick fights, or lawsuits either. I lead a normal life with normal people; I recognise my friends, and talk to them. Must be that *they're* crazy, the ones that say I am. What do I do now? I want to go home, but my wife won't have it. And I can't get in here. (*He points to the house of* EROTIUM.) A nice situation! I'll be stuck here forever! Well, maybe I'll get in at home by nightfall.

[ACT FIVE: SCENE 6]

(*Enter* MESSENIO.)

MESSENIO (*to himself, not seeing* MENAECHMUS I):
    It's a proof of an excellent slave,
    If, his master's belongings to save,
        He'll use as much care
        When his master's not there

As when master is watching the slave.
For his back and his shins he must fear,
The demands of his stomach not hear,
   And the punishment know
   Of the slothful and slow—
This servant whose conscience is clear.
There are beatings, and chains, and the mills,
Hunger, weariness, terrible chills—
   The reward of the lazy;
   But since I'm not crazy
I'm good, and avoid all these ills.

I can stand a tongue-lashing, but I don't like a whip-lashing; and
I'd rather eat the meal than turn the mill. So I obey my master;
it's worth my while. Others can take the easy way if they want
to; I'll take the hard way. I'll keep out of trouble by worrying
about being on the spot wherever my master needs me. Slaves
who worry while they're *out* of trouble are the ones that serve
their masters best: because the ones who don't worry then still
have plenty to worry about when they're *in* trouble, but then the
harm's done. But I don't have to worry much—my master will
reward me before long. Beware of a beating, that's my motto. I've
left the baggage and the slaves at an inn as he ordered, and now
I'm back to meet him. I'll knock and let him know I'm here, in
hopes I'm in time to get him safely out of this pirate lair. But I'm
afraid the fight may be over already. (*He goes toward* EROTIUM'S
door.)

[ACT FIVE: SCENE 7]

(*Enter* FATHER *with* SLAVES. MESSENIO *withdraws to one side.*)

FATHER (*to* SLAVES): Now by all that's holy, don't bungle
your orders. I repeat: pick that man up and carry him to the
doctor's, or your shanks and sides will smart for it. Pay no attention to his threats. Why do you stand there? What are you
waiting for? You should have had him up and off already. I'm
going to the doctor's; I'll be there when you come. (*He departs.*)

MENAECHMUS I (*finding himself surrounded*): Good lord, what's going on here? Why are these men making for me? What do you want? What are you after? Why are you surrounding me? Why are you grabbing me? Where are you taking me? Murder! Help! Good folk of Epidamnus, help! Let me go!

MESSENIO: Great heaven, what is this I see? A gang of strangers carrying off my master! Shame!

MENAECHMUS I: Doesn't anybody dare help me?

MESSENIO: I do, master, I dare most daringly! (*To the audience*)

> Oh! What an outrageous crime I see!
> Epidamnians, this man was free,
> My master, when he came today;
> And now they're carrying him away,
> While you're at peace, by light of day!

(*To the* SLAVES) Let go of him!

MENAECHMUS I: I implore you, stranger, help me! Make them stop this criminal outrage!

MESSENIO: You bet I will! I'll be your helper, your defender, your ally! I won't let them murder you; better me than you. That one who has you by the shoulder, gouge out his eye. I'll garden up these fellows' faces and plant my fists there. (*General scuffle*) Try to kidnap him, would you? This is what you get for it! Hands off him!

MENAECHMUS I: I've got him by the eye.

MESSENIO: Gouge it out! (*To* SLAVES) Villains! Robbers! Bandits!

SLAVES: Murder! Stop, for God's sake!

MESSENIO: Then let go of him! (*The* SLAVES *drop* MENAECHMUS I.)

MENAECHMUS I: Take your hands off me! (*To* MESSENIO) Keep on hoeing with those fists.

MESSENIO: Go, beat it! Get the devil out of here! Here's a prize for *you,* for being the last to go! (*The* SLAVES *run off.*) I mapped out those faces pretty well, I think! Well, master, I got here just in time, didn't I?

MENAECHMUS I: May heaven reward you, young man. If it

hadn't been for you, I'd never have lived to see the sun go down today.

MESSENIO: Well then, if you did the right thing, you'd set me free.

MENAECHMUS I: I'd set you free?

MESSENIO: Yes master, because I saved your life.

MENAECHMUS I: What is this? Young man, you are mistaken.

MESSENIO: What do you mean?

MENAECHMUS I: By father Jupiter, I swear I am not your master.

MESSENIO: You're joking!

MENAECHMUS I: No, I mean it. And no slave of mine ever served me as well as you have.

MESSENIO: Then if you say I don't belong to you, let me go free.

MENAECHMUS I: So far as I am concerned, I declare you free to go anywhere you want.

MESSENIO: My Patron! "Congratulations on your freedom, Messenio." "Thank you." But please, Patron, I'm still at your service just as much as when I was your slave. I'll live with you and go with you when you go back home.

MENAECHMUS I (to himself): I guess not!

MESSENIO: I'll go to the inn now and get your baggage and the money. The purse and the passage-money are sealed up safely in your bag. I'll have it all here right away.

MENAECHMUS I: Do, by all means.

MESSENIO: I'll give it back to you all safe, just as you gave it to me. Wait for me here. (He departs.)

MENAECHMUS I (to himself): A lot of strange things have certainly been happening to me today in strange ways. People denying that I am I, and locking me out of the house; and then this fellow saying he was my slave, and I set him free; and now he says he'll bring me a bag of money. If he does, I'll tell him he's free to go wherever he wants, so that when he comes to his senses he won't try to get the money back. And my father-in-law and the doctor saying I was insane! Heavens knows what it all means; it all seems like a dream.—Well, I'll try at Erotium's again. I suppose she's still angry at me, but I've got to try to get that dress and take it home. (He goes into the house of EROTIUM.)

[ACT FIVE: SCENE 8]

(*Enter* MENAECHMUS II *with* MESSENIO.)

MENAECHMUS II: You brazen rascal, you dare tell me you've seen me anywhere today since I told you to come here?

MESSENIO: Why, I rescued you just a few minutes ago, when four men were carrying you off bodily, right in front of this very house. You were yelling for help to all heaven and earth, and I ran up and rescued you with my fists, in spite of them. And you set me free, because I saved your life. I said I'd get the money and the luggage, and then you doubled round the block so you could meet me and deny the whole thing!

MENAECHMUS II: I set you free?

MESSENIO: You did.

MENAECHMUS II: I'd turn slave myself sooner than free you. And that's that!

[ACT FIVE: SCENE 9]

(*Enter* MENAECHMUS I *from the house of* EROTIUM.)

MENAECHMUS I (*to those within*): Swear by your eyes if you want to, but you did *not* give me the dress or the bracelet either, you trollops!

MESSENIO: Immortal gods, what's this I see!

MENAECHMUS II: What do you see?

MESSENIO: Your mirror!

MENAECHMUS II: What's this?

MESSENIO: He's the very image of you, as like as can be.

MENAECHMUS II: Well! He's certainly not unlike me, now that I take stock of myself.

MENAECHMUS I (*catching sight of* MESSENIO): Oh, the young man who saved my life. How are you?

MESSENIO: Please sir, if you don't mind, tell me what your name is, for goodness sake!

MENAECHMUS I: Indeed I don't mind, after what you did for me. My name is Menaechmus.

MENAECHMUS II: No, that's *my* name.

MENAECHMUS I: I am a Sicilian, from Syracuse.

MENAECHMUS II: That's where *I* come from.

MENAECHMUS I: What's that?

MENAECHMUS II: That's the truth.

MESSENIO (*pointing to the wrong man,* MENAECHMUS I): This is the man I know, of course, this is my master. I'm his slave, but I thought I was that other man's. (*To* MENAECHMUS I) I thought he was you, and bothered him. (*To* MENAECHMUS II) Please excuse me if I said anything foolish without realising it.

MENAECHMUS II: You must be crazy. Don't *you* remember leaving the ship with me today?

MESSENIO (*to* MENAECHMUS II): You are right. *You* are my master. (*To* MENAECHMUS I) *You* must look for another slave. (*To* MENAECHMUS II) Greetings to you. (*To* MENAECHMUS I) Good bye to you. (*Pointing to* MENAECHMUS II) I say *this* man is Menaechmus.

MENAECHMUS I: But I say *I* am.

MENAECHMUS II: What is this nonsense? *You* Menaechmus?

MENAECHMUS I: Yes; Menaechmus, son of Moschus.

MENAECHMUS II: The son of my father?

MENAECHMUS I: No, sir, mine, not yours. You may have your father; I don't want to deprive you of him.

MESSENIO (*to himself*): Immortal gods, fulfil this unhoped-for hope! Unless my mind has failed me, these are the two twin brothers! Both of them claim the same father and country. I'll tell my master about it first. (*Aloud*) Menaechmus!

MENAECHMUS I *and* II (*together*): What is it?

MESSENIO: I don't want both of you; just the one that came with me on the boat.

MENAECHMUS I: I didn't.

MENAECHMUS II: I did.

MESSENIO: Then it's you I want. (*Drawing him to one side*) Come over here.

MENAECHMUS II: Well, what is it?

MESSENIO: That man is either a swindler or your twin brother! I never saw two men look so much alike. You're as hard to tell apart as two drops of water or two drops of milk. And besides, he claims the same father and the same country. We'd better ask him about this.

MENAECHMUS II: That's good advice, and thanks! Keep on helping, do! If you prove he is my brother, you shall be a free man.

MESSENIO: That's what I hope.

MENAECHMUS II: I hope so too.

MESSENIO (to MENAECHMUS I): You, sir: you said your name was Menaechmus, I believe.

MENAECHMUS I: Yes, it is.

MESSENIO: His name is Menaechmus too. You said you were born at Syracuse in Sicily; that's where he was born. Moschus was your father, you said; his too. Now both of you can help me, and help yourselves too.

MENAECHMUS I: I am in your debt; ask me whatever you want, and you shall have it. I'm at your service, just as if you had bought and paid for me.

MESSENIO: I hope to prove that you two are twin brothers, born on the same day to the same father and mother!

MENAECHMUS I: Amazing! I certainly wish you could prove that.

MESSENIO: I can. But come now, both of you, answer my questions.

MENAECHMUS I: Ask away, I'll answer; I won't conceal anything I know.

MESSENIO (questioning each in turn): Your name is Menaechmus?

MENAECHMUS I: It is.

MESSENIO: And yours too?

MENAECHMUS II: Yes.

MESSENIO: You say you are the son of Moschus?

MENAECHMUS I: Quite so.

MENAECHMUS II: So am I.

MESSENIO: You are from Syracuse?

MENAECHMUS I: Yes.

MESSENIO: And you?

MENAECHMUS II: Of course.

MESSENIO: It checks very well so far. Now to proceed: what is the earliest thing you can remember of your life in Sicily?

MENAECHMUS I: Going with my father to the market in Tarentum; and then getting separated from him in the crowd, and being brought here.

MENAECHMUS II: God save us!

MESSENIO (*to* MENAECHMUS II): What are you shouting for? Be quiet. (*To* MENAECHMUS I) How old were you when you went on this trip with your father?

MENAECHMUS I: Seven: I was just beginning to lose my teeth. I never saw my father again.

MESSENIO: Now then: how many sons did your father have at this time?

MENAECHMUS I: To the best of my recollection, two.

MESSENIO: Which was the older, you or the other one?

MENAECHMUS I: Both the same age.

MESSENIO: How is that possible?

MENAECHMUS I: We were twins.

MENAECHMUS II: Thank God!

MESSENIO (*to* MENAECHMUS II): If you interrupt, I'll stop.

MENAECHMUS II: No, no, I'll be quiet.

MESSENIO (*to* MENAECHMUS I): Tell me, did you both have the same name?

MENAECHMUS I: Oh, no. I was the one who was called Menaechmus then, as I still am. His name was Sosicles.

MENAECHMUS II: That's proof enough! No more delay! O my own twin brother, come to my arms! I am Sosicles!

MENAECHMUS I (*doubting*): Then how does it come you're named Menaechmus?

MENAECHMUS II: After we got the news that you were lost . . .[13] and that our father was dead, our grandfather changed my name and gave me yours.

MENAECHMUS I: I believe you. But one more question.

MENAECHMUS II: Ask it.

MENAECHMUS I: What was the name of our mother?

MENAECHMUS II: Teuximarcha.

MENAECHMUS I (*convinced*): Exactly so! Oh, welcome, beyond all hope, after all these years!

MENAECHMUS II: Welcome, dear brother! Sought with such misery and toil, and found with joy at last! (*They embrace.*)

---

[13] Lindsay indicates a lacuna of one verse here.

MESSENIO (*to* MENAECHMUS II): So that's why the woman here called you by name! She took you for him, and asked you to dinner.

MENAECHMUS I: Yes, I told her to have a dinner for me there today (putting one over on my wife), and I gave her a dress that I'd stolen from my wife too.

MENAECHMUS II (*producing the dress*): Do you mean this dress?

MENAECHMUS I: That's the one! How did you get it?

MENAECHMUS II: The woman dragged me in to dinner and said the dress was mine, I'd given it to her. So after some excellent wine, women, and song, I took it away with me, and a gold bracelet too.

MENAECHMUS I: She thought she was getting *me* in, of course. But I'm certainly glad I got you fixed up so well.

MESSENIO: I suppose you're still willing to set me free as you promised?

MENAECHMUS I: A very good and fair request, brother; grant it for my sake.

MENAECHMUS II (*complying, with the correct legal formula*): I declare you free.

MENAECHMUS I: Congratulations on your freedom, Messenio.

MESSENIO: I hope it lasts better this time.

MENAECHMUS II: Well, brother, now that everything has turned out the way we wanted, let's both go back to Syracuse.

MENAECHMUS I: Agreed! I'll have an auction and sell all my Epidamnus property. In the meantime, brother, won't you come in?

MENAECHMUS II: Good. (*They move towards the house of* MENAECHMUS I.)

MESSENIO: Do me a favour!

MENAECHMUS I: What is it?

MESSENIO: Give me the job of auctioneer.

MENAECHMUS I: You shall have it.

MESSENIO: You want the auction cried at once?

MENAECHMUS I: Yes, for a week from today. (*The brothers go into the house.*)

MESSENIO: EXTRAORDINARY AUC—TION
                  WEEK FROM TODAY

MENAECHMUS SELLS HIS PROPERTY
CASH AND NO DELAY
ALL MUST GO—HOUSE AND LOT
SLAVES AND FURNITURE
WIFE GOES TOO IF ANY ONE
TAKES A FANCY TO HER

He'll be lucky if he gets a quarter of a million for the whole lot.
(*To the audience*) And now, spectators, fare ye well, and lustily
applaud us all.

PLAUTUS

THE ROPE (RUDENS)

TRANSLATED BY CLEVELAND K. CHASE

ACROSTIC ARGUMENT (NOT PLAUTINE)

Right from the sea a fisherman a hamper drew;
Unlocked, it showed the tokens of his master's child:
Daughter she was, though servant to procurer vile,
Established, after shipwreck, as her father's ward—
Now safe, though still unknown. At last, his daughter proved,
She weds her erstwhile lover, Plesidippus true.

CHARACTERS IN THE PLAY

ARCTURUS, *prologue, "Warder of the Bear"*
SCEPARNIO, *slave of Daemones, "Ax"*
PLESIDIPPUS, *a young man, in love with Palaestra*
DAEMONES, *an old man, from Athens, driven by fortune to live near Cyrene, in Africa*
PALAESTRA, *a young woman, daughter of Daemones, but kidnapped when a child; now owned by Labrax, "Sport"*
AMPELISCA, *a young woman in the possession of Labrax, "Vinette"*
PTOLEMOCRATIA, *elderly priestess of Venus*
FISHERMEN, *poor men from Cyrene who make a meagre living by fishing along the shore*
TRACHALIO, *slave of Plesidippus, "Bull-necked"*
LABRAX, *pander and slave dealer, "Bass" (a voracious fish)*
CHARMIDES, *an old man, friend of Labrax*
SLAVES, *belonging to Daemones*
GRIPUS, *fisherman, and slave of Daemones, "Fisher"*

The characters are listed in the order of their appearance in the play, according to the Latin custom.

The scene is laid near Cyrene, in northern Africa, and remains the same throughout the play.

THE ROPE

ARCTURUS: Compatriot am I, from the realms of the immortals, of him who shakes all lands and seas. I am, as you may see, a gleaming constellation bright; and ever in due season I rise. Arcturus am I called, both here and in heaven, and fair I shine at night among the gods; by day I pass the time with mortals, I and other stars that make their way to earth. Our supreme commander, Jove, stations us about the world, to note the ways and deeds of men, their faith, their reverence, to give them aid. Whoever falsely swears, to win his suit, or forswears his obligations, his name is entered forthwith in Jove's book of accounts. And however great his perjured gains, the judge on high reopens the case, and reverses; and soon he loses more than in the courts of men he falsely made. And Jove knows each day whose heart desires the evil course. But virtue finds its name in another column entered. And the evil wretch who hopes by gift and victim to appease the god has his toil for his pains. For Jove cares naught for the perjured offering; while he who keeps faith will ever find leniency from him. One word of advice then, to those who know yourselves good, who keep faith with men and show reverence to the gods: stand steadfast, that hereafter you may reap due reward.

Now hear the reason why I've come. It was the poet's will that the town here be Cyrene; and here too, in a house on a farm hard by the sea, dwells Daemones, an old man far from his native Athens, whose exile here was through no fault of his, for his life was blameless. Rather does he suffer the penalty of a kindly heart, his property lost in the service of his friends. He had a daughter once, but the wretch who stole her, a mere child, sold her to a vile pander, who hither brought her. And now a youth from

Athens, sojourning here, seeing her as she returned home from her music school, fell in love with her, approached her master, and for thirty minas bought her. And straightway he made ample deposit upon the purchase and bound the pander by an oath to complete the transfer. But that vile fellow, as one might know, cared nothing for plighted word or oath.

It chanced a friend of his from Sicily, old, vicious, a man who well his own country might betray, was visiting him. He praised the girl's beauty, and likewise that of the other women in the pander's train, and urged to take them all to Sicily, where, thus he declared, men were so given to pleasure that such trade as his would reap great profit. He gained his point. A ship was chartered and all the pander had was secretly placed by night upon it. To the youth who had bought the girl, he told of a vow to Venus (note here her shrine) and bid him to a breakfast here; then clapped sail upon his ship, and cleared the harbor with his women, leaving it to others to let the youth know what had befallen. Who, seeking him at the port, found the ship far out at sea.

Now I, when I saw the maiden's plight, thus stolen, brought aid to her, but ruin to the pander. With wintry blast I raged, and roughened all the surface of the sea. For know that I am Arcturus, of all the constellations none more fierce, whether at the rising, or when, at my course's end, in storm I hide my light. Look you now, both pander and his Sicilian friend cast forth upon the rocks, shipwrecked. But the young girl and a little maid, her friend, all trembling have leaped from the waves into a tiny boat, and the flood bears them landward from the rocks, towards this very cottage, where dwells the old man from Athens; his cottage too, and roof have suffered from the storm. The slave who now comes out is his slave, and soon you shall see with your own eyes the youth who bought the girl. Farewell now, and may your enemies give way before you.

[ACT ONE: SCENE I]

(SCENE: *A road, leading from Cyrene and its harbor, on the right, to the sea-shore, on the left. In the near background is a small area, raised slightly above the shore line, with a small tem-*

ple of Venus facing it diagonally, on the right, and the cottage
of DAEMONES, *in a corresponding position, on the left. Between*
the two buildings, in the center, there is a clear glimpse of the
sky line above the sea, extending half the width of the stage; the
altar in front of the temple shows against the sky line. At the left
front, flanking the side of the cottage, is thick foliage, including
bulrushes; the temple, on the other side, is correspondingly flanked
by rocks. It is thus possible for persons at the opposite sides of
the stage to be visible to the audience, and yet be out of sight
of each other, and of the area proper. It is a clear morning after
a hard storm, and SCEPARNIO *comes out of the cottage, carrying*
a spade, ready to begin the work of the day.)

SCEPARNIO: Ye gods! What a storm on the sea last night! And
how the winds raised the roof! In fact, it was no mere wind, but
what Euripides sent to Alcmene; for see how all the tiles are loose
or gone: the storm has made windows to let in light!

[ACT ONE: SCENE 2]

(*Enter, from the right* PLESIDIPPUS *with three friends.*)

PLESIDIPPUS: I have brought you from your affairs, and yet
have failed in what I sought: the procurer we couldn't catch at
the harbor. But I could not bear to lose my hopes through lack
of effort, and so have kept you with me all this while. I want now
to visit this shrine of Venus, where he said he had a vow to pay.
SCEPARNIO: If I'm wise, I'll be getting this confounded clay
dug.
PLESIDIPPUS: Somebody's talking here.

(*Enter* DAEMONES, *from cottage.*)

DAEMONES: Hello, Sceparnio!
SCEPARNIO: Who's calling?
DAEMONES: The man who paid for you.
SCEPARNIO: Hm! You'll be calling me your slave next, Dae-
mones.
DAEMONES: Well, we shall need a lot of clay, so dig the earth

up thoroughly. I see the whole house will have to be patched over . . . hm! "whole" is good; it's all holes.

PLESIDIPPUS (*advancing*): Good morning, good father—and to both of you.

DAEMONES: Good morning, sir.

SCEPARNIO: I say, are you a man or a woman, to be calling him father?

PLESIDIPPUS: Why, I am a man.

SCEPARNIO: Then go look for another father.

DAEMONES: I did have a daughter once, you see, but I lost her when she was young; I never had a son.

PLESIDIPPUS: But the gods will surely give you—

SCEPARNIO (*interrupting, to* PLESIDIPPUS): Well, if you ask me, they'll surely give *you* the devil for coming here, whoever you are, to trouble those who've got troubles of their own.

PLESIDIPPUS: Do you live here?

SCEPARNIO: What do you want to know for? Looking up places to rob?

PLESIDIPPUS: That slave of yours must be a privileged character, to talk so much in the presence of his master, and to address a gentleman so uncivilly.

SCEPARNIO: And you must be a bold, nervy fellow, to be butting into other people's houses, where no one owes you anything.

DAEMONES: Keep quiet, Sceparnio. What is it you wish, young man?

PLESIDIPPUS: Well first, a curse on this fellow for not letting his master get in a word first. But, if it is not too much trouble, I should like to ask you a few questions.

DAEMONES: Certainly, although you find me in the midst of work.

SCEPARNIO: Say, why don't you go down to the marsh instead, while the weather's clear, and cut reeds to thatch the house?

DAEMONES: Be quiet. (*To* PLESIDIPPUS) If I can be of assistance, let me know.

PLESIDIPPUS: Please tell me whether you have seen a rascally looking chap, with curly, gray hair, a false, fawning sort of a scoundrel.

DAEMONES: I've seen many of that breed, and it's thanks to such that I lead an unhappy life.

PLESIDIPPUS: I mean *here*—a man who was bringing two women with him to the shrine of Venus, to offer a sacrifice either yesterday or today.

DAEMONES: Emphatically not. I've seen no one sacrificing here for several days, and it would be impossible to do so without my knowledge. For they are always asking at the house for water, or coals, or a knife, or a spit, or a dish, or something—in fact one would think my utensils and well belonged to Venus and not to me.

PLESIDIPPUS: You pronounce death sentence upon me by those words.

DAEMONES: Not I, sir: you may live as long and happily as you wish, as far as I am concerned.

SCEPARNIO: I say, you, who make the rounds of the temples to get your belly full, why don't you have your meals served at home?

DAEMONES: Perhaps you've been invited here to a breakfast, and he who invited you hasn't come?

PLESIDIPPUS: Exactly.

SCEPARNIO: There's no harm, then, in your going home without breakfast. You ought to pray to Ceres rather than to Venus; for she gives you grub, and Venus only love.

PLESIDIPPUS (*to his friends*): That scoundrel, Labrax, has fooled me shamefully.

DAEMONES: By the gods! Sceparnio, what's that down by the shore?

SCEPARNIO: That's a party invited to a farewell breakfast, I should say.

DAEMONES: How so?

SCEPARNIO: Because they took their bath after dinner yesterday, a sea-bath that is, and so are ready for lunch today.

DAEMONES: Their ship has been wrecked on the sea.

SCEPARNIO: That's true; but so has our house been wrecked on land, by Jove, and the roof too.

DAEMONES: Ah, poor creatures! See how they swim from the wreck!

PLESIDIPPUS: Where are they, pray?

DAEMONES: Off here to the right, along the shore.

PLESIDIPPUS: I see. (*To his friends*) Come on. I hope the man we're looking for is there, curse him. (*To the others*) And you, farewell.

(*Exeunt* PLESIDIPPUS *and friends, to the right.*)

SCEPARNIO: We can fare well without any help from you. But holy Palaemon, partner of Neptune and Hercules, what a sight!

DAEMONES: What do you see?

SCEPARNIO: Two women sitting alone in a little skiff. How the poor things are tossed about! . . . Good! good! that's fine! The waves have driven the boat off the rocks towards the shore; a pilot couldn't have done better. I never saw the sea so high; but they're safe, if they escape the breakers. . . . Now, now's the danger. One of them is overboard, but she's in shallow water, and will easily get out. Oh, great! Did you see how the waves washed her out? But she's up and coming this way. It's all right now. But the other has jumped from the boat. She's so frightened, she's down on her knees in the waves. No, she's safe now, and out of the water. There, she is safe on the shore. . . . But she's turning now towards the right, to sure death. Oh, she'll be lost there.

DAEMONES: Well, that's no concern of yours.

SCEPARNIO: If she falls down on those rocks where she's headed, it will be the last of her wanderings.

DAEMONES: See here, Sceparnio, if you're going to have your dinner at their expense this evening, it's all right to worry about them; but if you eat here, I want you to get to work.

SCEPARNIO: All right; that's a fair demand.

DAEMONES: Follow me then.

SCEPARNIO: I'm coming. (*Exeunt* DAEMONES *and* SCEPARNIO *into cottage.*)

[ACT ONE: SCENE 3]

(*Enter* PALAESTRA, *by the road from the left. She is wet and exhausted, after having been shipwrecked, and unable to go farther, stops at the extreme left of stage, out of sight of the temple area. She sings plaintively.*)

PALAESTRA: Ah, how much more bitter is life than the tales men weave about it. And here am I, left like this (*looks at her dress*), in terror, cast upon an unknown shore, at the will of heaven. Was it for this I was born? Is this the reward of a life without offense? If in piety to parents or to gods I have been lacking, this would be no injustice. But if exactly in this I have been most careful, then you are wrong, immortals, and most unfair. For how will you repay hereafter the impious, if so you honor the innocent? I should not feel so sorry for myself, if either my parents or I were to blame. But it's my vile master, and his impiety, that have got me into this trouble. Well, he has lost everything, his ship included; I am the last remains of his fortune. She who was with me on the boat is gone; I am alone. If only she were left, it would not be so hard. Where shall I turn for help? Alone, by lonely sea and rocks, meeting no one, what I wear my only fortune; no roof, no food, why should I hope to live? Will there be no one who lives nearby to show me a road or pathway out, to relieve me from my uncertainties? Cold, and fear, and all distractions overwhelm me. My poor parents, you know not how wretched is your daughter—in vain born free; for how am I other than slave, or of what help have I ever been to you? (*She sinks down exhausted.*)

[ACT ONE: SCENE 4]

(*Enter, from the right,* AMPELISCA, *in the same state of exhaustion as* PALAESTRA. *She has climbed the bluff on the other side of the temple, and stops before catching sight of the area.*)

AMPELISCA: What better can I do than end it all with death? So wretched I am, so consumed by anxiety! I care no longer to live; I have no hope. All the shore along I have searched, and the undergrowth; calling, looking, listening; but no trace of her. And there is none to ask, and I know not where to turn. There never was desert so deserted as this spot. And yet, if she lives, while I live, I shall never stop until I find her.

PALAESTRA (*rising*): Whose voice is that so near? I am afraid.

AMPELISCA: Who's speaking there?

PALAESTRA: Oh, dear hope, do not forsake me.

AMPELISCA: Away from me, fear!

PALAESTRA: It's surely a woman's voice.

AMPELISCA: It's a woman; it's a woman speaking.

PALAESTRA: Can it be Ampelisca?

AMPELISCA: Oh, is it you, Palaestra?

PALAESTRA: Why don't I call out her name? (*She calls.*) Ampelisca!

AMPELISCA: Who is it?

PALAESTRA: It's I, Palaestra.

AMPELISCA: Oh, where are you?

PALAESTRA: Alas, I am in deep trouble.

AMPELISCA: In that I am with you, but I long to see you.

PALAESTRA: That is my one wish too.

AMPELISCA: Then let our voices lead our steps. . . . Now where are you?

PALAESTRA: Here; come over to me.

AMPELISCA: How eagerly I come. (*Crosses quickly over to* PALAESTRA.)

PALAESTRA (*almost too overcome to stand*): Your hand!

AMPELISCA: Take it.

PALAESTRA: Tell me; is it you, and alive?

AMPELISCA: At last I have the will to live, now that I can hold you—or do I hold you? Take me to your arms. My only hope for life is the comfort you give me.

PALAESTRA: How quick you are to outstrip me; your words speak all my thought. Now we have only to leave this place.

AMPELISCA: But how? By what path?

PALAESTRA: We'll follow the shore.

AMPELISCA: I'll follow you anywhere. Shall we go as we are, with our clothing drenched?

PALAESTRA: We shall endure what we must. But do see there, my dear Ampelisca!

AMPELISCA: What?

PALAESTRA: Don't you see the shrine?

AMPELISCA: Where?

PALAESTRA: Back, to the right.

AMPELISCA: I see—a place worthy of the gods.

PALAESTRA: Some one must live near by; it's such a charming spot. (*They advance supplicatingly to the altar, by which they kneel.*) To this divinity, whoever he be, I pray for help from their troubles, for two poor women in want and despair.

[ACT ONE: SCENE 5]

(*Enter* PTOLEMOCRATIA, *aged priestess of Venus, from temple.*)

PTOLEMOCRATIA: Who asks a boon here of my patron goddess? I heard the voice of supplication. They entreat a patron kind and indulgent, who does not grudge her favors.

PALAESTRA: We give you greetings, mother.

PTOLEMOCRATIA: My greetings to you, maidens; and whence come ye in your dripping weeds, so dismally clad?

PALAESTRA: From the sea nearby; but far away is the port from which we sailed.

PTOLEMOCRATIA: You journeyed then over the darkling paths of ocean on the sea-swung wooden steed?

PALAESTRA: Yes, mother.

PTOLEMOCRATIA: It is scarce seemly to approach the shrine as you are, without white garments or victims.

PALAESTRA: I pray you, where should we, but lately cast up from the sea, find victims? (*They embrace the priestess' knees.*) Behold, we who clasp your knees are strangers in an unknown land, hopeless, and in want; we pray for protection and shelter. Take pity on those who need it; we have lost our all, our goods, our homes, our hope even.

PTOLEMOCRATIA: Do not kneel; give me your hands. No one ever had a heart more compassionate than mine. But you will find me poor. My service of Venus here does not give me enough to support life.

AMPELISCA: This is a shrine of Venus, then?

PTOLEMOCRATIA: It is, and I am her priestess. But all I have is at your service. Come with me.

PALAESTRA: You honor us most generously, mother.

PTOLEMOCRATIA: It is my duty. (*Exeunt all into temple.*)

[ACT TWO: SCENE 1]

(*Enter three* FISHERMEN *from the right, roughly clad, carrying rod and line. They chant their chorus in unison, as they step about the stage.*)

FISHERMEN: In all ways poor folk have a sorry lot,
Especially they who lack both trade and skill.
The little that they have must them content.
Take us—from our equipment you can tell
How poor we are—these hooks and lines our all.
For wrestling and gymnastics we have this:
To exercise the while we fish the sea.
Sea-urchins, limpets, star-fish, mussels, shells,
Sea-nettles, fluted scallops, with our hands
We catch, and from the rocks too cast our lines.
Our larder is the sea, but when unkind
He gives no catch, ourselves, well cleaned and salt,
Are all the catch we carry sadly home,
While tired and supperless to bed we go.
Small hope for us today; the sea's too rough;
We've dined already, should we find no clams.
Our Lady Venus we'll now beg for aid.

(*They approach the shrine and pray.*)

[ACT TWO: SCENE 2]

(*Enter* TRACHALIO *from right.*)

TRACHALIO: I've been careful not to pass my master on the way, for when he left a little ago, he said he would stop at the harbor, and that I should meet him here at the temple of Venus. (*Sees the* FISHERMEN.) But good luck! here's a chance to ask; I'll speak to these fellows. Good day to you, thieves of the sea, Messrs. Hooker and Shelly! How fare you, or, since you have no fare, how starve you, comrades of the empty gut?

FISHERMEN: We fare as our calling allows—hunger, thirst, and false hopes, fisherman's luck.

TRACHALIO: Have you seen, while standing about here, a bold, determined young chap, with a ruddy countenance?

FISHERMEN: There's been no one here like that, we know.

TRACHALIO: Well then, have you seen a frowning, big-bellied old Silenus, hobbling about on a stick; with a bald forehead and twisted eyebrows? a cheating, scoundrelly, vicious-looking devil, a plague of gods and men; with a couple of pretty girls with him?

FISHERMEN: A man of such character would better go to the gallows than to a temple of Venus.

TRACHALIO: But have you seen him?

FISHERMEN: He's not been here. (*Going*) Well, good day to you.

TRACHALIO: Good bye (*Exeunt* FISHERMEN.) That's what I thought. I always suspected him. The rascally procurer has fooled us, and cleared out. He's sailed away with his women. I'm a wizard, I am. Didn't I say so all along? And then invited us here to breakfast, the cheat! I might as well wait now until the master comes. But perhaps the priestess will know something more. I'll go in and find out.

[ACT TWO: SCENE 3]

(*Enter* AMPELISCA; *she talks back into the temple.*)

AMPELISCA: Yes, I understand—to knock at the cottage next door and ask for water.

TRACHALIO: Now whose voice is that?

AMPELISCA: Who's that man talking there?

TRACHALIO: Is that Ampelisca coming out of the temple?

AMPELISCA: Why, that's surely Plesidippus' man, Trachalio.

TRACHALIO: It is.

AMPELISCA: Of course it is; welcome Trachalio.

TRACHALIO: Well, well, Ampelisca, what are you doing here?

AMPELISCA: I'm passing most unhappily what should be my time of happiness.

TRACHALIO: Don't say that; it will bring bad luck.

AMPELISCA: If we are wise, we admit the truth. But tell me please, where is your master, Plesidippus?

TRACHALIO: As if he were not there with you!

AMPELISCA: Faith, he is not; he hasn't been here.

TRACHALIO: He hasn't?

AMPELISCA: It's the truth you're speaking.

TRACHALIO: That wouldn't be like me, would it, Ampelisca? But I say, when will the breakfast be ready?

AMPELISCA: What breakfast, pray?

TRACHALIO: Aren't you sacrificing here?

AMPELISCA: You're dreaming.

TRACHALIO: Your master, Labrax, certainly invited my master, Plesidippus, to sacrifice and breakfast.

AMPELISCA: Now, isn't that like him? To cheat both gods and men is in his line of business.

TRACHALIO: Neither you nor your master is sacrificing here?

AMPELISCA: Right you are!

TRACHALIO: Then what are you doing here?

AMPELISCA: We have suffered many misfortunes and have been in great danger and fear of our lives, and in our need we were welcomed by the priestess, Palaestra and I.

TRACHALIO: Is Palaestra here, the girl my master loves?

AMPELISCA: Certainly.

TRACHALIO: Oh, that's good news; my dear Ampelisca, that's splendid. But tell me about your hard luck.

AMPELISCA: Our ship was wrecked by the storm last night, Trachalio.

TRACHALIO: What ship? What are you talking about?

AMPELISCA: Haven't you heard how Labrax tried to carry us off secretly to Sicily, along with all his property? And now he's lost everything.

TRACHALIO: Good boy, Neptune! I always said you were a fine dicer; that was a master throw; you've dished the procurer. But where is he?

AMPELISCA: Dead drunk, I think. Too many drinks of sea water last night.

TRACHALIO: Well, he didn't choose the drink, if there was water in it. Ampelisca, your words are a real treat; what a dear you are! But how did you and Palaestra escape?

AMPELISCA: I'll tell you. Although we were terribly afraid, we jumped into the little lifeboat, when we saw the ship making for the rocks, and quickly untied the rope; the men were too frightened to do anything. The storm drove our boat off here to the right. We pitched about in a rough sea all night, in the greatest distress, until the wind at last drove us ashore; we were nearly dead, I can tell you.

TRACHALIO: I know; that's the way of the old sea dog; Neptune is some market inspector, when he gets started—he throws out any goods he doesn't like.

AMPELISCA: Go on now; don't be impudent.

TRACHALIO: Apply that to yourself, please. I told you so! I knew the slave dealer would be acting that way. I think I'll let my hair grow, and set up for a prophet.

AMPELISCA: Well, if you knew so much, why didn't you and your master prevent his getting away?

TRACHALIO: What should he have done?

AMPELSICA: What should he have done? He should have been on the watch day and night. But on my word, I think his care was the exact measure of his regard for her.

TRACHALIO: What do you mean?

AMPELISCA: It's clear enough.

TRACHALIO: See here, Ampelisca; when a man goes to the bathhouse, no matter how sharply he watches out, he sometimes loses his clothing. It's hard to catch the thief when you don't know whom to suspect. But take me to her.

AMPELISCA: Just go into the temple; you'll find her sitting by the statue of Venus, in tears.

TRACHALIO: Oh, that's too bad; what is she crying for?

AMPELISCA: I'll tell you. She had a little casket containing the tokens of identification by which she hoped sometime to find her father. The procurer had taken this from her, and now she's afraid it's lost; that's why she is so distressed.

TRACHALIO: Where was the casket?

AMPELISCA: On the ship with him; he had locked it away in his luggage, just to make sure she shouldn't find her father.

TRACHALIO: What a scurvy trick, to try to keep in slavery a girl who by rights should be free.

AMPELISCA: And now it's gone to the bottom, along with all his gold and silver.

TRACHALIO: Some one has probably gone in by this time and got it.

AMPELISCA: That's why she's so sad; it's the loss of her tokens.

TRACHALIO: All the more reason for my consoling her. She shouldn't distress herself so; things are always happening to people beyond their expectations.

AMPELISCA: And on the other hand, so many people indulge in false hopes.

TRACHALIO: The more need then of keeping up your spirits in the face of troubles. I'll go in, unless you've something else in mind.

AMPELISCA: Go; I'll meanwhile get the water from the house here, as the priestess wished. (*Exit* TRACHALIO *into temple.*) She said they would give it, if I asked in her name. There never was a woman who deserved better of gods and men. How sweetly and kindly and generously she received us, like daughters; and we were so destitute, wet, dejected, and frightened. And then the way she tucked up her dress and warmed the water for our bath! I must not keep her waiting; it's high time to get the water. (*Knocks at door of cottage.*) Hello, is there any one at home? Won't some one come to the door? . . . Is anyone coming out?

[ACT TWO: SCENE 4]

(*Enter* SCEPARNIO *from cottage.*)

SCEPARNIO: Who's battering in the door?

AMPELISCA: It is I.

SCEPARNIO: I say! Here's luck. On my word, a likely wench!

AMPELISCA: Good day to you, young man.

SCEPARNIO: A very good day to you, young lady.

AMPELISCA: I was coming to your house.

SCEPARNIO: I'd treat you royally, if you'd only come a little later; I'm busy this morning. But what a pretty baggage it is! (*Chucking her under the chin*) There's a dear!

AMPELISCA: Not so familiar, *if* you please.

SCEPARNIO: By gad, she's a love—a twinkle in the eye, too. A sweet confection—complexion, I mean! and some figure! and a classy little mouth, to top it off!

AMPELISCA: I'm no dish for the village, young man; kindly keep your hands off.

SCEPARNIO: But a sweet kiss for a sweet girl is surely not amiss.

AMPELISCA: None of your merry pranks now, if you please; there will be time for that later, perhaps. Will you give me what I'm sent for? Say yes or no.

SCEPARNIO: What do you want?

AMPELISCA: You can tell by looking at me what I want. (*Holds out her pitcher.*)

SCEPARNIO: Yes, and you can tell by looking at me what I want.

AMPELISCA: The priestess has asked me to get water from your house.

SCEPARNIO: But I'm the king around here, and if you don't beg very prettily, not a drop will you get. I had to work hard on that well, at some risk, and the water will not come without rare coaxing.

AMPELISCA: Why do you refuse to give what any enemy would give to another?

SCEPARNIO: And why do you refuse to give what any friend would give to another—a bit of encouragement?

AMPELISCA: Very well, my dear; anything you want.

SCEPARNIO: Oh, joy! she calls me her dear. You shall have your water; it shall never be said a lady loved me in vain. Give me the pitcher.

AMPELISCA: Here; hurry now; there's a love.

SCEPARNIO: Wait here, my dear; I'll be back directly. (*Exit into house.*)

AMPELISCA: What shall I say to the priestess for staying so long? (*Looks toward the sea.*) Ah me, how I shudder every time I look at the sea. But what's that on the shore? Alas, my master, Labrax, and his Sicilian friend, whom I thought at the bottom of the sea, both of them! There's more trouble in store for us now than we thought. I'll fly to the shrine to let Palaestra know, that we may take refuge at the altar before the villain comes and carries us off. Run, Ampelisca; the crisis is at hand.

[ACT TWO: SCENE 5]

(*Enter* SCEPARNIO *from cottage.*)

SCEPARNIO: Gad, I never knew there was so much pleasure in mere water. How I enjoyed filling the pitcher! The well didn't seem deep at all today; it came up easy. What a devil of a fellow I am, to start this love affair today! Here's your water, dearie; I want you to take it prettily, as I give it to you, so that I'll be pleased with you. . . . Where is the jade? Come now, take the water, please. Where are you? By Jove, she must be in love with me! the little witch wants to play peek-a-boo. I say, where are you? Won't you be taking the water now? You're pretending very nicely to be afraid of me; but seriously, will you please take the pitcher? Where in the world is she? By Jove, I can't see her anywhere; she's making fun of me. I'll just set this pitcher down in the middle of the road. But what if it should be stolen? it's sacred to Venus. That would get me into a pretty pickle. I'm afraid it's a frame-up to get me caught with stolen goods. I'd get a proper jail sentence, if I were seen with it. The inscription on it would give me away. I'll just go up to the door and call the priestess out, and let her take it. (*Calls aloud.*) If you please, Ptolemocratia! Will you take your pitcher, left with me by some woman from the temple? Oh, I'll have to go in with it. I've found a job with a vengeance, if I've even got to carry their water to them. (*Exit into temple.*)

[ACT TWO: SCENE 6]

(*Enter, from the left,* LABRAX, *followed by* CHARMIDES, *wet and shivering.*)

LABRAX: If you want to be a beggar and down on your luck, just trust yourself to Neptune; after a mixup with him you will look like this. (*Looks at his clothing.*) By Jove, Liberty, you were a bright lass, never to set foot on ship with your pal, Hercules. But where's that friend of mine who played the devil with me so? Here he comes.

CHARMIDES: Where in the deuce are you going in such a hurry, Labrax? This pace is too swift for me.

LABRAX: I wish you'd been hanged in Sicily before I ever set eyes on you. All this trouble comes from you.

CHARMIDES: I wish the day you were bringing me to your house, I had slept in jail instead. I hope to heaven that after this, all your guests will be like yourself; it's no place for an honest man.

LABRAX: It was Bad Luck I had for a guest, when you came. I was a cursed fool when I listened to you. Why did we go away, or get on the ship, where I lost all I had—and more, too?

CHARMIDES: Any ship would sink that carried a rogue like you, and your rogue's fortune.

LABRAX: You got me in bad with your flatteries.

CHARMIDES: That last dinner I had with you was worse than the one served up to Thyestes.

LABRAX (coughing): I feel sick myself; hold my head, will you?

CHARMIDES: I hope you'll cough your lungs up.

LABRAX: O Palaestra, Ampelisca, where are you?

CHAMIDES: They're food for the fishes at the present moment.

LABRAX: It's your fault I'm a beggar; it's all from listening to you and your big lies.

CHARMIDES: On the contrary, it's due entirely to me that a man as insipid as you has had a little salt put in him.

LABRAX: Will you get to hell out of here?

CHARMIDES: I'll just return that advice; go to the devil yourself.

LABRAX: Was there ever a man had worse luck than I?

CHARMIDES: I have; much worse.

LABRAX: How do you make that out?

CHARMIDES: Because you deserve it, and I do not.

LABRAX (going up to bulrushes growing near): O enviable, water-shedding bulrush, I would I were as dry as you!

CHARMIDES (his teeth chattering): Brr! I'm trembling for a skirmish; even my words are jumping about.

LABRAX: Yes, confound it, Neptune does run a cold bathhouse. With all my clothes on I'm cold.

CHARMIDES: He doesn't even serve hot drinks when you go out; nothing but ice water.

LABRAX: Lucky fellows, these blacksmiths; they've always got a fire.

CHARMIDES: Well, I'd like to be a duck myself, so as to be dry after coming out of the water.

LABRAX: I think I'll go to the country fairs and hire out as an ogre.

CHARMIDES: Why so?

LABRAX: Because I'd need no hinge to work my jaws; my chattering teeth would do it.

CHARMIDES: Do you know, I deserved to be cleaned out in this deal.

LABRAX: Why?

CHARMIDES: For daring to get into a boat with a Jonah like you; you're enough to stir up any sea.

LABRAX: It all came from listening to you. Didn't you promise me that a man could pile up wealth there in my business?

CHARMIDES: Did you expect, like a greedy shark, to swallow up the whole island of Sicily?

LABRAX: Well, I'd like to know what shark swallowed up my hamper, with all my gold and silver stored away in it.

CHARMIDES: Probably the same one that got mine, with a purse full of money.

LABRAX: All I've got left is this one shirt and cloak. Oh, me!

CHARMIDES: Well, I'm your partner in that, on even shares.

LABRAX: If I could at least have saved my girls, there'd be some hope. If I ever meet that chap Plesidippus, who gave me part payment for Palaestra, I'll catch it. Oh-h-h!

CHARMIDES: What are you crying about? As long as you've a tongue in your head, you'll never get caught.

[ACT TWO: SCENE 7]

(*Enter* SCEPARNIO *from temple.*)

SCEPARNIO: What a to-do is this? with two young women in the temple weeping, and clasping the statue of the goddess, frightened out of their wits at somebody or other; shipwrecked last night, and cast up on the shore today, they say.

LABRAX: Look here, young man, where are those two young women you are talking about?

SCEPARNIO: In the temple.

LABRAX: How many are there?

SCEPARNIO: As many as you and I together would make.

LABRAX: They surely are mine.

SCEPARNIO: I surely don't know anything about that.

LABRAX: What do they look like?

SCEPARNIO: Not half bad; I could love either one of them, if I were drunk.

LABRAX: They're certainly the girls, aren't they?

SCEPARNIO: I know you're certainly a bore. Go and see them, if you wish.

LABRAX: My dear Charmides, those women of mine must be here.

CHARMIDES: A plague on you, whether they are or not.

LABRAX: I'll break into the temple. (*Exit into temple.*)

CHARMIDES: I wish you would break into jail instead. (*To* SCEPARNIO) I say, friend, could you give me a place to sleep?

SCEPARNIO: Sure! sleep anywhere here; it's a public road.

CHARMIDES: But see how wet my clothes are; can't you take me into the house, and give me others, while mine are drying out?

SCEPARNIO: Take this covering of mine; that's all I need to keep dry. If you want, I'll give you this. When I've got it on, the rain can't touch me. Just give me your clothes and I'll have them dried out.

CHARMIDES: See here, because I've been cleaned out by the sea, do you want to clean me out again on land?

SCEPARNIO (*angrily*): I don't care whether you are cleaned out or steamed out. I wouldn't trust you with a penny, unless I had good security. Freeze or sweat, be sick or well; I don't care. I haven't any use for foreigners anyway. 'Nough said. (*Exit into cottage.*)

CHARMIDES: Wait a moment! . . . He's no more sense of pity than a slave driver. But why do I stand around in these cursed wet clothes? I'll go into the temple and sleep off the drinks I took so unwillingly last night. Like some of the Greek wines, we've had salt water poured into us, enough in fact to get us well diluted. If Neptune had treated us to one more drink, we'd be dead drunk now; it was with difficulty we got home from that spree at all. Now I'll go and see what my friend the procurer is up to. (*Exit into temple.*)

[ACT THREE: SCENE 1]

(*Enter* DAEMONES *from cottage.*)

DAEMONES: What a plaything of the gods we men are! not even in our sleep will they give us peace. That was an uncanny dream I had last night—an ape trying to climb up to a swallow's nest; and when the beast was unable to reach the birds, coming to me and demanding a ladder. Then I remember my reply: that the swallows are descended from Philomela, of Attica, and that I would never harm one of my compatriots. How fierce the beast became and seemed to threaten me, and called me to court. Whereupon, becoming suddenly angry, I seemed to seize the ape about the middle and thrust the vile beast into chains. But I can't get any inkling of what the dream may mean. But what's the racket, I wonder, in the temple?

[ACT THREE: SCENE 2]

(*Enter* TRACHALIO, hastily, from temple.)

TRACHALIO: Men of Cyrene, farmers hereabout, neighbors, I beg you to bring aid to virtue and utterly confound villainy. Show that the power of the notoriously wicked shall not be greater than that of the innocent. Make an example of impudence, and put a premium on modesty. Prove that law is of more value here than mere force. All you who are within the sound of my voice, hasten to the shrine of Venus, I implore you, and help those who have entrusted their lives, as is their right, to Venus and her servant. Choke to death wrong and aggression before they lay hold upon you.

DAEMONES: What's the trouble here?

TRACHALIO (*running up to him*): By your knees, which I embrace, I implore you, good father, whoever you are—

DAEMONES: Let go my knees, and tell me what this uproar means.

TRACHALIO: —and entreat you, and beg you, as you hope this year for a good crop of asafetida and silph, and for the safe arrival of your exports at Capua, and for freedom from sore eyes—

DAEMONES: Are you crazy?

TRACHALIO: —and for plenty of silph seed, be willing, aged sir, to grant my request.

DAEMONES: And I beg of you, by your legs and ankles, and by this back of yours, as you hope for a large harvest of rods upon it, and for a generous crop of punishments this year, tell me the meaning of all this commotion you are raising.

TRACHALIO: Why do you speak so harshly, when I hoped for fair words only from you?

DAEMONES: On the contrary, I speak you fair, since I wish for you what you deserve.

TRACHALIO: Then please attend to this matter.

DAEMONES: What is it?

TRACHALIO: There are two women inside who are innocent of all wrong and need your help. Contrary to law and justice, they are being infamously handled in the temple of Venus; and the priestess is no less shamefully mistreated.

DAEMONES: Who would dare offer violence to her? But tell me who the women are, and the wrong done them.

TRACHALIO: Just listen: they were clasping the very statue of the goddess, and this man has the audacity to take them away forcibly; and they both really should be free women.

DAEMONES: Who is it, who so defies the gods?

TRACHALIO: A cheat, a rogue, a murderer, a law-breaker without sense of shame or honor, a perjured scoundrel—in short, to describe him in one word, a procurer.

DAEMONES: A man like that deserves the severest punishment.

TRACHALIO: Yes, and he choked the priestess too.

DAEMONES: Well, by Jove, he'll pay for it. (*Calls his slaves out of cottage.*) Come out there, Turbalio, Sparax! Where are you?

TRACHALIO: Now go in and help them.

DAEMONES: Don't let me have to call you again. (*Enter huge slaves from cottage.*) Follow me.

TRACHALIO: Have them smash his eyes in as the cooks do a cuttlefish.

DAEMONES: Drag him out by the legs like a butchered hog. (*Exeunt* DAEMONES *and slaves into temple.*)

TRACHALIO: I hear a racket; they're landing with their fists. I hope they knock the scoundrel's teeth out. But here are the women running out, scared to death.

[ACT THREE: SCENE 3]

(*Enter* PALAESTRA *and* AMPELISCA, *in great fear, from temple.*)

PALAESTRA: Now we are utterly lost; there is no help for us. All hope of safety has disappeared, and in our fright we know not where to turn. What outrage we have suffered from this vile master of ours, who has shamefully maltreated the priestess and dragged us from the very statue of the goddess. We can endure no more; death is the only resort from such misery.

TRACHALIO: This is sad language; I must try to console them. Palaestra!

PALAESTRA: Who calls? Who is it?

TRACHALIO: Ampelisca!

AMPELISCA: Who's that? Who's calling me?

TRACHALIO: Look and see.

PALAESTRA: O Trachalio, you are our only hope.

TRACHALIO: Keep calm and don't make a noise; just leave it to me.

PALAESTRA: If only we can escape his violence! I should lay violent hands upon myself, rather than submit to that.

TRACHALIO: Don't be foolish.

PALAESTRA: There is no use in trying to comfort us with mere words. Unless you can give us real help, we're done for.

AMPELISCA: For my part, I'd rather die than submit to the procurer's anger. But my heart fails me when I think of death, and a chill fear creeps over my body at the very mention of it; I am only a woman. Ah, bitter, bitter day!

TRACHALIO: Keep up your courage.

PALAESTRA: Courage? where shall we find it?

TRACHALIO: There, there; don't be afraid; sit down by the altar.

AMPELISCA: How shall the altar help us more than the statue of Venus, from which he tore us violently?

TRACHALIO: Just the same, sit down. I'll protect you from here. This altar will be your walled camp, your fortifications; and I'll be your defender. With the help of Venus, I'll resist the cunning of your master.

(*Both girls kneel at altar.*)

PALAESTRA: Kind Venus, to thee we hearken; and on our knees, embracing this altar, we beseech thee with our tears, that thou vouchsafe to help us. Punish the wicked who have set at naught thy sanctuary, and suffer us in peace to remain at thy altar. We were stripped of all we had by the storm last night. Hold it not against us, if thus unkempt we approach thy holy shrine.

TRACHALIO: I think that is a fair request, Venus, and that you should grant it. Their fears have driven them to it. If you came yourself from a sea shell, as they say, you should not object to these beached blonds. But good! here comes that excellent old man, your patron and mine.

[ACT THREE: SCENE 4]

(*Enter* DAEMONES, *with slaves thrusting* LABRAX *from temple.*)

DAEMONES: Come out of the temple, most sacrilegious of men. And you (*addressing women*), sit down by the altar. But where are they?

TRACHALIO: See! here.

DAEMONES: That's good; that's what I wanted. (*To his slaves*) Tell him to come nearer. (*To* LABRAX) Do you think you can thus defy the gods in our presence? (*As* LABRAX *fails to move*) Give him a punch.

LABRAX: You'll pay for what I'm suffering.

DAEMONES: He dares to threaten us!

LABRAX: You are robbing me of my rights, and taking my slaves against my will.

TRACHALIO: Choose as arbitrator any respectable man from the senate of Cyrene, and let him decide whether they should belong to you, or whether they ought not rather to be free women, and you oughtn't to be clapped into jail, to spend the rest of your life there, until you have worn the pavement through.

LABRAX: I don't propose to talk with a gallows-bird; I'm talking to you, sir.

DAEMONES: Talk first with the man who knows you.

LABRAX: My business is with you.

TRACHALIO: It will have to be with me. You say these are your slaves?

LABRAX: They are.

TRACHALIO: Well then, just touch either one of them with the tip of your little finger.

LABRAX: What then?

TRACHALIO: Then I'll at once make a punching bag of you, you perjured scoundrel.

LABRAX (to DAEMONES): Can't I take my own girls away from the altar of Venus?

DAEMONES: You may not; that's the law here.

LABRAX: What have I to do with your laws? I'll take them both away at once. But, I say, old man, if you're in love with them, you may have them, for spot cash; or if they've found favor with Venus, she may have them, if she will pay the price.

DAEMONES: The gods pay money to you? Now understand me clearly; just start, even in joke, to offer them violence, and I'll send you away with such a dressing-down that you won't know yourself. And if you (to slaves), when I give you the signal, don't gouge his eyes out, I'll wrap the whip around your legs, as tightly as they wrap a bundle of sticks into a faggot.

LABRAX: This is violence.

TRACHALIO: And you reproach us with that, you sink of iniquity?

LABRAX: Do you dare, you double-dyed scoundrel, to speak uncivilly to me?

TRACHALIO: I'm a double-dyed scoundrel all right, and you are a highly moral party; but just the same oughtn't these women to be free?

LABRAX: Free?

TRACHALIO: Yes; and instead of your being master, they should be; for they come from the mother country, and one of them was born at Athens of free parents.

DAEMONES: What's that?

TRACHALIO: She (*pointing to* PALAESTRA) was born free and at Athens.

DAEMONES: Is she a compatriot of mine?

TRACHALIO: Aren't you from Cyrene?

DAEMONES: I was born and bred at Athens, and brought up there.

TRACHALIO: Then defend your fellow citizens, worthy sir.

DAEMONES: O my daughter, when I look upon this young girl, how I am reminded of what your loss makes me suffer! She who was taken from me when only three years old, if she now lives, would be like this girl, I know.

LABRAX: I paid their former owner for them, and it makes no difference to me whether they were born at Athens or Thebes, so long as they obey me.

TRACHALIO: Is that so, impudence? Are you, like a cat, to be pouncing on young girls stolen from their parents, to ruin them in your disgraceful profession? I don't know about the birthplace of this other girl, but I do know that she is far above you, you vile scoundrel.

LABRAX: Apply your abuse to yourself.

TRACHALIO: Shall we prove by the trial of backs which of us is the cleaner? If your back isn't cut into as many ribbons as a man-of-war has nails, I'm the worst of liars. Then, after I've looked at your back, you look at mine; and if it isn't clean and whole, so that any flask-maker would say it was a perfect hide for his business, what reason is there why I shouldn't baste you until I'm tired of it? What are you looking at them for? I'll gouge your eyes out if you touch them.

LABRAX: And just because you forbid me, I'll take them both off with me directly.

DAEMONES: What are you going to do?

LABRAX (*starting towards cottage*): I'm going to fetch Vulcan; he's opposed to Venus.

TRACHALIO: Where's he going?

LABRAX: Hello there, any one here?

DAEMONES: By Jove, if you touch that door, I'll harvest a crop of hay on your face, with my fists as pitchforks.

SLAVES: We don't use fire here; we live on dried figs.

TRACHALIO: I'll give you fire, if you'll let me apply it to your head.

LABRAX: I'll get fire somewhere else.

DAEMONES: What will you do when you have found it?

LABRAX: I'll make a big blaze.

DAEMONES: With which to burn the meanness out of yourself?

LABRAX: No; I'll burn these two alive at the altar.

TRACHALIO: And, by gad, I'll throw you by the beard into the fire, and when you're half-done give you to the vultures for food.

DAEMONES (aside): When I come to think of it, this is the ape that in my dream tried to steal the swallows from their nest, against my will.

TRACHALIO: Do you know what I should like you to do, worthy sir? guard these girls until I fetch my master.

DAEMONES: Go and get him.

TRACHALIO: But don't let this fellow—

DAEMONES: It will be at his peril, if he touches them.

TRACHALIO: Be on your watch.

DAEMONES: I will see to that; be off.

TRACHALIO: And don't let this fellow get away, for we are engaged to deliver him to the hangman today, or forfeit a talent of silver.

DAEMONES: Be off now; I'll take care of him until you return.

TRACHALIO: I'll be back shortly. (*Exit* TRACHALIO *towards shore*.)

[ACT THREE: SCENE 5]

DAEMONES: See here, pander; would you rather keep quiet with a beating or without one, if you could choose?

LABRAX: I don't care a fig for what you say, old man. I'm going to take them away from the altar, in spite of you, or Venus, or Jove himself.

DAEMONES: Just touch them.

LABRAX: Sure, I'll touch them.

DAEMONES: Very well; try it.

LABRAX: Tell these fellows to retreat a bit.

DAEMONES: On the contrary, they will advance.

LABRAX: I don't think so.

DAEMONES: If they advance, what will you do?

LABRAX: Oh, I'll—retreat. But see here, old chap, if I ever catch you in town, if I don't have sport with you before you get away, never call me pimp again.

DAEMONES: Threaten away, but meanwhile, if you so much as touch them, I'll give you the devil of a punishment.

LABRAX: How much will that be?

DAEMONES: Enough for even a procurer.

LABRAX: A fig for your threats; watch me take them both in spite of you.

DAEMONES: Again I say, just try it.

LABRAX: I will, by Jove.

DAEMONES: Yes, you will; but do you know at what cost? (*To one of the slaves*) Turbalio, go into the house and get two clubs; run.

LABRAX: Clubs?

DAEMONES: Yes, and big ones. (*To slave*) Hurry now. (*To* LABRAX) I'm going to give you the reception you deserve.

LABRAX: And I unluckily left my helmet on the ship; it would come in handy now. May I at least speak to them?

DAEMONES: You may not. Ah, here comes the cudgel-bearer.

LABRAX: Which means a tingling for my ears.

DAEMONES: Here, Sparax, take the other club. You stand here, and you there, one on either side; so. Now listen to me. If he lays a finger on them, against their will, and you don't give him such a reception that he won't know where he's at, it will be the end of you both. If he addresses either one, you reply for them; and if he tries to get at them, wrap your cudgels about his legs.

LABRAX: Won't they even let me go away?

DAEMONES: I've said enough to you. (*To slaves*) And when that slave returns with his master, go into the house at once. I want you to show the greatest vigilance. (*Exit into cottage.*)

LABRAX: I say, this temple's changing hands; it formerly belonged to Venus, and now Hercules is in charge. The old man has set up two statues of Hercules and his club! Now in very truth, I don't know which way to turn; everything's against me, on land, as well as on sea. Palaestra!

SLAVE (*gruffly*): What do you want?

LABRAX: Get out now; I protest. That was not my Palaestra who answered. Ampelisca!

SLAVE: Look out for trouble.

LABRAX (*aside*): As well as they can, these cowardly fellows give me good advice. See here, you, will it cause any trouble if I go a bit nearer to them?

SLAVE: No—not to us.

LABRAX: To me?

SLAVE: Not if you take care.

LABRAX: Take care for what?

SLAVE: A sound beating.

LABRAX: But I entreat you to let me go closer to them.

SLAVE: Very well, if you wish.

LABRAX: Oh, that's good; I am much obliged to you. (*As he starts forward, they threaten with clubs.*) No, no, I won't go; stay where you are. Oh, how wretchedly everything turns out! But I'll get them yet, if I have to lay seige to them.

[ACT THREE: SCENE 6]

(*Enter* PLESIDIPPUS *with* TRACHALIO, *from the shore, stopping at extreme left.*)

PLESIDIPPUS: And the pimp tried to take my mistress away by force from the altar of Venus?

TRACHALIO: Exactly.

PLESIDIPPUS: Why didn't you kill him?

TRACHALIO: I had no sword.

PLESIDIPPUS: Why didn't you take a club or a rock?

TRACHALIO: Should I have stoned him to death like a mad dog?

LABRAX: The jig's up; here's Plesidippus. He'll mop up the earth with me.

PLESIDIPPUS: And were they still by the altar when you left?

TRACHALIO: They're there now.

PLESIDIPPUS: Who is guarding them?

TRACHALIO: An old man who lives next to the temple, and his slaves; I told him what to do.

PLESIDIPPUS (*advancing towards area*): Take me to the pimp; where is he?

LABRAX: Good morning.

PLESIDIPPUS: I don't want any of your "good mornings." Make your choice quickly. Would you rather be taken away with a rope around your neck; or be dragged off by the heels? Decide while you can.

LABRAX: Neither.

PLESIDIPPUS: Run to the shore, Trachalio, and tell those men whom I brought to take this fellow to the hangman, that they're to meet me at the harbor. Then return and keep guard here. I'm going to take this rascal to court. (*Exit* TRACHALIO, *left.*) Come along with you.

LABRAX: What have I done that's wrong?

PLESIDIPPUS: Do you ask me that? Didn't you accept part payment from me for this girl, and then take her away?

LABRAX: I didn't take her away.

PLESIDIPPUS: Why do you deny it?

LABRAX: Because I only tried, but couldn't get her away, unfortunately. And besides, didn't I tell you I would be here at the shrine of Venus? Did I break my word? Am I not here?

PLESIDIPPUS: Tell that to the judge; we've had talking enough. (*Throws rope over his head.*) Come on here.

LABRAX: Help, dear Charmides; they're dragging me off with a rope.

CHARMIDES (*coming out of temple*): Who's calling?

LABRAX: Don't you see how they're taking me away?

CHARMIDES: Yes, and glad to see it too.

LABRAX: Won't you please help me?

CHARMIDES: Who's taking you?

LABRAX: The young man, Plesidippus.

CHARMIDES: Make the best of a bad business, and go to jail cheerfully. In this way you will attain what many desire.

LABRAX: What's that?

CHARMIDES: The goal you've always headed for.

LABRAX: Do please follow me.

CHARMIDES: Your advice is as bad as you are; they are taking you to jail and you ask me to follow you.

PLESIDIPPUS (*to* LABRAX): Are you still holding back?

LABRAX: I'm lost.

CHARMIDES: I hope you are.

PLESIDIPPUS (*turning to the two women*): And you, Palaestra dear, and Ampelisca, remain where you are until I return.

SLAVE: I suggest that they go to our house until you return.

PLESIDIPPUS: I like that; that's an excellent offer.

LABRAX: Oh, you thieves!

SLAVE: "Thieves"! is it? Jerk him along.

LABRAX: I beg of you, Palaestra!

PLESIDIPPUS: Come along, jail-bird.

LABRAX: My friend!

CHARMIDES: I'm no friend of yours; I repudiate your friendship.

LABRAX: Do you so spurn me?

CHARMIDES: I do; I've had one drink with you already.

LABRAX: A curse on you then.

CHARMIDES: On your own head, rather. (*Exeunt* PLESIDIPPUS *and slaves with* LABRAX.) I suppose men are changed into all sorts of animals, as the philosophers say. This procurer, for instance, will be turned into a stock dove; his neck will shortly be in the stocks; and the jail will be his dovecot. But just the same I'll go and act as his counsel, so that, if possible, he'll be the more quickly—sentenced.

[ACT FOUR: SCENE 1]

(*Enter* DAEMONES *from cottage.*)

DAEMONES: It's a pleasure to have done a good turn to these young women, and to have them as my wards, both young and pretty, too. But my wife, confound her, is always on the watch for fear I'll have some understanding with them. . . . But I wonder what in the world that slave of mine, Gripus, is doing. He left last night to fish in the sea. He would have been wiser to sleep at home; the rough weather, last night and this morning, must have played the deuce with his fishing, and his nets, too. I can fry on my fingers all he'll catch, with a sea running like this. But there's my wife calling luncheon; I'll go and have my ears filled with her idle talk.

[ACT FOUR: SCENE 2]

(Enter GRIPUS from the left. From his shoulder he drags a net, in which is secured a traveling hamper. The hamper is tied about with a rope, one end of which goes, with the net, over his shoulder, while the other trails lengthily behind him. He sings.)

GRIPUS: To Neptune, patron of fishermen, who dwells in the salt domain of the finny tribe, all thanks for this, in that he has sent me back from his realms so well supplied, with so rich a booty, and my fishing boat safe. In spite of rough seas, in strange and marvellous way, he has prettily enriched me with a haul the like of which none other has ever seen. And not a pound weight of fish have I caught this day, except what is here in this net. By rising in the middle of the night. I preferred gain to peaceful sleep, tried in the face of storm to relieve my poor master and my own slave's lot. I spared not myself. A lazy man is a man of naught, and I despise the tribe. He who would do his tasks in good season, should be awake, nor wait till his master stir him up. He who prefers sleep, takes his rest, to be sure, but without gain, and he suffers for it.

Now I, who have always worked hard, have found the means be idle, if I will. For this, whatever it is, I have found in the sea; and whatever it is, it's heavy. There's gold without doubt; and no one knows. The time has come to be free, Gripus. . . . I have a plan: I'll approach my master cunningly and shrewdly. I'll offer little by little small sums for my freedom. And when I am free, I'll have me an estate and house to match, my own property. I'll do merchandizing in great ships, and be the mightiest of the mighty. And then for my own pleasure I'll build me a ship, and like Stratonicus sail from port to port. When my fame is complete, I'll build a great city, and call it Gripus, a monument to my fame and fortunes. I shall then become king of the country. I have in mind to do mighty things. But first I'll hide this hamper. To think that I, this great king, must go without dainties for my breakfast, and be content with sour wine, and salt for relish. (*Moves toward cottage.*)

[ACT FOUR: SCENE 3]

(TRACHALIO, *who has been watching for some time from the left, now advances.*)

TRACHALIO: Wait there.

GRIPUS: What for?

TRACHALIO: While I coil up this rope you're dragging. (*He begins to coil it up.*)

GRIPUS: Just let that go.

TRACHALIO: But I'm helping you; favors done good men don't go unrewarded.

GRIPUS: The weather was stormy yesterday, and I haven't a fish; so don't expect anything. Don't you see I'm bringing back only a wet net, with no haul?

TRACHALIO: It isn't fish I want; but only a little talk with you.

GRIPUS: You bore me to death. (*Starts to go.*)

TRACHALIO (*grasping rope*): You shall not go; hold on.

GRIPUS: You look out for trouble. What the devil are you holding me back for?

TRACHALIO: Listen.

GRIPUS: I won't.

TRACHALIO: By George, you will.

GRIPUS: Well, later.

TRACHALIO: No, now.

GRIPUS: What do you wish, then?

TRACHALIO: It will pay you to hear what I have to say.

GRIPUS: Then why don't you talk?

TRACHALIO: See if anyone's following us.

GRIPUS: Does that interest me at all?

TRACHALIO: Certainly it does. Could you give me a little good advice?

GRIPUS: Speak up; what is it?

TRACHALIO: Be quiet now—I'll tell you, if you'll pledge your word to keep faith with me.

GRIPUS: I will, whoever you are.

TRACHALIO (*impressively*): Listen.
I saw a man steal something.
I knew the man from whom he stole it.
I went to the thief and made him an offer, like this:
"I know the man from whom you have stolen;
Divide the loot with me, and I'll keep quiet."
But he wouldn't give me any answer.
How much do you think I should get out of him?
I hope you'll say "a half."

GRIPUS: On the contrary, more than half; and if he doesn't give it to you, I advise you to inform the original owner.

TRACHALIO: I'll follow your advice. Now pay attention, for this concerns you.

GRIPUS: Why so?

TRACHALIO: I've known for a long time the man to whom that hamper belongs.

GRIPUS: What do you mean?

TRACHALIO: And how it was lost.

GRIPUS: You do, do you? Well, I know how it was found, and I know the man who found it, and who now owns it. How does this fact concern you, any more than the other concerns me? I know whose it is now; you know whose it was before. No one shall ever get it from me; don't you hope to.

TRACHALIO: If the owner should turn up, wouldn't he get it?

GRIPUS: Don't fool yourself; there's no man alive that will ever own it except me, who took it in my catch.

TRACHALIO: Is that so?

GRIPUS: You'll have to admit, won't you, that the fish I catch are mine? I treat them as mine, and no one else ever claims them or any part of them. I sell them openly in the market as mine. The sea is surely common to all.

TRACHALIO: I admit that; but why then should this hamper not be common to me, as well as to you? it was found in the common sea.

GRIPUS: Of all the impudence! If what you say is true, it's the end of all fishermen. For as soon as they offered fish in the market, no one would buy. They would say they were caught in the common sea, and each demand his share.

TRACHALIO: Talk about impudence! Have you the nerve to compare a hamper with a fish? Do they seem the same thing to you?

GRIPUS: I'm not responsible for the catch; I drop in my net and hooks, and draw in whatever's caught. And all that I take in that way is most decidedly mine.

TRACHALIO: Quite the contrary, by Jove, if what you've caught is a hamper.

GRIPUS: You're some shyster, you cut-throat!

TRACHALIO: But have you ever seen a fisherman catch and bring a hamper into market? You can't follow all the trades at once; you can't be a maker of hampers, and a fisherman at the same time. You'll have either to prove to me that a hamper's a fish, or else give up your claim to what's not raised in the sea, and has no scales.

GRIPUS: What! Have you never seen a hamper-fish?

TRACHALIO: There's no such thing, wretch.

GRIPUS: Sure, there is. I'm a fisherman, and ought to know. But they're rare, and you don't often land them.

TRACHALIO: Get out, thief. Do you think you can fool me? What color is it?

GRIPUS: The smaller ones are of this color (*points to hamper*). The big ones are red; and then there are some that are black.

TRACHALIO: I know; and you'll be turning into one yourself, if you don't look out; first *your* hide will be red, and then black.

GRIPUS (*aside*): What a rascal it is!

TRACHALIO (*aside*): We're wasting time; the day's going. (*To* GRIPUS) See here, at whose arbitration do you want this settled?

GRIPUS: At the arbitration of the hamper.

TRACHALIO: So?

GRIPUS: Yes, so!

TRACHALIO: You're a fool.

GRIPUS: My compliments, Philosopher!

TRACHALIO: You'll not get away with this today, without either a trustee or an arbitrator, at whose decision the matter will be settled.

GRIPUS: You must be crazy.

TRACHALIO: I do need hellebore.

GRIPUS: I'm cracked, myself; but nevertheless I'll not let this go.

TRACHALIO: Say another word, and I'll beat your head in with my fists; I'll squeeze the juice out of you like a new sponge.

GRIPUS: Just touch me; I'll smash you to the ground like an octopus.* You want to fight?

TRACHALIO: Oh, what's the use? Why don't we divide up instead?

GRIPUS: The only thing you can get here is trouble. I'm going.

TRACHALIO (*jerking him around by the rope*): I'll put the ship about, so that you can't go. Heave to, now.

GRIPUS: If you man the prow, I'll take the tiller. Avast on that rope, lubber.

TRACHALIO: Avast yourself; let go the hamper, and I'll let go the rope.

GRIPUS: You'll not be a penny the richer from coming here.

TRACHALIO: Well, you can't satisfy me by refusals; either give me a share, or else agree to an arbitrator or trustee.

GRIPUS: Even though I caught it in the sea?

TRACHALIO: But I saw it from the shore.

GRIPUS: It was my boat and net and work.

TRACHALIO: But if the true owner should appear, would I, who saw the act, be any less a thief than you?

GRIPUS: Not at all.

TRACHALIO: Wait then, you crook; how do you prove that I share in the theft and yet not in the booty?

GRIPUS: I can't say, and I don't know about your city laws; but I do know that this is mine.

TRACHALIO: And just as emphatically I say it's mine.

GRIPUS: Wait a minute; I've found a way for you not to share in the theft.

TRACHALIO: How?

GRIPUS: Let me go away; then you go away quietly. Don't you tell on me, and I'll not tell on you. You keep quiet, and I'll be mum.

TRACHALIO: Come, won't you make me an offer?

GRIPUS: I've made one: be off; drop that rope, and stop bothering me.

---

* Small octopuses are frequently caught in the Mediterranean. They are thrown on the ground and beaten long and lustily to make them tender—a table delicacy.—*Editor P. W. H.*

TRACHALIO: Wait until I make *you* an offer.

GRIPUS: Clear out instead.

TRACHALIO: Do you know anyone in these parts?

GRIPUS: I should know my neighbors.

TRACHALIO: Where do you live hereabouts?

GRIPUS: Off over there, by that further farm.

TRACHALIO: Are you willing that the man who lives here (*pointing to the cottage*) be arbitrator?

GRIPUS: Ease off on that rope a bit, while I step aside and consider.

TRACHALIO: All right.

GRIPUS (*aside*): By George, it's all safe now; this haul is mine for ever. He offers me my master as judge and my own home as the court; and *he* will never award a penny of that away from me. I'll accept him. This fellow doesn't know what he's offering.

TRACHALIO: Well, what do you say?

GRIPUS: While I know I'm absolutely in the right, yet rather than fight, I'll give in.

TRACHALIO: I'm glad to hear it.

GRIPUS: Although you are offering me an unknown arbiter, if he's an honorable man, a stranger is as good as one who is known; but even one's friend, if not honest, is utterly unsatisfactory.

[ACT FOUR: SCENE 4]

(*Enter* DAEMONES, *with* PALAESTRA *and* AMPELISCA, *from cottage.*)

DAEMONES: Seriously now, although I wish you very well, I fear my wife will drive me out of the house on your account; she will say I brought rivals in under her eyes. You must take refuge again at the altar, or I must.

PALAESTRA and AMPELISCA: Alas! we are lost.

DAEMONES: I'll place you here in safety; don't fear. But (*to the slaves*) what are you following for? No one will harm them, while I am here. Go home, both of you; you're no longer on guard.

GRIPUS: Good morning, master.

DAEMONES: Good morning, Gripus; how are things?

TRACHALIO (*to* DAEMONES): Is he your slave?

GRIPUS: Yes, and not ashamed to admit it.

TRACHALIO (*to* GRIPUS): I've nothing to do with you.

GRIPUS: Then please leave.

TRACHALIO: Tell me, worthy sir, is he your slave?

DAEMONES: He is.

TRACHALIO: Well, I'm very glad he is. For the second time, I give you good day.

DAEMONES: Good day to you. Wasn't it you who left here, a little while ago, to fetch your master?

TRACHALIO: Yes.

DAEMONES: What do you want now?

TRACHALIO: But is he (*pointing to* GRIPUS) really yours?

DAEMONES: He is.

TRACHALIO: Well, I'm very glad.

DAEMONES: What's the trouble?

TRACHALIO: He's a rascal.

DAEMONES: What's the rascal done to you?

TRACHALIO: I want you to crack his shins for him.

DAEMONES: What is it you two are quarreling about?

TRACHALIO: I'll tell you.

GRIPUS: Let me tell.

TRACHALIO: I'm doing this, I believe.

GRIPUS: If you had any shame, you'd get out of here.

DAEMONES (*to* GRIPUS): Pay attention, and keep quiet.

GRIPUS: Shall he speak first?

DAEMONES: Hear him. (*To* TRACHALIO) Speak on.

GRIPUS: Will you let an outsider speak first?

TRACHALIO: Can nothing shut him up? As I was about to say: this slave of yours has the hamper which belongs to the procurer you drove away from the temple.

GRIPUS: I don't have it.

TRACHALIO: Do you deny what I see with my own eyes?

GRIPUS: But I wish you couldn't see. What difference does it make to you whether I have it or don't have it?

TRACHALIO: It makes a great deal of difference whether you have it rightly or wrongly.

GRIPUS: You may hang me, if I didn't catch it in the sea, with my own net; how is it then yours rather than mine?

TRACHALIO: He's only bluffing; it's just as I tell you.

GRIPUS: What's that?

TRACHALIO: Can't you shut him up, until his betters have spoken?

DAEMONES: See here, what do you want?

TRACHALIO: I don't ask for any share in the hamper, and I haven't said it was mine. But there is in it a little casket, belonging to the woman I told you was free-born.

DAEMONES: The one you said was a compatriot of mine?

TRACHALIO: Yes; and the trinkets which she had as a little child are in that casket inside the hamper. This is of no use to him (*pointing to* GRIPUS), but, if given to her, would help the poor girl identify her parents.

DAEMONES: I'll see that he gives it to her. (*To* GRIPUS) Be silent.

GRIPUS: By Jove, I'll not do it.

TRACHALIO: I ask for nothing but the casket and trinkets.

GRIPUS: What if they are gold?

TRACHALIO: That would not affect you. You will receive your equivalent, gold for gold.

GRIPUS: Let me see the gold first; then you may take the casket.

DAEMONES: Take care now; and keep quiet. (*To* TRACHALIO) Go on with what you were saying.

TRACHALIO: I entreat you to have pity on the poor girl, if the hamper does belong to the slave dealer, as I suspect; of course I don't speak from certainty.

GRIPUS: You see? he's setting a trap for us.

TRACHALIO: Let me continue. If it does belong to the pander, as I suggest, these two will be able to tell. Let him show it to them.

GRIPUS: Show it?

DAEMONES: That's not unfair, Gripus—to show them the hamper.

GRIPUS: On the contrary, it's most unfair.

DAEMONES: How?

GRIPUS: Because, if I show it to them, they'll of course say, at once, it's theirs.

TRACHALIO: You scurvy knave! Do you think everybody's like yourself?

GRIPUS (*to* TRACHALIO): I don't mind all this, so long as he's on my side.

TRACHALIO: He may be on your side now, but he's going to hear the evidence.

DAEMONES: Gripus, pay attention. (*To* TRACHALIO) State briefly your demand.

TRACHALIO: I've told you, but I'll tell you again, if you didn't understand. Both of these women, as I've just said, ought to be free. This one was stolen from Athens, when a child.

GRIPUS: What's it got to do with the hamper, whether they're slaves or free?

TRACHALIO: Are you trying to kill time, you piker, by having everything told twice?

DAEMONES: Stop your abuse, and answer my question.

TRACHALIO: There should be a willow casket in that hamper, in which are the tokens by which she can identify her parents; she had them when she disappeared from Athens, as I have told you.

GRIPUS: Oh, you be damned! Look here, you body-snatcher, what's the matter with these women? are they dumb? can't they speak for themselves?

TRACHALIO: They're silent because a woman is good when she's quiet, not when she's talking.

GRIPUS: Then you are neither man nor woman.

TRACHALIO: Why is that?

GRIPUS: Because, whether talking or quiet, you're never good. But (*to* DAEMONES) when will you give me a chance to say something?

DAEMONES: If you add another word, I'll break your head.

TRACHALIO: As I was about to say, sir, I wish you'd tell him to return the casket to them; and if he wants a reward, he shall have it. And let him keep the rest for himself.

GRIPUS: You're saying that at last, because you recognize my rights; a while ago you demanded a half share.

TRACHALIO: And so I do now.

GRIPUS: I've seen a hawk swoop down, and yet, like you, get nothing.

DAEMONES: Can't I shut you up except by a beating?

GRIPUS: I'll be quiet, if he will; if he talks, then let me.

DAEMONES: Give me that hamper, Gripus.

GRIPUS: I'll give it to you, but on the condition that it be returned to me, if these things are not in it.

DAEMONES: Very well.

GRIPUS: Here it is.

DAEMONES: Palaestra, you and Ampelisca, listen carefully. Is this the hamper, in which you say your casket was?

PALAESTRA: It is.

GRIPUS: I lost out there; almost before she saw it, she said it was.

PALAESTRA: I will tell you all about it. There should be a wicker casket in the hamper; and I will name everything in it without looking. If I make a mistake, it will be my loss, and you may keep everything. If I am right, then please give it to me.

DAEMONES: Very well; that's mere justice.

GRIPUS: Mere injustice, by Jove. What if she's a witch, or fortune-teller, and knows everything in it? Will she get it just the same?

DAEMONES: She'll not get it without telling the truth; there's nothing in this fortune-telling business. Untie it, that we may know the facts as soon as possible.

TRACHALIO (*aside, exultingly*): That does for him!

GRIPUS: It's untied.

DAEMONES: Open it. . . . I see the casket. (*Lifting it out*) Is this it?

PALAESTRA: It is. O my father and my mother! In this little box I hold you; here is my one hope of finding you.

GRIPUS: The gods must be angry with you for getting your parents into such a tight box.

DAEMONES: Step here, Gripus; your interests are at stake. And you, girl, keep back, and describe every article here; everything, remember. If you should make the slightest mistake, something you'd like later to correct, it will be in vain.

GRIPUS (*emphatically*): That's right.

TRACHALIO: Then it's nothing to do with you; for you're all wrong.

DAEMONES: Speak now, girl. Gripus, keep quiet, and pay attention.

PALAESTRA: There are tokens.

DAEMONES: Yes, here they are.

GRIPUS: Down and out in the first round! (*As* DAEMONES *begins to lift out tokens*) Stop! don't show them to her.

DAEMONES: Describe them one after another.

PALAESTRA: First, there is a little sword of gold, with an inscription on it.

DAEMONES: What does the inscription say?

PALAESTRA: It gives my father's name. Next, there is a little double-headed battle-axe, also of gold, with my mother's name on it.

DAEMONES: Stop! what's the name of your father, on the sword?

PALAESTRA: Daemones.

DAEMONES (*in a low voice*): Good heavens! where are my hopes now?

GRIPUS: Rather, where are mine?

TRACHALIO: Go on; don't stop.

GRIPUS: On the contrary, go slow—or go to the deuce.

DAEMONES: What's the name of your mother here?

PALAESTRA: Daedalis.

DAEMONES: The gods wish me saved.

GRIPUS: And me, ruined.

DAEMONES: This must be my daughter, Gripus.

GRIPUS: She may be, for all of me. But (*shaking his fist at* TRACHALIO) curses on you for seeing me, and on myself, for not looking around a thousand times before drawing the net out of the water.

PALAESTRA: Then there's a little silver sickle, with two hands clasped about it; and then a crane—

GRIPUS: The devil take you and your cranes—I think you're a cormorant, yourself.

PALAESTRA: And a gold amulet, that my father gave me the day I was born.

DAEMONES: Without doubt it is she; I can wait no longer. (*Holds out his arms.*) Come to me, my daughter! I am Daemones, your own father; and your mother Daedalis is within the house.

PALAESTRA: O my father unexpected!

DAEMONES (*embracing her*): Find welcome in your father's arms.

TRACHALIO: It's a pleasure to see a daughter's piety so rewarded.

DAEMONES: Come, Trachalio, take this hamper, if you can, and carry it inside.

TRACHALIO (*to* GRIPUS): Here's a blow for you, Gripus; congratulations on your luck.

DAEMONES: Let us go, my dear, to your mother. She had more to do with you, and is acquainted with the tokens; and she will know the proofs better than I.

PALAESTRA: Let us all go in, as we have a common interest. Come, Ampelisca.

AMPELISCA: I am so pleased that fortune favors you at last.

(*Exeunt all but* GRIPUS *into cottage.*)

GRIPUS: Am I not a block-head to have fished up this hamper, or, having caught it, to fail to hide it? A troubled sea was certain to bring a troublesome catch; and it was sure full of gold and silver. I might as well go in and hang myself—for a little while, at least, until I stop feeling so bad. (*Exit* GRIPUS *into cottage.*)

[ACT FOUR: SCENE 5]

(*Enter* DAEMONES *from cottage, much pleased with himself.*)

DAEMONES: By the gods, was ever man more fortunate? I, who had neither hopes nor expectations, have suddenly found a daughter. When the gods wish us well, in some way our piety is rewarded by the granting of our hopes. And she shall marry this young man, of a good family, an Athenian gentleman, and, as it turns out, even a connection of ours. And I want his slave to summon him from town immediately. But I wonder where he is. I'll go to the door and see. Now look there—my wife with her arms still about her daughter's neck! There is almost too much of this affection; it's a bit boring. [SCENE 6] (*Calls into the house.*) It's time to put a stop to the kissing now, and prepare for the sacrifices which I shall offer, as soon as I return, to the gods of this house for their aid to us; we have sacrificial lambs and pigs all ready. But why do you women keep Trachalio so long? (*A moment later*) Good; here he comes.

TRACHALIO (*coming out of cottage*): I'll find Plesidippus and bring him back with me, wherever he is.

DAEMONES: Tell him about my daughter; ask him to drop everything and come.

TRACHALIO: Sure.

DAEMONES: Tell him he's to marry her.

TRACHALIO: Sure.

DAEMONES: And that I know his father, and find him a connection of mine.

TRACHALIO: Sure.

DAEMONES: But hasten.

TRACHALIO: Sure.

DAEMONES: So that we may have dinner ready for him soon.

TRACHALIO: Sure.

DAEMONES: Are you so *sure* of everything?

TRACHALIO: Sure. But do you know what I want of you? To remember your promise, so that I may get my freedom today.

DAEMONES: Sure.

TRACHALIO: Persuade Plesidippus to free me.

DAEMONES: Sure.

TRACHALIO: And get your daughter to urge him; she'll easily have her way with him.

DAEMONES: Sure.

TRACHALIO: And have Ampelisca marry me, when I'm free.

DAEMONES: Sure.

TRACHALIO: And let me find you grateful.

DAEMONES: Sure.

TRACHALIO: Are *you* so sure of everything?

DAEMONES: Sure; I'm just returning in kind. But go quickly to the city, and be back again.

TRACHALIO: Sure; I'll be back immediately. You, meanwhile, attend to the rest.

DAEMONES: Sure. (*Exit* TRACHALIO *to the town.*) The curse of

Hercules be on him and his sureness. He has split my ears with his continual "sure" to everything I said.

[ACT FOUR: SCENE 7]

(*Enter* GRIPUS *from cottage.*)

GRIPUS: How soon may I speak to you, Daemones?

DAEMONES: What's the matter, Gripus?

GRIPUS: About that hamper—a word to the wise! Keep what the gods have given you.

DAEMONES: Shall I claim what belongs to another?

GRIPUS: But I found it in the sea!

DAEMONES: All the better for the man who lost it; it doesn't make it any more yours on that account.

GRIPUS: This is why you're poor, Daemones; you're too good.

DAEMONES: O Gripus, Gripus, we find many pitfalls in this life, and traps to ensnare us; and the bait is so cunningly placed, that while in our greed we reach for it, we are caught. When a man is very careful, and clever, he may enjoy for a long time that which is honestly his. But this appears to be plunder that will soon be plundered from you again, wherein you lose more than you get. Shall I conceal what you have brought here, when I know it belongs to another? Your master will never do that. The wise man will always find it best to have no part in another's wrong. I don't care for wealth gained by deception.

GRIPUS: I've often gone to the play and heard talk like that, with the audience applauding the words of wisdom. But when we went back home, no one acted on the advice he had heard.

DAEMONES: Hold your tongue, and don't be troublesome; you may go inside. I'll not give it to you; don't deceive yourself.

GRIPUS: I hope to heaven everything in that hamper, whether gold or silver, turns to ashes. (*Exit.*)

DAEMONES: That's the reason we have such dishonest slaves. If he had applied to one of his fellows, he would have implicated both himself and the other in theft. While he would think to gull some one else, he would himself be gulled; one act would bring on the other. But I will go in and sacrifice, and then order dinner. (*Exit into cottage.*)

[ACT FOUR: SCENE 8]

(Enter PLESIDIPPUS *and* TRACHALIO *from right.)*

PLESIDIPPUS: Tell me that again, my dear Trachalio, my freedman, nay rather my patron, my father. Has Palaestra really found her parents?

TRACHALIO: She has.

PLESIDIPPUS: And is an Athenian?

TRACHALIO: I understand so.

PLESIDIPPUS: And will marry me?

TRACHALIO: I suspect as much.

PLESIDIPPUS: Do you think he will betroth her today?

TRACHALIO: I reckon.

PLESIDIPPUS: Shall I congratulate her father on finding her?

TRACHALIO: I reckon.

PLESIDIPPUS: And her mother?

TRACHALIO: I reckon.

PLESIDIPPUS: What is it then you reckon?

TRACHALIO: I reckon on what you ask.

PLESIDIPPUS: Do you reckon up the amount then?

TRACHALIO: Oh, I reckon.

PLESIDIPPUS: But I am here in person; so will you not close your reckoning?

TRACHALIO: I reckon.

PLESIDIPPUS: Would you say the same, if I ran?

TRACHALIO: I reckon.

PLESIDIPPUS: If I walked slowly, like this?

TRACHALIO: I reckon.

PLESIDIPPUS: Shall I salute her when I see her?

TRACHALIO: I reckon.

PLESIDIPPUS: And her father?

TRACHALIO: I reckon.

PLESIDIPPUS: And her mother, too?

TRACHALIO: I reckon. What next?

PLESIDIPPUS: Well then, shall I embrace her father when I see him?

TRACHALIO: I reckon not.

PLESIDIPPUS: Her mother?

TRACHALIO: I reckon not.

PLESIDIPPUS: But the girl herself?

TRACHALIO: I reckon not.

PLESIDIPPUS: The devil! he has stopped the review; just when I want him to go on, he puts an end to his reckonings.

TRACHALIO (*laughing*): What a fool you are! Come on.

PLESIDIPPUS: My dear patron, take me where you will. (*Exeunt into cottage.*)

[ACT FIVE: SCENE 1]

(*Enter* LABRAX *from right.*)

LABRAX: I am certainly the unluckiest man alive; I'm ruined, with the court deciding in favor of Plesidippus, and awarding Palaestra tò him. Your procurer is the only real son of joy: he gives such joy to others, when he gets into trouble. I'll try at least to get the other girl away from the temple of Venus; she's all that's left of my property.

[ACT FIVE: SCENE 2]

(*Enter* GRIPUS, *carrying a spit; he talks back into cottage.*)

GRIPUS: You'll not see Gripus alive by evening, unless you return me the hamper.

LABRAX: The devil! Every time I hear the word "hamper", it's like driving a stake through my heart.

GRIPUS: That scoundrel is free, while I, who fished the hamper out of the sea with my net, get nothing.

LABRAX: That puts a flea in my ear, by Jove.

GRIPUS: I'll put up a sign, I will, with letters a yard high telling anyone who has lost a hamper full of gold and silver to see Gripus. You'll not get away with that as you think.

LABRAX: This fellow apparently knows who has my hamper; I'll speak to him. (*Approaching* GRIPUS) Help me, ye gods.

GRIPUS: What are you calling for now? I want to clean this,

outside. (*To himself*) Jove! There's no iron left; it's all rust. The more I rub, the thinner and rustier it gets; it's bewitched, and dissolves in my hand.

LABRAX: Good day, young man.

GRIPUS: Lord bless you, you of the bald forehead.

LABRAX: How do you find yourself?

GRIPUS: Busy cleaning this spit.

LABRAX: How are you, I mean?

GRIPUS: Are you a doctor?

LABRAX: No, but I'm what comes from having one.*

GRIPUS: A beggar?

LABRAX: That strikes the nail on the head.

GRIPUS: Well, you look the part. What's happened to you?

LABRAX: Shipwrecked last night, and lost all I had.

GRIPUS: What did you lose?

LABRAX: A hamper full of gold and silver.

GRIPUS (*jumping up in great excitement*): Do you remember what was in the lost hamper?

LABRAX: What's the difference, now that it's lost?

GRIPUS: And yet—

LABRAX: Excuse me; let's talk of something else.

GRIPUS: Perhaps I know who found it. How can it be identified?

LABRAX: There were eight hundred gold pieces in it, in a purse, and a hundred Philippic pieces, in addition, in a leather bag.

GRIPUS (*aside*): Here's plunder for you; there will be a large reward. I'm a favorite of the gods, and will just annex this plunder. It's his hamper, all right. (*To* LABRAX) Go on with the rest.

LABRAX: Then you'll find a full-weight talent of silver, in a money-bag, and besides that, a drinking-bowl, a tankard, a pitcher, a jug, and a ladle.

GRIPUS: My! but you had a rich pile!

LABRAX: That's a miserable and cursed word, to say I "had".

GRIPUS: What would you care to give to the man who discovered this and showed it to you? Tell me quickly.

---

* The joke in the original is quite different—a word play on *medicus* and *mendicus* (beggar).—*Editor* P. W. H.

LABRAX: Three hundred drachmas.

GRIPUS: Stuff and nonsense!

LABRAX: Four hundred then.

GRIPUS: A dirty bagatelle!

LABRAX: Five hundred.

GRIPUS: Nuts!

LABRAX: Six hundred.

GRIPUS: That's weevil talk.

LABRAX: I'll give eight hundred.

GRIPUS: Your mouth's hot, and you're trying to cool it off.

LABRAX: Make it a thousand, then.

GRIPUS: You're dreaming.

LABRAX: I'll not add another penny.

GRIPUS: Good-bye, then.

LABRAX: Hold on; if I go away from here, I'll be gone. Do you want eleven hundred?

GRIPUS: You're asleep.

LABRAX: Tell me how much you do want.

GRIPUS: A talent of silver; and you needn't add to that unless you wish to—but nothing less. Say yes or no.

LABRAX: Well, as I see it's necessary, I'll give the talent.

GRIPUS (going to the altar): Come here; I want Venus to hear your oath.

LABRAX: Anything you wish; give me your orders.

GRIPUS: Touch the altar.

LABRAX: I'm touching it.

GRIPUS: Swear before Venus, here.

LABRAX: Swear what?

GRIPUS: What I tell you.

LABRAX: Dictate any oaths you want; but, as I am never at a loss for them, I don't need help.

GRIPUS: Now touch the altar.

LABRAX: I'm touching it.

GRIPUS: Swear that you will give me the money, as soon as you get your hamper.

LABRAX: Very well.

GRIPUS: Repeat after me: Venus of Cyrene, I call thee to witness,

LABRAX: Venus of Cyrene, I call thee to witness,

GRIPUS: If I find the hamper full of gold and silver, which I lost in the sea,

LABRAX: If I find the hamper full of gold and silver, which I lost in the sea,

GRIPUS: then I to this Gripus—(When you say that, touch me.)

LABRAX: then I to this Gripus—(I say this that thou mayest hear, O Venus.)

GRIPUS: will at once give to him an Attic talent.

LABRAX: will at once give to him an Attic talent.

GRIPUS: Pray also that if you cheat me, Venus shall curse you and your profession, root and branch. (*Aside*) And I pray that she does this anyway, exactly as you swear it.

LABRAX: If, O Venus, I fail in my oath in any respect, I pray that all procurers may suffer.

GRIPUS (*aside*): They will, even if you keep your oath. (*To* LABRAX) Wait here; I'll bring the old man out. Then you ask at once for the hamper. (*Exit into cottage.*)

LABRAX: Even if he does return, he'll never get a penny out of me. It's for me to decide what I shall swear to. But soft, here he comes with the old man.

[ACT FIVE: SCENE 3]

(*Enter* GRIPUS *with* DAEMONES, GRIPUS *carrying the hamper.*)

GRIPUS: This way.

DAEMONES: Where's the procurer?

GRIPUS (*to* LABRAX): Here's your man; he has the hamper.

DAEMONES (*to* LABRAX): I acknowledge that I have; if it is yours, you may have it. You will find the contents untouched. Take it, if it is yours.

LABRAX: Immortal gods, it's mine. (*Kissing and embracing it*) Welcome back, my hamper.

DAEMONES: It's yours then?

LABRAX: Even if it were Jove's, it's mine just the same.

DAEMONES: Everything is there safe, with the exception of the little casket containing tokens by which I have discovered my daughter.

LABRAX: Your daughter?

DAEMONES: The girl whom you knew as Palaestra has proved to be my daughter.

LABRAX: That's good, by Jove; I'm glad things have turned out so well for you.

DAEMONES: I can't readily believe that.

LABRAX: Well, by Jove, to make you believe it, don't give me a penny for her; she's yours, free.

DAEMONES: That's certainly very generous.

LABRAX: On the contrary, you are the generous one.

GRIPUS: I say, you've got your hamper now.

LABRAX: I have.

GRIPUS: Then hurry up.

LABRAX: Hurry up about what?

GRIPUS: To hand over the money.

LABRAX: I'll give you nothing, nor do I owe you anything.

GRIPUS: What does this mean? You don't owe me anything?

LABRAX: No, by Jove.

GRIPUS: Didn't you just swear to me?

LABRAX: Yes, and I'll swear again, if I please. Oaths were invented to save property, not to lose it.

GRIPUS: Come, hand that Attic talent over, oath-breaker.

DAEMONES: What's this talent you're demanding, Gripus?

GRIPUS: The one he swore he would give me.

LABRAX: I make an oath when I please; are you my father confessor?

DAEMONES (to GRIPUS): For what did he promise you the money?

GRIPUS: He swore to give me a full silver talent, if I returned his hamper.

LABRAX: Come, name me some patron with whom I may go to court, to prove that you made the bargain under false pretenses, and that I am not yet of legal age.

GRIPUS (pointing to DAEMONES): Take him.

LABRAX: I'd rather have some one else.

DAEMONES: Did you promise him this money?

LABRAX: I confess I did.

DAEMONES: What you promised my slave, you owe me. Don't think you can be using a procurer's honor with me; you can't do it.

GRIPUS (to LABRAX): Did you think you had found a man you could cheat? You'll have to pay this in full; then I'll give it to him for my freedom.

DAEMONES: Since this was saved for you by my kindness and assistance—

GRIPUS: By mine; don't say by yours.

DAEMONES (to GRIPUS): If you're wise, you'll keep quiet—(to LABRAX) You will do well to repay my kindness by kindness on your part.

LABRAX: You recognize my rights then by your request?

DAEMONES: It would be strange if I should risk trying to take your own rights from you.

GRIPUS (aside, as LABRAX hesitates): It's all safe; the procurer is wavering; freedom is at hand.

DAEMONES: He found the hamper, and he is my property. I've saved this for you, with all the money in it.

LABRAX (after further hesitation): I'm obliged to you, and as to the talent I swore to give him, you may have it.

GRIPUS: Here, give that to me, please.

DAEMONES: Will you keep quiet?

GRIPUS (to DAEMONES): While pretending to look after my interests, you're looking after your own. You'll not beat me out of this, by Jove, if I did lose the other.

DAEMONES: You'll get a thrashing, if you say another word.

GRIPUS: Beat me to death, but you'll never shut me up except with a talent.

LABRAX (to GRIPUS): Keep quiet; he's doing this in your interest.

DAEMONES: Step over this way, Labrax.

LABRAX: Very well.

GRIPUS: No, do it openly; I don't like this secret diplomacy.

DAEMONES: Shall I make you a first-rate offer?

LABRAX: By all means.

DAEMONES: I'll divide that talent with you.

LABRAX: That's very kind.

DAEMONES: Take one half of the talent yourself for the freedom of that other girl, and give the other half to me.

LABRAX: By all means.

DAEMONES: With this half, I'll free Gripus, through whom you found your hamper, and I my daughter.

LABRAX: That's all right, and I'm very much obliged.

(*They now turn toward* GRIPUS.)

GRIPUS: How soon will the money be paid me?

DAEMONES: It's all paid, Gripus; I have it.

GRIPUS: Yes, by Jove, but I prefer to have it myself.

DAEMONES: There's nothing here for you; don't expect it. I want you to acquit him of his oath.

GRIPUS: Curse the luck; I'm damned if I don't hang myself. You'll never cheat me again after today.

DAEMONES: Labrax, dine with me.

LABRAX: Very well; I should be pleased.

DAEMONES: Follow me in. (*To the audience*) I should invite you in the audience also, except that we're going to have nothing worth eating, and if I didn't think you all had dinner invitations anyway. But if you are willing to applaud the play heartily, come and make a night of it with me—sixteen years from now. (*To* LABRAX *and* GRIPUS) You two will dine here.

LABRAX and GRIPUS: Very well.

DAEMONES: Now, your applause.

TERENCE

THE PHORMIO

TRANSLATED BY WILLIAM ABBOTT OLDFATHER

CHARACTERS IN THE PLAY

DAVOS, *a slave, friend of Geta*

GETA, *a slave belonging to Demipho*

ANTIPHO, *son of Demipho*

PHAEDRIA, *son of Chremes, and cousin of Antipho*

DEMIPHO, *an elderly man, father of Antipho, brother of Chremes, and uncle of Phaedria*

PHORMIO, *a man about town, technically called a "parasite"*

HEGIO ⎫
CRATINUS ⎬ *legal counsel for Demipho*
CRITO ⎭

DORIO, *a slave dealer*

CHREMES, *an elderly man, brother of Demipho, married to Nausistrata, father of Phaedria, and uncle of Antipho*

SOPHRONA, *the nurse of Phanium, the illegitimate daughter of Chremes and a woman in Lemnos, recently married to her cousin, Antipho. "Modesty"*

NAUSISTRATA, *wife of Chremes*

Note: The two young women about whose fortunes the plot revolves do not appear.

THE PHORMIO

[ACT ONE: SCENE 1]

(SCENE: *A street in Athens; three house-doors.*)

DAVOS (*coming in from one side and at once taking the audience into his confidence*): My good old friend and fellow countryman, Geta, was around to see me yesterday. For some time I'd been owing him a trifle on a bit of an account. I was to get it together. Get it together I did, and here it is. (*Holding up a bag of money*) The fact is, they say his young master has gone and got married. I suppose it's for the bride he's scraping up this wedding present. What a crying shame that those who have little enough to start with must always be adding something to rich folks! What he's had hard work to save, a speck at a time, out of his daily rations, by fairly starving himself, poor fellow, all that she'll grab off, without ever a thought about what it cost him. What's more, they'll strike Geta for another present when the first baby comes, another on his birthday, another when he gets initiated into the mysteries. All this the mother will walk off with; the baby's merely an excuse for sending presents. (*As* GETA *comes out*)— But, I say, isn't that Geta coming out now?

[ACT ONE: SCENE 2]

GETA (*to some one in the house*): If any red-headed fellow asks for me—

DAVOS (*tapping his shoulder*): Never mind, I'm right here.

GETA (*glancing around*): Oh, I was just starting to look you up, Davos.

DAVOS (*giving over the bag*): There you are; take it; it's good, no counterfeit coins; you'll find it's the exact amount I owe.

GETA: That's very kind of you, and thanks for not forgetting me.

DAVOS: You'd better thank me, the way things are now. Why, they've got to such a pass, if anybody pays anything back you ought to be good and grateful! But why are you so down in the mouth?

GETA: Me? You don't know all the fear and danger we're in.

DAVOS: And what's that?

GETA: I'll tell you, if only you can keep it to yourself.

DAVOS: Get out, you simpleton! When you've tested a fellow's honesty in a business transaction, are you afraid to trust him with mere words? Besides, what's there in it for me, even if I *should* play you false?

GETA: Well, listen then.

DAVOS (*in mock politeness*): I guarantee you my careful attention.

GETA: Well, Davos, you know Chremes, the brother of our old man, don't you?

DAVOS: Sure.

GETA: All right, and his son, Phaedria, too?

DAVOS: As well as I know you.

GETA: Both old gentlemen went off on a trip at the same time, as luck would have it, Chremes to Lemnos, our old man to Cilicia, to visit an old friend. That friend had sent him a letter inviting him to come, promising him all but mountains of gold.

DAVOS: What? When he had already so much and to spare?

GETA: Don't get excited, that's just his way.

DAVOS: Oh, if only I had been born a millionaire!

GETA: The two old men when they went away left me behind here as a guardian for their sons.

DAVOS: A right tough proposition, eh, Geta?

GETA: I found that out, all right, by experience, too. As I think it over now, my guardian angel must surely have had it in for me. I started in at first trying to hold them down (*with an expressive gesture*); to make a long story short, being true to the old man meant *my* taking it on the chin.

DAVOS: Yes, I was thinking about that! It's foolish, you know, kicking against the pricks.

GETA: Then I began to do everything they wanted, to indulge them in every humor.

DAVOS: You knew how to play the market, all right.

GETA: Our young man didn't do anything bad to begin with. But that fellow, Phaedria, the first thing *he* did was to tie up with a little chit of a chorus-girl; went just crazy about her. She belonged to the filthiest kind of slave dealer, and Phaedria didn't have a penny to give him—the old gentleman had looked out for that, all right. There was nothing left for him to do but feast his eyes, tag around after her, take her to the music school, and then back home again. We weren't very busy either, and so helped him out.

Now, right across the street from her music school there was a barbershop. We usually loafed around there, waiting for her until she got ready to go home. Well, one day as we were sitting in the shop, up came a boy with tears in his eyes. We were surprised; and asked him what was up. "I never realized before," said he, "what a miserable, crushing burden poverty is. Right around the corner here, a moment ago, I saw a girl crying her eyes out over her dead mother. There she was without a friend, without an acquaintance, without even a neighbor,—nobody, but one little old woman, to help her with the funeral. It was really pitiful; a pretty girl, too." Well, of course, he made a great impression on us. Antipho blurts out: "Why not go and see her?" Some one else says: "All right, let's go; lead the way, won't you?" We went, we got there, we took a look. She *was* a pretty girl, and you could put it all the stronger, too, because she didn't have *any* make-up. Hair down her back, barefoot, frowsy, weepy, and a shabby dress on. Why, if her beauty hadn't been the real thing, all that would have simply ruined it. The one that was in love with the chorus-girl merely said: "Not so bad, at that"; but *my* young master!

DAVOS: *I* know; Antipho fell in love with her.

GETA: Well, rather! But look what came of it. The next day he goes straight to the old woman and begs for an introduction. She wants to know if he has honorable intentions; the girl was a citizen of Athens, of good character, and from a good family. If he wanted to, he could make her his lawful and wedded wife.

Anything else, no, no! Our young man was utterly nonplussed. He would have married her, all right, but he was afraid of his father, who was out of town.

DAVOS: Well, wouldn't his father have forgiven him, when he got back?

GETA: What? *He* allow *him* to marry a girl without any dowry, that nobody knew anything about? He would never do it.

DAVOS: Well, what next?

GETA: What next? There's a man about town here by the name of Phormio; he's got more *gall;* (*in a sudden fit of anger*) damn him!

DAVOS: What did *he* do?

GETA: He put them up to this: Says he: "There's a law that orphan girls must marry their next of kin, and the same law goes on to compel the kinsmen to take them, or else furnish a dowry. Now, I'll claim that you're her cousin, and sue you. I'll make it out that I'm an old friend of the girl's father; we'll come to court; who her father was, and her mother, and just how she's related to you, I'll make all that up, and it will be a good and easy thing for *me*. Of course you won't deny a thing I say, and so I'll win the case. Your father gets back; I'll have trouble on my hands; who cares? By that time we'll have the girl."

DAVOS: What a jolly piece of impudence!

GETA: The young man fell for it; the deed was done; we went to court and lost the case; he married the girl!

DAVOS: You don't say!

GETA: I certainly do.

DAVOS: Oho, Geta, what's going to happen to you?

GETA: Heavens, don't ask me! (*A pause, and then a bit grandiloquently*) Yet this one thing I know: Whatever fortune chance may bring, we'll bravely bear the blow!

DAVOS: That's right. (*Patting him on the back*) There, there! That's showing them you can take it.

GETA (*still somewhat exalted*): This courage of mine is my only hope!

DAVOS: That's fine!

GETA: Of course I might apply to a professional peacemaker. He would intercede for me like this: "Now, please, let him off this time; if he ever does anything again, I won't have a word to say"; all but adding: "Kill him, for all I care, as soon as my back is turned."

DAVOS (*insinuatingly*): What about the chorus-girl's "chaperon"? How's he getting along?

GETA (*with a shrug*): So-so; pretty slim pickings for him.

DAVOS: Hasn't a great deal to give her, perhaps?

GETA: Worse than that; he hasn't anything at all but sheer—hopes.

DAVOS: Is his father back?

GETA: Not yet.

DAVOS: When are you looking for your old man?

GETA: Don't know for sure; but I just heard a while ago that a letter from him had come and had been taken to the customs house; I'm going after it now.

DAVOS: Well, Geta, there's nothing more I can do for you, is there?

GETA: Only be good to yourself. (*Exit* DAVOS. GETA *walks back to the door of* DEMIPHO's *house, knocks, and calls.*) Hey there, boy! (*Slave appears.*) Take that and give it to my Dorcium. (*Exit.*)

[ACT ONE: SCENE 3]

(ANTIPHO *and* PHAEDRIA *enter.*)

ANTIPHO (*dejectedly*): That it should have come to this, Phaedria! I simply shudder when I think of my father coming home, and yet everything he does is meant for my best interests. If I hadn't been so thoughtless, I'd be looking for him now the way I ought to be.

PHAEDRIA (*impatiently*): What's all this now?

ANTIPHO: *You* ask that, when you were in on the whole wild scheme? Oh, how I wish it had never entered Phormio's head to put me up to that, and that he hadn't driven me to take that first step which started all this trouble! I wouldn't have the girl of course; that *would* be pretty tough—for a few days, at least; but then I wouldn't be so everlastingly worried—

PHAEDRIA: Yes! Yes!

ANTIPHO: While I'm wondering how soon father's going to come and take away my wife.

PHAEDRIA (*seriously*): See here, Antipho, some people feel bad because they don't possess the object of their affections; you seem to be suffering because you've got too much of yours. You're simply embarrassed with bliss, Antipho. So help me Heaven, I swear, this life of yours is what all men covet and desire. Bless *me!* I'd sell my life right on the spot if I could have *my* sweetheart as long as you've had yours already. Just you try to imagine the other side of the picture, all that I'm suffering now from privation, and all that you're enjoying from possession; to say nothing of the fact that, without any expense, you've found a well-born and well-bred lady, that you can acknowledge her openly as your wife, without any scandal—a perfectly happy man but for one thing, a disposition to take it all and be content. Why, if you had anything to do with a slave dealer like mine, then you'd find out! But that's the way most all of us are made; always feeling sorry for ourselves!

ANTIPHO: Quite the contrary, Phaedria; you're the one that looks lucky to me. You have perfect liberty to change your mind all over again, and decide what you'd rather do: keep her, love her, or let her go. But as for me, poor devil, I've got into such a jam that there's no chance of letting her go, or of keeping her, either. (*Surprised*) But what's that? Isn't this Geta coming here on the dead run? It's the very man himself. I'm dreadfully afraid to hear the news he's bringing.

[ACT ONE: SCENE 4]

GETA (*excited, to himself*): You're a dead duck, Geta, unless you find some way out, and mighty quick, too; such a cloud of trouble has all of a sudden gathered over your unprotected head; I don't see how I'm going to dodge it or get out from under. These wild doings of ours can't possibly be kept dark any longer.[1]

ANTIPHO (*to* PHAEDRIA, *aside*): What is it he's come here in such a fright about?

---

[1] Line 181a in Kauer-Lindsay has been omitted here.

GETA: Besides, I've only a moment for the whole business; master's right on my heels!

ANTIPHO: What *can* the matter be?

GETA: As soon as he gets wind of it, what remedy have I to cool off his rage? Talk? That would be simply setting fire to him. Hold my tongue? That would be just egging him on. Excuse myself? Might as well launder a brickbat. I'm frightened for myself, of course, but it's the thought of Antipho that fairly wrings my heart. He's the one I feel sorry for, he's the one I'm afraid for, and he's the one, too, that's keeping me back. If it weren't for him, I'd have looked out for myself all right, and got even with the old man for his nasty temper. I'd have bundled up a few old traps, and taken to my heels, right straight out of here.

ANTIPHO: What's he getting ready to steal and run off with?

GETA: But where shall I find Antipho? What street'll I take to go and look for him?

PHAEDRIA: He mentioned your name.

ANTIPHO: I'm afraid this messenger has news of some awful trouble for me.

PHAEDRIA: Oh, pull yourself together!

GETA: I guess I'll go into the house; he's most always there.

PHAEDRIA: Let's call the fellow back.

ANTIPHO (*to* GETA): Stop there, you, right where you are!

GETA (*without looking around*): Huh! Pretty peremptory tone you take, whoever you are.

ANTIPHO: Geta!

GETA (*turning*): He's just the man I was looking for.

ANTIPHO: Come, what's the news? And if you can, tell it in a word.

GETA: I'll do so—

ANTIPHO: Well, out with it!

GETA: I just saw at the harbor—your—

ANTIPHO (*in dismay*): What, mine?

GETA: You've hit it.

ANTIPHO: Dead and done for!

PHAEDRIA (*excited*): W-h-e-w! (*Whistling*)

ANTIPHO: What *am* I to do?

PHAEDRIA (*to* GETA): What's that you say?

GETA: I've seen the man that's *his* father and *your* uncle.

ANTIPHO: Oh, how can I get out of this sudden jam? (*Addressing* PHANIUM, *his wife, who is indoors*) Oh, my dear Phanium, if fortune comes to such a pass that I must be torn from you, life will no longer be worth living.

GETA: Well, if that's the case, Antipho, you ought to be all the more alert. Fortune favors the brave.

ANTIPHO (*weakly*): But I'm all upset.

GETA: And yet this is the time of all times, Antipho, when you ought to be in complete control of yourself; for if your father sees you're scared, he'll think you're guilty.

PHAEDRIA: That's so.

ANTIPHO: I can't change my character.

GETA: What would you do, if you had something even harder than this to do?

ANTIPHO: As I can't do this, I'd be still less able to do the other.

GETA (*irritated*): This is all nonsense, Phaedria; it's no use; let's go. What are we wasting our time *here* for? *I'm* going into the house.

PHAEDRIA: So am I. (*Starts.*)

ANTIPHO (*frightened*): Oh, please don't! What if I put up a bluff? (*Makes an effort.*) How's that?

GETA (*without looking around*): Drivel!

ANTIPHO: Look at my face. There! Won't that do?

GETA (*indifferently*): No!

ANTIPHO (*even bolder*): How about this?

GETA: *Almost.*

ANTIPHO (*folding arms with great dignity*): How's this, then?

GETA (*enthusiastically*): That's the stuff. Now, keep looking like that, and mind you answer him word for word, tit for tat, so he won't blast you off the field of battle with his violent language when he gets all wrought up.

ANTIPHO (*weakly*): Yes, I know.

GETA: Tell him you were compelled to do it, against your will.

PHAEDRIA: By due process of law, by a judgment of the court.

GETA: Do you get that? But who's that old man at the end of the street? Why, its Demipho himself!

ANTIPHO (*frantically running off*): I *can't* stay.

GETA: Hey, what are you up to? Where are you going, Antipho? Wait, I say!

ANTIPHO (*as he disappears*): I know myself and all my faults. I entrust Phanium and my life to you two boys. (*Exit.*)

PHAEDRIA: What will happen now, Geta?

GETA: *You'll* get a calling down; I'll be strung up and whipped, if I don't miss my guess. But, Phaedria, we ourselves now will have to take the advice we were giving Antipho a moment ago.

PHAEDRIA: Get out with your "have to." Just give me your orders about what I'm going to do.

GETA: Do you remember, when you started in with this affair, how you and he used to argue, by way of protecting yourselves from trouble, that the case was just, easy, in the bag, the best ever?

PHAEDRIA: I do.

GETA: Very well, that's exactly the kind of talk we need now, or rather, if possible, even better and smarter talk than that.

PHAEDRIA: I'll do my best.

GETA: Now you begin the assault. I'll stay here in ambush, and play first reserves, in case you need any help (*ducking into an alleyway*).

PHAEDRIA: All right, go to it. (*Retiring a little to one side.*)

[ACT TWO: SCENE I]

DEMIPHO (*enters, muttering to himself*): Well, well, well, so Antipho has gone and got married without consulting me, has he? The very idea of his not respecting my authority—but dropping that—no consideration for my displeasure! Utterly lost to shame! Oh, what an outrage! Oh, Geta! You put him up to it!

GETA (*aside*): I'm in for it at last.

DEMIPHO: I wonder what they'll say, what excuse they'll find. I should *really* like to know.

GETA: *I'll* find one, don't *you* worry about *that.*

DEMIPHO: Will he say, "I did it against my will, the law compelled me"? (*Ironically*) Oh, yes! Of course!

GETA: You old dear!

DEMIPHO: Yes, but with your eyes wide open, and without saying a single word, simply to give the case to the other side? Did the law compel you to do that, too?

PHAEDRIA: That's a hard nut to crack.

GETA: I'll crack it, all right; leave that to me.

DEMIPHO: I don't know what to do, it's taken me all in a heap. I never looked for anything like that, and now I can't believe it. I'm so annoyed I can't collect myself and think the thing out. (*Moralizing*) So ought all men, at the very height of their good fortune, consider how they are going to bear the bitterness of suffering, peril, loss, and exile. When a man comes home from foreign parts he ought to expect that his son has got into a scrape, his wife died, his daughter fallen sick—these things happen to everybody else, why not to him?—so that nothing catches him off his guard. As a result, whatever takes you by surprise, you can set down as so much clear profit.

GETA (*aside*): O, Phaedria, you can hardly believe how much smarter I am than the boss! *I've* thought over every one of the misfortunes waiting for me when he got back. I'll have to turn the grist mill, take a flogging, wear chains, work on the farm; no one of these things will catch *me* off my guard. Whatever surprises *me*, I'll set down as just so much velvet. But why don't you run up to the fellow and give him the glad hand as a starter?

DEMIPHO (*as* PHAEDRIA *hurries out*): There's my nephew, Phaedria, coming to meet me.

PHAEDRIA (*cheerfully*): Well, well, uncle, how *do* you do, anyway?

DEMIPHO (*brusquely*): How do you do? Where's Antipho?

PHAEDRIA: Now that you've got back safe and sound, I—

DEMIPHO (*impatiently*): Oh yes, of course, but answer my question.

PHAEDRIA: Antipho? Why, he's well, he's here in town. But do you find that everything has been going to suit you, now you're back?

DEMIPHO: I wish it had.

PHAEDRIA (*in affected surprise*): What do you mean by that?

DEMIPHO: Have you got the gall to ask me such a question, Phaedria? (*Sarcastically*) That's a nice mess of a marriage you've cooked up here while I was away.

PHAEDRIA: What? Are *you* angry at *him* now for *that*?

GETA (*aside*): This is what I call really artistic.

DEMIPHO: Why shouldn't I be angry at him? I'm just aching to catch sight of him, and let him know that good-natured old dad of his has turned into a regular savage, and he's nobody to blame for it but himself, either.

PHAEDRIA: And yet, uncle, he hasn't given you the *least* ground for getting angry.

DEMIPHO: Just listen to that, will you! All of one piece; they're in cahoots. If you know one, you know 'em all.

PHAEDRIA (*with an air of injured innocence*): It's not so.

DEMIPHO: A's in trouble; B pleads his case; B's in trouble; A's right there to help him. Mutual Protective Association!

GETA (*aside*): The old man hardly realizes it himself, but he has certainly drawn them to the life!

DEMIPHO: Why, if it weren't so, Phaedria, you wouldn't be taking his side now.

PHAEDRIA (*with a serious air*): Now, uncle, if it is *really true* that Antipho has made a mistake at some point in which he hasn't been careful enough about his property or his reputation, I haven't a word to say against his suffering all he deserves. *But,* if someone, counting on his malicious cunning, set a trap for our youthful innocence and caught us in it, whose fault is it, ours or the judge's? You know yourself they often rob the rich because they have it in for them, and give something to the poor out of mere sympathy.

GETA (*aside*): If I didn't know the facts in the case, I'd swear he was telling the truth.

DEMIPHO: Why, is there any judge on earth that can recognize the justice of your case when you yourself do as he did, and never say a word?

PHAEDRIA (*with great dignity*): He acted exactly as a young gentleman should. When he got to court he simply was unable to recite his little piece. He was so modest he was just struck dumb with stage-fright.

GETA (*aside*): Three cheers for him! But why not hustle out and greet the old man myself? (*Eagerly*) Hello, master, I'm awfully glad to see you back safe and sound!

DEMIPHO (*in disgust*): Oh, how do *you* do, noble guardian, mainstay of my family, my personal representative while I was away!

GETA (*injured*): I have heard already how you have been accusing us, when we were perfectly innocent, and me, too, especially, the *most* innocent of them all. Why, what did you expect *me* to do for you? The law won't let a slave plead a case; *he* can't even give testimony.

DEMIPHO: Oh, I waive all that; I grant your excuse: "The innocent boy got stage-fright"; of course you're a slave, but, even if she'd been the very nearest and dearest kin to him, there wasn't any need of *marrying* the girl. Why *didn't* you take the alternative that the law provides? Give her a dowry and let her go and hunt up some other husband? On what account *ever* did he choose to bring home a *pauper*?

GETA (*sarcastically*): It wasn't an *account* at all, they wanted spot cash.

DEMIPHO: He should have *got* it somewhere or other.

GETA (*ironically*): "Somewhere or other"! Nothing more easily *said!*

DEMIPHO: At the very worst, if he couldn't get it any other way, from some loan shark.

GETA: Huh! Fine idea, that! As if anybody would trust *him* as long as you were yet alive!

DEMIPHO: No, no! I *won't* have it that way! It *can't* be! Do you think I'll let him keep *her* as his wife a single day? The case doesn't call for kindness. I want you to bring that fellow here to me, or else show me where he lives.

GETA: Who? Phormio?

DEMIPHO: That guardian of the girl.

GETA: I'll have him here in a jiffy.

DEMIPHO: Where's Antipho now?

GETA: He's out.

DEMIPHO: Phaedria, you go hunt him up and bring him here.

PHAEDRIA: All right. I'll make a beeline. (*Exit.*)

GETA (*aside*): Yes, a beeline to go see his Pamphila. (*Exit, grinning.*)

DEMIPHO: I'll turn into the house now and salute the gods of my hearth and home. Then I'll go on downtown and get a few friends together to stand by me in this affair. I won't be caught napping, then, if Phormio should come

[ACT TWO: SCENE 2]

(PHORMIO *and* GETA *enter.*)

PHORMIO: And so he got scared when he heard his father was back, and ran off, did he?

GETA: Exactly.

PHORMIO: Phanium left all alone?

GETA: Just so.

PHORMIO: The old man furious?

GETA: Precisely.

PHORMIO: The whole thing's up to *you*, Phormio, old boy, and you alone. You mixed up this mess, now you've got to eat it. Roll up your sleeves and spit on your hands.

GETA: Oh, please!

PHORMIO (*too intent to notice*): Supposing he asks—?

GETA: You're our only hope.

PHORMIO (*triumphantly*): There you are! But if he retorts—?

GETA: You got us into this.

PHORMIO: That'll fix him, I guess.

GETA: O, help us out!

PHORMIO: Trot out your old gentleman. I've got my plans all drawn up in battle array, right here in my head.

GETA: What will you do?

PHORMIO: What do you want? Let Phanium stay here, clear Antipho of any blame, and turn the torrent of the old man's wrath upon myself.

GETA: Oh, you dear, brave man! But, Phormio, I'm often afraid that those daredevil ways of yours will land you in the stocks some day.

PHORMIO: Not a bit of it! I've run the gauntlet before. I know how to watch my step. How many fellows, would you guess, I've beaten up to the very point of death, down to date, regular citizens, too, as well as mere foreigners? The oftener I do it, the easier it goes. But say, did you ever hear of anybody suing me for assault and battery?

GETA: No, I never did. What's the answer?

PHORMIO: Why, because we never set a trap for hawks and buzzards that will play hob with us, if we catch them; but we *do* set traps for harmless birds. The fact is, you can pluck a dove, but when you catch a buzzard you've merely got your trouble for your pains. Men who have anything they can get skinned out of, are likely to find trouble almost anywhere. Everybody knows *I* haven't anything to lose. Perhaps you'll say: "If you lose your case and can't pay your fine, the court will put you into your enemies' custody, until you do." Granted. But *they're* not anxious to feed a ravenous appetite like mine, and right there's where they're wise, if *I* know anything about it. Of *course* they don't want to return good for evil.

GETA: Antipho never can thank you as much as you deserve.

PHORMIO: Quite the contrary. No parasite can ever thank his patron as much as *he* deserves. (*Losing himself in a dream*) Just think of it! You come to the dinner table scot free, all perfumed, straight from the bath, never a care on your mind, while the patron is just being eaten up with worry and expense. While you're having the time of your life, he's fairly snarling. You're wreathed in smiles, begin the drinking, sit near the head of the table; before you is placed a puzzling repast.

GETA: What do you mean by that expression?

PHORMIO: "A puzzling repast"? Oh, that's where you're puzzled to know what to eat first. Why, when you reckon up all this, how *good* it *tastes* and how *much* it *costs*, don't you feel that the man who is setting you up is a regular manifestation of divine providence?

GETA: Here's the old man! Ready! Get set! The first attack is always the fiercest. If you can take that, why, in a few minutes, you'll be just kidding him along. (*Both step aside.*)

[ACT TWO: SCENE 3]

(DEMIPHO *enters with* HEGIO, CRATINUS, *and* CRITO, *his battery of attorneys. During this scene there is opportunity for much humorous byplay on the part of the attorneys as they snicker at* PHORMIO'S *thrusts.*)

DEMIPHO: Did you ever hear of anybody suffering such an outrageous piece of injustice as I have to suffer now? Stand by me, I beg of you.

GETA (*aside*): He's mad, all right.

PHORMIO (*aside*): Just watch me now. *I'll* touch him up. (*To* GETA *very loud*) Immortal Gods! Does Demipho actually *deny* that Phanium is related to him? What, *Demipho* says she's no kin?

GETA: That's what he says.

PHORMIO: And he doesn't know who her father was?

GETA: That's what he says.

DEMIPHO (*noticing them*): I'll bet that's the man I was talking about. Follow me!

PHORMIO: Because she's been left a poor friendless orphan, her father is disowned; she's neglected. That's what *greed* makes of a man!

GETA (*threateningly*): If you make any insinuations against my master, you'll hear something!

DEMIPHO: The gall! He's *actually* got the impudence to come and accuse *me*.

PHORMIO: Why, I've no reason to get angry at the *young* man because he didn't know her father very well. The fellow *was* pretty well along in years; he was poor, *he* had to *work* for *his* living; spent most of his time on the farm. There my own father let him have the use of one of *our* farms. I've often heard the old man tell how his kinsman, Demipho, highhatted him. (*Pathetically*) And every inch a *man* he was, too! I never saw his like.

GETA (*sarcastically*): Yes, you might very profitably compare him with your own self!

PHORMIO: Oh, go to hell! If I hadn't thought so highly of him, I'd never have got into such a quarrel with you folks, all for the sake of this girl that he's now treating so shabbily.

GETA: Are you going to keep on insulting my master behind his back? You dirty pup!

PHORMIO: It's just what he deserves.

GETA: Still talking, you jail-bird?

DEMIPHO: Geta!

GETA (*pretending not to hear*): You blackmailer! You shyster!

DEMIPHO (*still louder*): Geta!

PHORMIO (*whispering aside*): Answer him.

GETA (*turning*): Who's that? Aha!

DEMIPHO: Keep still.

GETA: Why, he's been abusing you no end here behind your back, saying things that *don't* apply to *you,* but fit *him* to a T.

DEMIPHO (*to* GETA): That will do. (*To* PHORMIO *with a great effort at controlling himself*) Young man, by your good leave I have a request to prefer. Will you be kind enough to answer me? Explain to me just who that man was that you call your friend, and how, as he claimed, he was related.

PHORMIO (*insolently*): Huh, fishing around, as if you didn't know him!

DEMIPHO: Know him?

PHORMIO: That's what I said.

DEMIPHO: I claim I don't know him. Since you claim that I do, just jog my memory.

PHORMIO: So! So! You didn't know your own cousin, eh?

DEMIPHO: You'll be the death of me yet. (*Still controlling himself*) Tell me his name!

PHORMIO: His name? Why, sure—(*hesitating*)

DEMIPHO: Why don't you speak?

PHORMIO (*confused, aside*): Oh, hell! I'm sunk! I've forgotten it!

DEMIPHO: Huh, what did you say?

PHORMIO (*aside*): Geta, if you remember the name we used a while ago, prompt me! (*clearing throat*) H-e-m! I won't tell you! You're trying to pump me, as if you didn't know it yourself.

DEMIPHO: *I* pump *you?*

GETA (*slipping around behind and prompting him as he goes by*): Stilpo!

PHORMIO: And yet, what do I care? His name was Stilpo.

DEMIPHO: Who's that you say?

PHORMIO: I say Stilpo was the man you know.

DEMIPHO: I did *not* know him, and I never had a relative by that name.

PHORMIO: Indeed? Aren't you ashamed in the presence of all these gentlemen here? If he'd left you a legacy to the tune of a hundred thousand—

DEMIPHO: Damn your cursed hide!

PHORMIO: You'd be the very first man to show up with a per-

fect memory; you'd bring out a family tree running clear back to
the father of your great-great-grandfather.

DEMIPHO: Have it your own way, of course. But when I showed
up, I would have explained just how the girl was related to me.
You do the same thing yourself. Come, how is she related?

GETA: Bravo, master, that was a home thrust! (*To* PHORMIO,
loudly) You there, watch out!

PHORMIO (*coolly*): *My* duty was to explain all that to the court,
and I did so with perfect lucidity. Besides, if it wasn't true, why
didn't your son deny it?

DEMIPHO: You're talking about my son, are you? The language
doesn't exist that's fit to describe his asininity.

PHORMIO (*with ironical deference*): All right, since *you're* so
wise, just go to court, and tell them you want to try the case all
over again. Why, you talk as if you were the lord paramount in
these parts, the only living man who can get a rehearing.

DEMIPHO (*momentarily calmed down*): Although you've done
me a wrong, yet rather than start a lawsuit, or listen to you any
longer, I'll act as *though* she were related. Take her away, and
I'll give you the legal dowry, one thousand cash down.

PHORMIO (*with a horse-laugh*): Haw! haw! haw! How sweet
of you!

DEMIPHO: What do you mean? Isn't that a fair proposition?
Can't I even get common justice?

PHORMIO (*with biting irony*): Indeed! And does the law re-
quire you to act as though you'd merely mistreated a common
prostitute? Pay her off, and let her go? Or is it precisely to prevent any free-born girl from being compelled to enter a life of
shame because of her poverty, that the law gives her to her nearest
relative, to live with her as his wife? And that is just what you
are trying to prevent.

DEMIPHO: Why, yes, of course, to her nearest relative. But how
or where do we come in?

PHORMIO: Oho! But, my dear sir, as they say, this incident is
closed.

DEMIPHO (*angrily*): It is, is it? I tell you what, I'm not going
to stop until I've had my way.

PHORMIO: You're a fool.

DEMIPHO: You just let me be!

PHORMIO: But, in any event, Demipho, we haven't a thing to do with *you*. It was your *son* that lost the case, not *you*. It's been some time since *you* were young enough to get married.

DEMIPHO: Take it from me, that son of mine will say just exactly what *I* do. If not, I'll turn him and his wife out into the street.

GETA (*aside*): He *is* angry.

PHORMIO: Better turn yourself out!

DEMIPHO: Do you intend to thwart me at every turn, you wretch?

PHORMIO (*aside, to* GETA): He's scared now, in spite of his efforts to hide the fact.

GETA (*aside, to* PHORMIO): You've made a good beginning.

PHORMIO: Why not take what you have to, anyway? You'll be living up to your reputation as a benevolent old gentleman, and we'll be good friends.

DEMIPHO: Do you think I want *you* for a friend, or ever want to see or hear of you again?

PHORMIO: If you make up with the girl, you'll have some one to cheer your declining years; just think how old you are.

DEMIPHO: She can cheer *you*, take her yourself!

PHORMIO: Come! Come! Calm down now!

DEMIPHO: Listen here! Enough's been said already. If you don't hurry up and take that woman away from here, I'll throw her right out into the street. And that's my last word, Phormio.

PHORMIO (*mimicking him*): And if you lay your little finger on that woman in any way that's unbecoming to a lady, I'll bring a great big smashing lawsuit against you. And that's *my* last word, Demipho. (*To* GETA) Say, there! If you need me, you'll find me at home. (*Exit.*)

[ACT TWO: SCENE 4]

GETA: I get you.

DEMIPHO (*pacing up and down*): What trouble and worry my son has got me into! Tangled me all up in this marriage. What's more, he won't come into my sight, so that at least I can learn what *he* has to say about the affair, and how he feels. (*To* GETA) Go and see if he has come back home yet.

GETA: I'm on my way.

DEMIPHO (*to his legal counsel*): Gentlemen, you see the situation. What am I to do? Tell me, Hegio.

HEGIO: Me? I suggest Cratinus, if you have no objection.

DEMIPHO: Speak, Cratinus.

CRATINUS: You mean me?

DEMIPHO: Yes, you.

CRATINUS: I should like to have you consult your own interest in the case. This is the way it looks to me. It is only right and fair that anything your son has gone and done here in your absence, should be rendered null and void; and you will carry the point. *That* is *my* judgment.

DEMIPHO: Now, Hegio, you speak.

HEGIO: I feel that my friend, Cratinus, here has delivered a very *weighty* opinion. But, you know how it is: "Many men of many minds." Every person has his own point of view. Now *I* feel that due process of law cannot be rescinded. And, more than that, it is disreputable to make the attempt.

DEMIPHO: Now you speak, Crito.

CRITO: *I* feel that we ought to take more time to think it over. It is a very serious matter.

HEGIO (*after an awkward pause, in which* DEMIPHO *expressively indicates his disgust*): There's nothing else we can do for you, is there?

DEMIPHO (*bitterly*): Oh no! You've done superbly! (*Adding, as the attorneys file out*) I'm a good deal more in doubt *now* than I was before.

GETA (*coming out of* DEMIPHO'S *house*): They say he isn't back yet.

DEMIPHO: I'll have to wait for my brother to return. Whatever advice *he* gives me in this affair, that's what I'll follow. And now I'm off down to the harbor to find out when they are going to start looking for him. (*Exit.*)

GETA: And I'm going to hunt up Antipho, to put him in touch with the latest developments. But there he is right now, in the very nick of time.

[ACT THREE: SCENE 1]

ANTIPHO (*finding fault now with himself*): There's no doubt about it, Antipho, but you and that panicky disposition of yours deserve a first-rate calling down. The idea of running off and leaving your very life in other people's hands! Did you imagine others would attend to your interests better than you would yourself? No matter what happened to the rest, you should at least have thought about your wife at home, to see that *she* didn't get into trouble from any misplaced confidence in you. Poor thing, every hope for safety that she has depends on you!

GETA: Yes, master, we too have been bawling you out behind your back, because you ran away.

ANTIPHO: I was looking for you.

GETA: But just the same we didn't fail you.

ANTIPHO: Please tell me, how are my fate and fortunes? Has father caught on yet?

GETA: Not yet.

ANTIPHO: Any hope for the future?

GETA: I don't know.

ANTIPHO: Oh!

GETA: Except that Phaedria never gave up the good fight for you.

ANTIPHO: Just like him.

GETA: And Phormio, in this as in everything else, gave a demonstration of his vim and vigor.

ANTIPHO: What did *he* do?

GETA: Absolutely bluffed the angry old man with his talk.

ANTIPHO: Bravo, Phormio!

GETA (*modestly*): And then *I* did what I *could*, myself.

ANTIPHO (*hugging him*): O you Geta! I just *love* you all!

GETA (*shaking himself free*): That's the way the first round went. At present, it's all quiet. Your father's going to wait till your uncle gets back.

ANTIPHO: And why for him?

GETA: Why, he said he'd prefer to take *his* advice in this case.

ANTIPHO: My word, how scared I'll be when I see my uncle back safe and sound! Life and death hang for me, as you say, in the balance of his judgment.

GETA: Here's Phaedria.

ANTIPHO: Where's that?

GETA: There, coming out of his "training quarters."

[ACT THREE: SCENE 2]

(*Enter* DORIO *and* PHAEDRIA *from* DORIO'S *house.*)

PHAEDRIA: Dorio! Please listen!

DORIO: I won't!

PHAEDRIA: Just a second. (*Laying a hand on him.*)

DORIO: Let go of me.

PHAEDRIA: Listen to what I have to say.

DORIO: But I'm *tired* of listening to the same thing a thousand times.

PHAEDRIA: But now I've something to say you'll be glad to listen to.

DORIO (*turning sharply*): Speak! I'm all ears.

PHAEDRIA: Can't I persuade you to give me three more days of grace? (*As* DORIO *starts off again*) *Where* are you going now?

DORIO: I could hardly believe, anyway, that you had a new proposal to offer.

ANTIPHO: Oh, I'm afraid that slave dealer will—

GETA: Get his foot in it, eh? So am I.

PHAEDRIA: Don't you believe me yet?

DORIO: The bunk!

PHAEDRIA: But if I pledge my sacred honor?

DORIO: Stuff and nonsense!

PHAEDRIA: You'll call it a good investment some day.

DORIO: Words, idle words!

PHAEDRIA: Upon my honor, you'll be glad you did it. By Heaven, it's the naked truth.

DORIO: Moonshine!

PHAEDRIA: Just *try* it once, it isn't long—

DORIO (*wearily*): The same old song and dance!

PHAEDRIA: You'll be nearer and dearer to me than my cousin, my father, my friend, my—

DORIO: Such rot!

PHAEDRIA: To think that you're so hard and cruel that neither prayers nor pity can soften your heart!

DORIO (*mockingly*): To think that you're so unreasonable and impudent, Phaedria, as to suppose that you can bamboozle me with all these fancy words, and walk off with my girl for nothing.

ANTIPHO (*aside*): What a shame!

PHAEDRIA: Alas, alas! It's only too true. I'm down and out.

GETA (*aside*): Each perfectly in character!

PHAEDRIA: Yes, and the blow didn't fall until just when Antipho has troubles of his own, too!

ANTIPHO: Ah there! What's the matter *now*, Phaedria?

PHAEDRIA: Oh, lucky Antipho!

ANTIPHO: Me lucky?

PHAEDRIA: Yes, you; you've got your sweetheart at home, and you've never had to struggle against a calamity like this.

ANTIPHO: Got mine at home, you say? Not much! I've got a wolf by the ears: Can't hold on much longer, and afraid to let go.

DORIO: Just the fix I'm in with Phaedria.

ANTIPHO: What's that? Better watch out or people may mistake you for a gentleman and not the pimp that you are. (*To* PHAEDRIA) What's he gone and done?

PHAEDRIA: He? Just what the veriest brute would do. Sold my Pamphila!

ANTIPHO: What? Sold?

GETA: You don't say so! Sold?

PHAEDRIA (*resignedly*): Yes. Sold!

DORIO (*sarcastically*): Regular outrage, isn't it, to sell a slave-girl that I've bought and paid for?

PHAEDRIA: And I can't persuade him to wait, and stand the other fellow off, until day after tomorrow, while I'm collecting what my friends have promised me. (*To* DORIO) If I don't pay it then, you won't need to wait a minute longer!

DORIO: You'll deafen me yet.

ANTIPHO: That's only a short while. Come, give in! *He'll* repay the favor a hundred percent.

DORIO: That's all idle talk.

ANTIPHO: Are you going to let Pamphila be taken out of town? Can you bear to see such a pair of loving hearts torn asunder?

DORIO (*ironically*): Of course not, any more than you!

PHAEDRIA: May all the gods conspire to see that you get yours some day!

DORIO (*to* PHAEDRIA): I've been waiting for you, though I hated to do it, several months already. Brimfull of promises and tears, but no cash. Now I've found your exact opposite, a man with plenty of cash and no tears. Make way for your betters!

ANTIPHO (*to* PHAEDRIA): But, by Heaven, unless I'm pretty badly mistaken, you set a day some time ago, before which you could pay this fellow.

PHAEDRIA: We did.

DORIO: You haven't heard *me* deny it either, have you?

ANTIPHO: Has that day passed yet?

DORIO: No, but today got in ahead of it.

ANTIPHO: Aren't you ashamed of such a swindle?

DORIO: Of course not, if there's anything in it for *me*.

GETA (*to* DORIO *excitedly*): You old manure-pile!

PHAEDRIA: Dorio, is that really a nice way to behave?

DORIO: That's me. If you don't like it, you can lump it.

ANTIPHO: Are you really cheating him that way?

DORIO: Quite the contrary, Antipho, he's been cheating me all along. He knew the sort of man I was, but I thought he was something very different. He's the one that has been putting it over on me. Right now I'm just what I've always been. Spite of all that, I'll do this much for you. The Colonel said he'd pay me tomorrow morning. If you bring me the money first, Phaedria, I'll follow my old rule: "First come, first served." Good afternoon. (*Exit.*)

[ACT THREE: SCENE 3]

PHAEDRIA: What shall I do? Where *am* I going to find the money for him, as fast as all that? In my present fix I've less than nothing myself. If only I could have got him to wait till day after tomorrow! I could have had it by then.

ANTIPHO: See here, Geta, are we going to allow him to be as

miserable as all that, when only a little while ago, as you yourself said, he did me such a good turn? Why not try to pay back the favor when he needs it most?

GETA: Sure enough, that's no more than the square thing to do.

ANTIPHO: All right. Come on! (*Slapping him on the back*) You're the only one that can save him.

GETA: What am I to do?

ANTIPHO: Find the money.

GETA: No objections, but where? Please specify.

ANTIPHO: Father's back home again.

GETA: Yes, and what of it?

ANTIPHO (*trying to look sagacious*): Ah, a word to the wise!

GETA: Is *that* what you're driving at?

ANTIPHO: Exactly.

GETA: That's a lovely idea, isn't it? *You're* going back on me too, are you? Isn't it as good as a victory if I get off *alive* after your marriage, without ordering me, when I'm in trouble already, to go crucify myself, simply to please Phaedria here?

ANTIPHO: There's truth in what he says.

PHAEDRIA: Why, Geta! Am I a perfect stranger to you fellows?

GETA: Of course not. But isn't it enough that the old man is red hot at all three of us, without our egging him on until he'd never forgive us?

PHAEDRIA (*sentimentally*): Shall another man take her away, before my very eyes, to foreign parts unknown? (*Sighing deeply*) Ah me! All right, Antipho, while yet you can, while I'm still here, talk with me, gaze upon my features.

ANTIPHO: Why? What are you to do? Tell me.

PHAEDRIA (*tragically*): It is my high resolve to follow her all over this wide world, or die in the attempt!

GETA: Heaven help you, if it's as bad as all that! And yet, you'd better go slow!

ANTIPHO: See if you can't help him out, somehow.

GETA: "Somehow?" Tell me just how!

ANTIPHO: Do think up a plan, Geta; I'm afraid he'll go and do something that we'll all regret when it's too late.

GETA: I'll think. (*Heavy business of thinking; after a long pause*) I believe we *can* save him, although I'm afraid it will make trouble.

ANTIPHO: Never fear. *We'll* stand by you through thick and thin.

GETA: Tell me, how much money do you need?

PHAEDRIA: Only six thousand.

GETA: Six thousand! Whee! She's "dear," all right, Phaedria.

PHAEDRIA (*indignantly*): That's dirt cheap for a girl like her.

GETA: All right, all right! I'll see that it's found.

PHAEDRIA (*hugging him*): That's an old dear!

GETA: Oh, go 'long!

PHAEDRIA: I need it right away.

GETA: You'll get it right away, too. But I'll have to have Phormio to help me out on this.

ANTIPHO: He's ready and waiting. Lay on him boldly what you will; he'll carry it off. He's the only fellow that's a real friend in need.

GETA: Well, then, let's hunt him up quick.

ANTIPHO: You don't need *me* any longer, do you?

GETA: No; go into the house and cheer up that poor wife of yours. I'm sure she's half scared to death by this time. Why don't you go?

ANTIPHO: Nothing would suit me better. (*Exit.*)

PHAEDRIA: How are you going to do it?

GETA: I'll tell you on the way; only clear out of here now. (*Exeunt.*)

[ACT FOUR: SCENE 1]

(DEMIPHO *and* CHREMES *enter from the harbor.*)

DEMIPHO: Well, Chremes, did you do what you went to Lemnos for? Bring your daughter back?

CHREMES: No.

DEMIPHO: Why not?

CHREMES: When her mother saw how I kept staying and staying here, while the girl was growing up just the same, and couldn't wait any longer on my negligence, they say she picked up bag and baggage and came here to hunt me up.

DEMIPHO: What made you stay there then so long, when you heard that, I'd like to know?

CHREMES (*evasively*): 'Gad, I was sick.

DEMIPHO: How so? What was the trouble?

CHREMES: The trouble, you say? (*Uneasily*) Old age itself is trouble enough. But the captain who brought them over said they got here safely.

DEMIPHO: Have you heard what my son has gone and done in my absence, Chremes?

CHREMES: Yes, and that's what upsets all my plans. For (*looking all around*) if I offer the girl in marriage to anyone outside of the family, I'll have to tell just how and by whom I came to be her father. I've always felt certain that you were as loyal to me as I was to myself. Now a stranger, if he wants to, will keep quiet just as long as we're good friends, but if we have a falling out, he'll know a good deal more than he ought to. Besides, I'm afraid my wife will somehow get wind of this. If she does, the only thing for me to do is to get up and get out, for I myself am all that I've got in the world I can call my own.

DEMIPHO: I know you're right, and that's just what worries me. But I'll never give up until I do what I promised.

[ACT FOUR: SCENE 2]

GETA (*entering, unaware of the presence of* CHREMES *and* DEMIPHO, *who keep on conferring; to the audience*): I never saw a smoother guy in all my born days than that man, Phormio! I found the fellow, told him we wanted the money, and how to get it. He saw the point before I was half through, began to laugh, said some nice things about me, and wanted to see the old gentleman right away. He thanked Heaven for giving him the chance to show he was just as good a friend to Phaedria as he had been to Antipho. I told him to wait downtown; I'd bring the old man along. But there he is now. Who's that on the other side? Whoo-wee! It's Phaedria's father. And yet, what were you afraid of *them* for, you dumb ox? Because you've got two men to cheat instead of one? Why, it's a good deal easier to have two strings to your bow. I'll try to get the money from the first one, just as I had planned; if he gives it, well and good. If there's nothing doing there, I'll go for the newcomer.

[ACT FOUR: SCENE 3]

ANTIPHO (*coming out of* DEMIPHO's *house*): I'm looking for Geta back any minute. But there's my uncle standing with my father. Dear me, how scared I am when I think of what *he* may put dad up to! (*Slips aside.*)

GETA (*aside*): I'll speak to them. (*Running up.*) Well! Well! My dear Chremes, how are you, anyway?

CHREMES: How are you, Geta?

GETA: I'm delighted to see you here safe and sound.

CHREMES (*coolly*): I dare say.

GETA: Anything doing? I suppose you've noticed a good many changes during your absence.

CHREMES (*dryly*): Yes, several.

GETA: To be sure! And have you heard what's happened to Antipho?

CHREMES: Everything.

GETA (*to* DEMIPHO): Ah, *you* told him, did you? Oh, Chremes! What an outrage to get taken in that way!

CHREMES: Just as I was saying.

GETA: Yes, and by Heavens, I've been thinking over this thing carefully, and I believe I've found a way out.

CHREMES: What is it, Geta?

DEMIPHO: "A way out," you say?

GETA: As I left you, I was lucky enough to run across Phormio—

CHREMES: Who's Phormio?

DEMIPHO: The fellow who was her—

CHREMES: I see.

GETA: I thought I'd like to test his real feelings. I took him around behind the corner. Says I, "Phormio, why not try to adjust our little difference in a friendly way, and stop quarrelling about it? My master's a gentleman and a peaceable fellow. For, I'd have you know, by Heaven, every single one of his friends has just been urging him to chuck the girl right out of the house."

ANTIPHO (*aside*): What's he getting into, and how's this going to come out?

GETA: "Perhaps you think he'll have to settle it in court, if he throws her out. He's looked into *that* already. I tell you, you'll sweat for it, all right, if you get into a scrap with him; he's that eloquent But even suppose you *should* win your case; after all, this is no capital offense for *him;* there's nothing but a little money involved." When I saw I'd made some impression on him by this kind of talk, I went on, "See here, we're all alone. How much would you take, cash down, on the understanding that my master won't be sued, the girl makes herself scarce, and you stop bothering us?"

ANTIPHO (*aside*): Has he gone crazy, or not?

GETA: "For I'm sure, if you make anything *like* a fair proposition, he's such a good-hearted fellow, you won't have to exchange three words in the whole affair."

DEMIPHO (*testily*): Who authorized you to talk like that?

CHREMES: Oh no! Don't bother him. We couldn't possibly get what we want more easily any other way.

ANTIPHO (*aside*): It's all over now!

DEMIPHO: Go on and get through!

GETA: At first the fellow was fairly crazy.

CHREMES: How much did he want?

GETA: Oh, a great deal too much.

CHREMES: Well, how much?

GETA: As if we'd offer him ten thousand!

DEMIPHO: Ten thousand damns, you mean! Such impudence!

GETA: *Exactly* what *I* said. "Why, look here," says I, "what if he were marrying off his only daughter? It hasn't done him any good not to have brought one up, now that some other girl's been found to demand a dowry." But, to cut the whole story short, and leave out all his silly talk, this was his last proposal. Says he, "From the very first I wanted to marry my friend's daughter myself, as I should have, had it been possible. I couldn't help but think how uncomfortable it would be for her to become some rich man's housemaid rather than his wife, just because she was poor. But, to be frank about it, I simply had to get a wife who would bring me in a little sum to pay off a few obligations. And so, even now, if Demipho's really *eager* about it, and willing to give me as much as the girl I'm engaged to *now* offers, I don't know anybody in the world I'd rather have as my wife."

ANTIPHO (*aside*): Is he talking that way because he's a fool or a knave, with knowledge or in ignorance? That's what I'd like to know.

DEMIPHO: What if he's up to his ears in debt?

GETA: "My farm," said he, "is mortgaged for a couple of thousand."

DEMIPHO: All right, all right! He can have the girl. I'll pay that.

GETA: "My bungalow, too, for another two thousand."

DEMIPHO: W-h-e-e! That's too much.

CHREMES: Don't carry on like that! *I'll* raise *this* two thousand for you.

GETA: "Then I'll have to buy a lady's maid, and get a little more furniture; besides, there are the expenses connected with the wedding; call all this a couple of thousand more, or six thousand in all."

DEMIPHO (*disgusted*): Why, he can bring six thousand suits against me before I'll ever pay that! Let that scoundrel get the laugh on me again?

CHREMES (*anxiously, for fear* NAUSISTRATA, *inside the house, might hear something*): Oh, keep still, won't you? *I'll* pay it. Just you get your son to marry (*significantly*) the girl—we want him to.

ANTIPHO (*wildly*): Woe's me! Geta, you certainly have wrecked me with your tricks!

CHREMES: You see you're throwing the girl out for my sake, so it's only fair that I pay the bill.

GETA: "Let me know as soon as you can," said he, "if you'll give me the girl, so that I can break my present engagement, and won't be left in suspense; you see her relatives had agreed to pay the whole sum down right away."

CHREMES: He can have it immediately. Tell him to break the engagement, and take the girl.

DEMIPHO (*sullenly*): Yes, and bad luck to him, too!

CHREMES: It's very lucky I brought that money along with me, the rent from my wife's estate in Lemnos. I'll turn that over, and tell my wife I've made you a loan. (DEMIPHO *and* CHREMES *go into the house of* CHREMES.)

[ACT FOUR: SCENE 4]

ANTIPHO (*wildly*): Geta!

GETA: What?

ANTIPHO: What have you gone and done?

GETA: Diddled these old duffers out of their money!

ANTIPHO: Is *that* all?

GETA: Heavens! I don't know. That's all I was *told* to do.

ANTIPHO (*striking him*): You damned scoundrel! Why don't you answer my question?

GETA: What are you talking about, then?

ANTIPHO: "What am I talking about"? Thanks to you, there's nothing left for *me* to do but go hang myself. May all the gods and goddesses there are in heaven above and hell below make an example of you! (*With great sarcasm*) If you want anything done, here's the man. When you're sailing smoothly along, he'll bring you all of a sudden bang up against a rock! What *could* have been worse than to touch that sore spot and begin to talk about my wife? You've encouraged the old man to think he can chuck her out. Worse than that, if Phormio takes the dowry he's got to marry the girl; what then?

GETA (*disgusted at such unimaginative incompetence*): He'll never marry her.

ANTIPHO (*sarcastically*): Of course not! But when they ask for the money back, he'll cheerfully walk off to jail just for *my* sake!

GETA: There's nothing, Antipho, you can't spoil by telling it badly. You leave out all that's good, and emphasize all that's bad. Listen to the other side. If he takes the money, it follows at once, of course, that he'll have to marry her, just as you say; I grant you that. In the meantime, however, they'll allow him a *little* time in which to prepare for the wedding, get out the bids, and make the necessary sacrifices. Before all *that's* done Phaedria's friends will have raised what they promised. Your man Phormio will take that and pay the old gentleman back.

ANTIPHO: What sort of excuses can he give?

GETA: Excuses? Plenty of them! Why, for example, he'll say: "After I got into this, I began seeing things at night. Somebody's black dog ran into the front of my house; a snake dropped through the skylight; a hen started to crow; the clairvoyant forbade it; the fortuneteller said 'No'; besides, to start anything new before the first of the year"—and this the best excuse of all. *That's* what he'll say.

ANTIPHO: If only he will.

GETA: Of course he will, trust me for that. There's your father. Go tell Phaedria we've got the money. (ANTIPHO *runs off*.)

[ACT FOUR: SCENE 5]

(DEMIPHO *and* CHREMES *come out*.)

DEMIPHO: Keep your shirt on! I'll see to it he doesn't give us the slip. I'll never let *this* go (*holding up the bag of money*) helter-skelter without witnesses. I'll have it nominated in the bond just who's to get the money, and for what purpose.

GETA (*aside*): How careful he is now, when there's no use!

CHREMES: That's just the thing to do; and hurry up, while he's still in the mood, for, if the other girl he's engaged to now is insistent, he may throw us down even *yet*.

GETA (*aside*): You're dead right about getting "thrown down."

DEMIPHO (*to* GETA): Take me to him, right now.

GETA: All ready.

CHREMES: When that's fixed up, come over and see my wife, so that she can have a talk with the girl before she leaves. Have Nausistrata tell her we're going to arrange to have her marry Phormio, and not to be angry about it; that he's a much better match for her, because she knows him already; and that we've done our full duty by giving him all the dowry he demanded.

DEMIPHO: Plague take it! What difference does *that* make?

CHREMES: A good deal, Demipho. It isn't enough to do your duty, unless people in general approve of what you've done. I want her to act voluntarily, so that afterwards she can't say she was thrown out.

DEMIPHO: I can do that myself.

CHREMES: Women understand each other better.

DEMIPHO (*still annoyed*): All right, I'll ask her.

(*Exeunt* DEMIPHO *and* GETAS)

CHREMES: I wonder where I can find my other wife and daughter.

(*Enter* SOPHRONA.)

SOPHRONA (*to herself*): What *shall* I do? Where *can* I find a friend in all this trouble? With whom can I consult, or where can I get any help? I'm afraid my innocent young mistress will come to grief; and I'm responsible for it all, too. I hear Antipho's father is carrying on something awful about the matter.

CHREMES (*aside*): Who's that old woman that's come out of my brother's house in such a state of excitement?

SOPHRONA: It was poverty that forced me to it. I knew such a marriage was a risky thing, but I simply had to see that she was sure of a living, for the time being, at least.

CHREMES: Upon my soul, unless my mind's going or my eyesight failing, that's my daughter's nurse.

SOPHRONA: And we can't find—

CHREMES: What shall I do?

SOPHRONA: Her father anywhere.

CHREMES: I wonder if I had better speak to her, or wait until I'm *certain* who she is?

SOPHRONA: But if I could only find *him*, there'd be nothing to fear.

CHREMES: That *certainly is* the woman. I'll call to her.

SOPHRONA: Who's that talking?

CHREMES: Sophrona.

SOPHRONA: He's using my name, too!

CHREMES: Look around here.

SOPHRONA: Goodness me! Is that Stilpo?

CHREMES: No.

SOPHRONA: What? No?

CHREMES (*in a low tone*): Move over in that direction a little, away from this door. (*After she has done so*) Don't you ever call me by that name again!

SOPHRONA: Why not, please? Aren't you the man you always said you were?

CHREMES: Shh!

SOPHRONA: What's there about that door that scares you so?

CHREMES: I've got a wife behind that shut door, and she's a perfect terror. Stilpo was a fictitious name I took in those days, so that you wouldn't blab out the truth, even though you didn't intend to, and my wife get to hear about it.

SOPHRONA: For pity's sake! *That's* why we poor women couldn't find you.

CHREMES: But say, tell me, what business do you have with these people inside here? Where are my wife and daughter?

SOPHRONA (*crying*): Oh dear me!

CHREMES: Ah! What's the matter? Are they dead?

SOPHRONA: Your daughter is still alive, but her mother, poor thing, died of a broken heart!

CHREMES (*mechanically and callously; obviously much relieved*): Too bad!

SOPHRONA: And I, a lone, lorn, poverty-stricken old woman, did the best I could, and got the girl married to the young man who lives in there.

CHREMES: To Antipho?

SOPHRONA: Yes, that's his name.

CHREMES (*unable to grasp it*): What, has he got *two* wives?

SOPHRONA: Mercy no! *She's* the only one.

CHREMES: What about the one they call his cousin?

SOPHRONA: Why, she's it.

CHREMES: What?

SOPHRONA: Why, yes. It was all a put-up job, so that he could marry her without a dowry.

CHREMES (*excitedly*): Heaven help us! How often we just blunder right into something that we wouldn't have even prayed for! Here I come back home to find my daughter married to *just* the husband I had picked for her, and *just* the way I wanted. The *very thing* we were both trying our level best to do, Antipho has gone and done all alone, without bothering us, and at no end of trouble to himself.

SOPHRONA (*not understanding*): Now see what we are going to do! The young man's father is back, and they say he's perfectly furious about it.

CHREMES: Not a *particle* of danger. But swear to me, by gods and men, that nobody will *ever* find out she's *my* daughter.

SOPHRONA: No one ever will from *me*.

CHREMES: Come on, I'll tell you the rest indoors.

[ACT FIVE: SCENE 2]

(*Enter* DEMIPHO *and* GETA *after the conference with* PHORMIO.)

DEMIPHO: It's all our own fault that it's a paying proposition to be a rascal these days. We're so anxious for everybody to call us "good" and "kind." "Don't run away so hard you can't stop at your own house," as the saying goes. Wasn't it enough to suffer an outrage from him in the first instance, without actually throwing away our money, and giving him something to live on till he springs some new skulduggery?

GETA: Right you are.

DEMIPHO: The man who can turn good into evil gets a bonus *these* days.

GETA: Sure enough.

DEMIPHO: And that all shows we've gone and made fools of ourselves in this business.

GETA (*dropping a precautionary suggestion, so as to keep the record straight, if need arises*): I only *hope* he doesn't change his mind, and refuse to marry her.

DEMIPHO: What? There's no doubt about that, is there?

GETA: Heavens, you never can tell! A fellow like him just *might* change his mind any minute.

DEMIPHO: Huh! Change his mind, you think?

GETA: I don't *know;* I'm only saying "you never can tell."

DEMIPHO (*reassured*): I'll take my brother's suggestion and bring his wife over to have a talk with the girl. You, Geta, go ahead and tell her Nausistrata's coming. (*Enters the house of* CHREMES.)

GETA (*a trifle apprehensively*): Phaedria's found his money! Not a word about the calling-down that's coming to us. For the time being, at least, the bride won't have to leave the house. But after that? What then? Stuck in the same mud-hole. Settling one debt by making another, Geta. You've put off today's evil until tomorrow. But there's a crop of switches growing for you, if you don't watch out. (*With a shrug*) I'll go in now and tell Phanium not to be afraid of Phormio, or of Nausistrata's talk. (GETA *goes.*)

[ACT FIVE: SCENE 3]

(DEMIPHO *and* NAUSISTRATA *come out of the other house.*)

DEMIPHO (*ingratiatingly*): Come now, Nausistrata, you have a way with you; just make her feel friendly toward us, and get her to do of her own free will what she *has* to do anyway.

NAUSISTRATA: Very well.

DEMIPHO: By so doing you'll be giving me quite as valuable a personal service as when you helped me in a financial way a little while ago.

NAUSISTRATA: You're perfectly welcome to *that,* and, sure as I live, it's all my husband's fault that I can't do as much as I ought to.

DEMIPHO: How do you mean?

NAUSISTRATA: Why, dear me, he lets the property that poor father worked so hard for, go at such loose ends; father used to get twenty thousand from these same estates, cash in full, too! That shows how much better one man is than another!

DEMIPHO: What, twenty thousand? You don't say!

NAUSISTRATA: Yes *sir,* and the cost of living wasn't near as high then as it is now.

DEMIPHO: Whee!

NAUSISTRATA: What do you think of that?

DEMIPHO: Why, of course!

NAUSISTRATA: I wish *I'd* been born a man, *I'd* have shown him how—

DEMIPHO: Oh, yes, I'm sure you would.

NAUSISTRATA: Just how I'd—

DEMIPHO: Now please, save your strength for this girl of ours. She's a young thing, and I'm afraid she'll wear you out.

NAUSISTRATA: Oh, very well, then, I'll do as you suggest. But that's my husband coming out of your house. (*Enter* CHREMES.)

CHREMES (*excitedly*): Hey there, Demipho, have you paid that fellow the money yet?

DEMIPHO: I attended to it right away.

CHREMES: I wish you hadn't. (*Suddenly catching sight of* NAUSISTRATA, *aside*) Hi! There's my wife! Almost said too much that time.

DEMIPHO: What makes you wish I hadn't?

CHREMES (*confused*): That's all right.

DEMIPHO: Well, what have you been doing? Did you tell the girl why we were bringing Nausistrata over to see her?

CHREMES: I've fixed it all up.

DEMIPHO: What does she say?

CHREMES: We can't possibly send her away.

DEMIPHO: Why not?

CHREMES: Why, because she and Antipho love each other so!

DEMIPHO: What's that to us?

CHREMES: A good deal. Besides, I've found out she really *is* related to us.

DEMIPHO: What?! You're crazy!

CHREMES: You'll find it's the truth, and I'm not just talking either. I remember now all about it.

DEMIPHO: Are you really in your right mind?

NAUSISTRATA: Now, now, for mercy's sake! Don't mistreat one of your own kin.

DEMIPHO: *She's* no kin of ours.

CHREMES: Don't contradict me. Her father went by another name. That's where *you* made your mistake.

DEMIPHO: Didn't she know her own father?

CHREMES: Yes.

DEMIPHO: Why didn't she call him by his right name, then?

CHREMES (*sidling over to him*): Won't you *ever* give in? *Can't* you catch on?

DEMIPHO: How *can* I, when you talk such nonsense as all this?

CHREMES: You'll be the ruination of me yet.

NAUSISTRATA: I wonder what's up.

DEMIPHO: By Heavens! I can't make out what you're driving at.

CHREMES: Do you really want to know? Very well then. And now, so help me Heaven, there's nobody in the wide world any closer kin to her than *I* am, in the first place, and *you* in the second place.

DEMIPHO: May the Lord help us! Let's go *right* in. I want all of us to know whether this is true or not.

CHREMES: Oh, no!

DEMIPHO: What is it?

CHREMES: To think you have so little confidence in me!

DEMIPHO: Do you want me to believe you? Consider it settled? All right, so be it! Well, then, (*slyly*) what are we going to do about our friend's daughter?

CHREMES (*embarrassed*): All right.

DEMIPHO: Let the one here go? (*With a slight gesture at* NAUSISTRATA)

CHREMES: Yes, of course.

DEMIPHO: And the *other* stay? (*With a slight gesture to his own house, where* PHANIUM *is living*)

CHREMES: Exactly.

DEMIPHO: All right, Nausistrata, you can go.

NAUSISTRATA: Mercy on me! *I* think it's much better for all concerned that she should stay here rather than be driven out. She struck me as being a perfect lady when I saw her. (*Goes into her own house.*)

DEMIPHO (*disgusted*): What sort of a mess is this?

CHREMES: Has she shut the door yet?

DEMIPHO: Yes.

CHREMES (*relieved*): Thank Heaven! The gods fairly smile upon us! I find my daughter in here married to your son.

DEMIPHO: Huh! How *could* that have happened?

CHREMES: This place isn't safe enough to tell you.

DEMIPHO: Come into the house, then.

CHREMES (*half-way into* DEMIPHO'S *house, and then suddenly stopping*): Look here! I sure don't want our sons to get word of this!

[ACT FIVE: SCENE 4]

(*Enter* ANTIPHO.)

ANTIPHO: I'm glad, whatever happens to me, that my cousin Phaedria's got his heart's desire. What a bright idea it is to have feelings of the kind that can easily be mended when things go wrong. As soon as Phaedria got the money he was perfectly happy, yet I can't think up any way of getting out of this trouble. Even if it *should* stay secret, I'd be in constant suspense; if it gets out, I'm disgraced. I wouldn't be coming back home even now, if it weren't for the hope of keeping Phanium. I wonder where I can find Geta, and learn from him just when he thinks it would be best to have my interview with father.

[ACT FIVE: SCENE 5]

(*Enter* PHORMIO.)

PHORMIO: I took the money, gave it to the slave-dealer, carried off the girl, and turned her over for keeps into Phaedria's hands; for she's been freed already. There's only one thing left to do now, and that's to get these old men to let me alone long enough to go off on a spree. For that's the way I'm going to spend the next few days!

ANTIPHO: But here's Phormio. Say, there!

PHORMIO: What?

ANTIPHO: What's Phaedria going to do now? How's he going to spend his honeymoon?

PHORMIO: He's going to play *your* part.

ANTIPHO: How so?

PHORMIO: Keep out of his father's sight. He sent word for you to play *his* part now, and beg him off; for he's coming to my house to get drunk. I'll tell the old men I've got to attend a county fair at Sunium, to buy the lady's maid Geta spoke about, so they won't think I'm blowing in all their money, when they don't see me around. But your door squeaked just then. (*Steps behind the corner.*)

ANTIPHO: Look who's coming out.

PHORMIO: It's Geta.

[ACT FIVE: SCENE 6]

GETA: O Fortune, lucky lady Fortune! What blessings you have showered on my master, Antipho, this day!

ANTIPHO (*aside*): What *does* he mean by that?

GETA: And you've taken off the back of his friends all the burden of our cares. But why don't I hoist my cloak upon this shoulder, hurry off to find the fellow, and let him know what's happened?

ANTIPHO (*aside, to* PHORMIO): You can't make out what he's up to, can you?

PHORMIO (*aside, to* ANTIPHO): No, can you?

ANTIPHO (*aside, to* PHORMIO): Not a bit.

PHORMIO (*aside, to* ANTIPHO): Same here.

GETA: I'll go off to the slave-dealer's. That's where they probably are now.

ANTIPHO: Hey there! Geta!

GETA (*slowing down, but without turning around*): Well, what do you know about that? Nothing strange or surprising, is it, for somebody to stop you before you get half started?

ANTIPHO (*louder*): Geta!

GETA: Bless me! He's keeping it up. (*Shouting back*) You'll never get the best of me with your stinking tricks.

ANTIPHO: Aren't you going to stop?

GETA (*crossly*): Oh, go take a licking!

ANTIPHO: You'll get a licking yourself, if you don't stop, you whipping post!

GETA (*surprised*): He must know me pretty well to threaten me like that. (*Turning*) But isn't it the very man I was looking for? It surely is. I'll up and speak to him at once.

ANTIPHO: What's the news?

GETA: Oh, blessedest of all living mortal men! There's no denying it, Antipho, you're the gods' own darling.

ANTIPHO: Hope so; but I'd like to know how you make that out.

GETA: Will it be enough if I fairly drown you in buckets of bliss?

ANTIPHO: You're killing me!

PHORMIO: Why don't you cut out all these promises, and tell him the news?

GETA: Oh, you're here, too, are you, Phormio?

PHORMIO: Yes, but hurry up.

GETA: All right, listen. When we paid you the money down-

town we came right back home. The master sent me in to see
your wife.

ANTIPHO (*nervously*): What for?

GETA: Never mind; I'll leave that out. It hasn't anything to do
with the story, anyway. As I was going into the ladies' apartments,
the slave boy, Mida, ran up, caught my coat-tail, and pulled me
back. I look around, and ask why he's delaying me. He says we
are not allowed to go in there. "Sophrona," says he, "has just
brought our old man's brother, Chremes, in." He was in there
right then. When I heard that, I began to slip up softly on tiptoe,
and got near, stood still, held my breath, applied an ear; and then
I began to listen to what they were saying, just this way. (*Going
through an elaborate pantomime*)

PHORMIO: Bravo, Geta!

GETA: Then and there I heard the best thing ever! By Heavens
I *almost shouted* for joy!

ANTIPHO: What about?

GETA: What do you suppose?

ANTIPHO: Can't imagine.

GETA: It's most amazing, too! Your father turns out to be
Phanium's own uncle!

ANTIPHO: What's that you say?

GETA: Her mother was a wife Chremes had without our knowing it, there in Lemnos.

PHORMIO: Nonsense! Wouldn't she know who her own father
was?

GETA: Take my word for it, Phormio, there's some good reason
for that. But you don't suppose I could have heard from the outside, *everything* they said on the inside, do you?

ANTIPHO: I've had an inkling about such a story, too!

GETA: I'll give you even better grounds for believing me. A
while ago your uncle came out; not long after that your father
got back, and then they went in together. Both of them say now
that you can keep your wife. In short, I was sent out to hunt you
up and bring you back.

ANTIPHO: Why don't you carry me off, then? What *are* you
waiting for?

GETA: I'll do it. (*Carrying* ANTIPHO *into the house in his arms*)

ANTIPHO (*kissing his finger-tips*): O, my dear Phormio, good-bye!

[ACT FIVE: SCENE 7]

PHORMIO: Good-bye, Antipho! For the love of Heaven, I'm glad it's turned out this way. (*Soliloquizing*) Such a great stroke of good luck has come to these young fellows, all so unexpectedly! And such a brilliant chance for me to gouge the old gentleman, and relieve Phaedria of all anxiety about the money, so that he won't have to go around and beg his pals for it. Because, the money the old men have paid down to him, for all their squirming, will stay paid exactly the same way. I know how I can put the screws on them for *that*.

Now I'll have to put on a new front, and change my expression. And so I'll sneak off here and confront them when they come out of the house. (*Slyly*) I guess I'll not attend the county fair at Sunium, as I had planned.

[ACT FIVE: SCENE 8]

(DEMIPHO *and* CHREMES *come out of* DEMIPHO's *house*.)

DEMIPHO: I'm full of gratitude to the gods, and wish to express it, too, for the blessing they've given us. It has all turned out so well for us, brother.

CHREMES: Isn't she a lady, just as I said? [2]

DEMIPHO: Through and through. Now we've got to find that fellow, Phormio, as soon as possible, before he starts to blow in our money, and get it back.

PHORMIO (*coming out and pretending not to see them*): I wonder if Demipho is at home. I'd like to—

DEMIPHO: Ah, we were just looking for you, Phormio.

PHORMIO: Probably for the same reason.

DEMIPHO (*excited, but still not quite certain how he is going to proceed*): Yes, by Heaven!

---

[2] Line 905 is transposed to this position.

PHORMIO: *I* thought so. (*An awkward pause, as they glare at one another*) Then *why* were you coming to look me up?

DEMIPHO: O, a small matter!

PHORMIO: You were afraid I wouldn't live up to my contract, eh? Look here! However poor I may be, there's one thing I have always been particular about, and that's my sacred honor. And so, Demipho, I've come to tell you I'm all ready. Whenever you wish, turn over my wife. I've put off all my other engagements; which was the only decent thing to do, as soon as I saw you two had your hearts so set on the matter.

DEMIPHO: Yes, but Chremes here has been persuading me not to do it. Says he, "How people *will* talk if you do that! A while ago, when you *might* have done it *decently*, you didn't come across with the girl's dowry, and marry her off to somebody else; it's a scandal to turn her out of doors now." In short, he made pretty much the same caustic comments that you yourself did, to my face, a little while ago.

PHORMIO (*with an injured air*): That's a mighty high-handed way you have of trying to put something over on me!

DEMIPHO: How so?

PHORMIO: "How so," you say? Why, *now* I won't be able to marry even the other girl. How can I have the gall to go back to her, when I've just thrown her down?

CHREMES (*prompting* DEMIPHO): "And besides, I notice that Antipho doesn't want to let her go." Say that.

DEMIPHO: And besides, I notice that my son is dead set against letting her go. But come on, my good sir, downtown with me, and give orders to have that money credited to my account again.

PHORMIO: What? The money I've already gone and paid around among my creditors?

DEMIPHO: What are you going to do about it, then?

PHORMIO: Just this. If you want to give me the wife you've promised, I'll marry her; but, if you should *prefer* to keep her in your own home, as for the dowry, why, that's going to stay right here, Demipho! (*Patting his chest*) It's not fair that I should stand to lose on your account, when it was just for your sake that I bundled the other girl off, who was offering me the same amount as a marriage portion.

DEMIPHO (*violently excited*): O, go to hell, with all that big talk of yours, you jail bird! Do you suppose we don't know you and what you're up to any better than that?

PHORMIO: Look out, now! I'm beginning to lose my temper.

DEMIPHO: Does anybody suppose *you'd* marry her, if you had the chance?

PHORMIO: Just try it and see.

DEMIPHO: You want to keep her at your house to be a mistress for my son, that's your little game.

PHORMIO (*dignified, and sinister*): Beg your pardon, what was that you said?

DEMIPHO (*bluffed, and afraid to repeat the libel*): You give me my money!

PHORMIO: Not much! You give me my wife!

DEMIPHO: Come on to court, then.

PHORMIO: See here, if you two *keep on* annoying me—

DEMIPHO: What will *you* do?

PHORMIO: Me? Perhaps you think I'm the patron saint only of beggar maids. (*Walking over to* CHREMES *and leering at him*) I've acquired the habit of championing ladies with dowries, in precisely the same way.

CHREMES: What's that to us?

PHORMIO: Oh, nothing!—(*Ostentatiously strolling over towards the front door of* CHREMES's *house.*) I used to know a lady in this part of town, whose husband had another—

CHREMES (*excitedly*): What?

PHORMIO: Wife at Lemnos—

CHREMES: I'm dead this time—

PHORMIO: And a daughter by her, too, that he's bringing up.

CHREMES: And buried, too.

PHORMIO: I've a notion to tell her all about it *now*. (*Starting to knock*)

CHREMES: Oh, don't! For mercy's sake!

PHORMIO (*sarcastically*): Oh, really! Were *you* the fellow?

DEMIPHO: How silly he's making us look!

CHREMES (*trying to be conciliating*): We'll let you off.

PHORMIO: Oh, drivel!

CHREMES: What do you want? You can keep the money you've got.

PHORMIO: Yes, yes. (*A pause, and then indignantly*) Damn

it all! Why are you trying to take me in with all your silly, childish, shilly-shallying? I won't, I will; I will, and then again, I won't; take it over, and give it back; agreed, disagreed; make a contract, break a contract!

CHREMES (*to* DEMIPHO): How did he get on to that?

DEMIPHO (*to* CHREMES): I don't know. I'm sure *I* never told anybody!

CHREMES: For the love of Heaven, it's like a freak of nature!

PHORMIO (*aside*): I've stuck a spoke in his wheel, all right!

DEMIPHO (*to* CHREMES): See here! Is this fellow going to walk off with all that money of ours, right out from under our very noses, and give us the merry ha! ha! too? By Heaven, *I'd* rather die! Brace up here, and be a man! Your little love affair has got out now, and you can't keep it from your wife any longer. The easiest way to get forgiveness, Chremes, is for us to tell her ourselves, what she'll be sure to hear from others, anyway. And then, best of all, we can wreak our vengeance on this dirty skunk here. (*They start for* PHORMIO, *with fists doubled up.*)

PHORMIO: Hi-yi! I'm in for it, If I don't look out! These fellows are making for me like a couple of gladiators.

CHREMES (*to* DEMIPHO, *suddenly stopping*): But I'm afraid she won't forgive me, after all.

DEMIPHO: Don't worry about that. I'll get you back into her good graces. It's easy enough, too, because the other woman, who bore you this daughter, is dead and out of the way now. (*They advance again.*)

PHORMIO: So *that's* what you're up to now, eh? Pretty bright idea, too! (*To* DEMIPHO) But I'll tell *you* something, Demipho; Chremes here won't be having a good time, now that you've made me lose my temper. (*To* CHREMES) You dare to peep? You, who have a jolly good time, when you're away from home, without any regard for this noble lady, but insult her in such outlandish ways? *You* think you'll wash away your guilt with prayers, do you? I'll have her in such a blazing fury against you with what I've got to tell her, that you'll *never* put out the conflagration, not even if you should simply melt away into tears.

DEMIPHO: Perdition! And may all the gods and goddesses visit it upon him, too! Did you ever hear of such impudence? Why doesn't the government deport a scoundrel like that to some desert island!

CHREMES (*to* DEMIPHO): I'm in such a jam I don't know what to do.

DEMIPHO: Yes, but *I* do. Let's go to court.

PHORMIO: "To court," you say? *Oh, no!* I'm going to go in *here.* (*Starting for the house of* CHREMES.)

CHREMES (*to* DEMIPHO): Follow him! Catch him! Hold on to him till I call the slaves!

DEMIPHO (*catching* PHORMIO *and being shaken off*): I can't hold him all by myself. Hurry up!

PHORMIO (*to* DEMIPHO): There's one suit for assault and battery against you, Demipho.

DEMIPHO: All right! Sue away! (CHREMES *jerks at him.*)

PHORMIO: One for you, too, Chremes.

CHREMES: Drag him off!

PHORMIO: That's your game, is it? I'll have to use my lungs. (*Yelling*) Nausistrata, come out!

CHREMES (*to* DEMIPHO): Shut his dirty mouth! Just see how strong he is!

PHORMIO (*louder*): Nausistrata, I say!

DEMIPHO: Won't you shut up?

PHORMIO: "Shut up," you say?

DEMIPHO (*to* CHREMES): Sock him a few in the belly, if he doesn't come along.

PHORMIO: Yes, or even gouge an eye out! There'll come a time some day when I'll get it back at you good and proper.

[ACT FIVE: SCENE 9]

(NAUSISTRATA *comes out. The two old men let go of* PHORMIO, *and fall back sheepishly.*)

NAUSISTRATA: Who's calling me? (*As no one answers, she turns to* CHREMES.) Why, what's all this racket about, my dear?

PHORMIO (*insolently to* CHREMES): Ahem! Struck dumb, are you?

NAUSISTRATA: Who's that person? (*Still no reply.*) Aren't you going to answer?

PHORMIO: He answer you? Lord, he doesn't even know where he's at!

CHREMES (*finally, and with a great effort*): Don't you believe a word he says.

PHORMIO (*to* NAUSISTRATA, *who looks in surprise at* CHREMES): Go up to him, touch him; you can kill me if he isn't absolutely frozen stiff.

CHREMES (*mumbling*): There's nothing the matter.

NAUSISTRATA: Well, then, what's he talking about?

PHORMIO: You'll find out. Listen!

CHREMES: Are you going to insist on believing him?

NAUSISTRATA: But, my dear, how *can* I *believe anything*, when he hasn't said a word yet?

PHORMIO: The poor thing! He's just delirious with fear.

NAUSISTRATA (*to* CHREMES): Upon my soul, you must have some good reason for being so scared!

CHREMES (*trying to bluff it out*): Me scared?

PHORMIO (*sneeringly*): Fine, indeed! All right, since you're not scared, and there's nothing in what I have to say, tell her the story yourself.

DEMIPHO (*to* NAUSISTRATA): Are you going to let that low-life talk to you?

PHORMIO (*to* DEMIPHO): Oho! Demipho! You *have* done nicely for your brother!

NAUSISTRATA: My dear, *aren't* you going to talk?

CHREMES: —But—

NAUSISTRATA: "But," what?

CHREMES: There's no need to tell.

PHORMIO: No, *you* don't need to *tell*, but *she* needs to *know*. (*To* NAUSISTRATA) In Lemnos—

DEMIPHO: What's that you're saying?

CHREMES: Shut up!

PHORMIO: Behind your back—

CHREMES: Woe's me!

PHORMIO: He kept another woman.

NAUSISTRATA (*staggering*): My husband! The gods forbid!

PHORMIO: It's the absolute truth.

NAUSISTRATA: Mercy! That's the death of me!

PHORMIO: Yes, and more than that. She had a baby girl, that he's been bringing up, while you were sound asleep.

CHREMES (*to* DEMIPHO): What *are* we to do?

NAUSISTRATA: Immortal Gods! A pitiful and wicked outrage!

PHORMIO (*to* CHREMES): "Do"? This is *done,* already.

NAUSISTRATA: Was ever anything as bad as this? When their wives are around, *then* they turn into tired old men. Demipho, I appeal to you, for it makes me sick to talk to this creature over here. Was *that* what all those business trips of his to Lemnos meant? Was *that* the reason he was always delayed there so long? Was *that* the "hard times" there which cut down my income?

DEMIPHO (*attempting to conciliate*): As for me, Nausistrata, I can't deny that Chremes is to blame in this affair. But why not forgive him?

PHORMIO (*aside*): This is the obituary for Chremes!

DEMIPHO: It wasn't out of disregard, or any lack of affection for you, that he behaved this way. Something like fifteen years ago he met this woman, when he was somewhat under the influence of wine. He did her wrong, and she had this girl in consequence. He never touched her again, though, and besides, she's dead now and out of the way, the one who was the only fly in the ointment. And so I beg of you to exhibit the sweet disposition here that you show everywhere else, and bear up under this cheerfully.

NAUSISTRATA (*thoroughly angry*): "Cheerfully," you say? Bless me! *I'm* eager enough to have the thing stop right here. But why expect anything like that? Because he's older, is he any less likely to go wrong again? Fifteen years ago he was an old man, if old age is enough to make men decent. And do my looks and years make me any more attractive now, Demipho, than I was then? What guarantee can you give me so that I can expect, or at least hope, it will never happen again?

PHORMIO (*proclaiming like a town-crier*): Oyez! Oyez! Oyez! If anybody wants to attend the funeral of Chremes, now's the time! That's the way I'll pour it into him. Come one, come all, that want to have a round with Phormio! I'll butcher them with trouble just the way I have Chremes here. (*Sneering at him for a moment in silence, then finally, to the audience*) Oh well, let him get back on good terms with her. I'm satisfied. She's got something now she can nag into his ears as long as he lives.

NAUSISTRATA: Perhaps I deserved it, I suppose they'll say. But, Demipho, why should I now tell the whole story, in all its details, of the kind of wife I've been to him?

DEMIPHO: I know it all perfectly.

NAUSISTRATA: Did I deserve it, or not?

DEMIPHO: Never, in the wide world. But you can't change what's gone and been done, simply by scolding. Do forgive him; he begs your pardon; confesses he was wrong; makes a clean breast of it; what more do you want?

PHORMIO (*aside*): Before she forgives him I'll have to look out for myself and Phaedria. Hold on there, Nausistrata! Listen to me a minute before you make any rash promises.

NAUSISTRATA: What is it?

PHORMIO: I beat him out of six thousand today, and gave the money to your son. He took it and bought his sweetheart from a slave-dealer.

CHREMES: Hey! What's that?

NAUSISTRATA (*with supreme contempt*): Indeed! And do *you* think it such a scandal if your son, in the first flush of youth, has *one sweetheart,* while *you* have *two* wives? Haven't you *any* sense of shame? How can *you* have the face to reprove him? Tell me that! (CHREMES *falls back crushed.*)

DEMIPHO: He'll do whatever you want him to.

NAUSISTRATA: No, it's not going to be as simple as that. To be explicit about it, I'll grant no pardon and make no promises, until I see my son, Phaedria. I'll let *him* decide, and I'll do whatever *he* says.

PHORMIO: You're a wise woman, Nausistrata.

NAUSISTRATA (*to* DEMIPHO): Will that suit you?

DEMIPHO: It will.

CHREMES (*aside*): As a matter of fact, it's a lot better than that! I'm getting off elegantly, splendidly; I never dreamed of anything like that.

NAUSISTRATA (*to* PHORMIO): And what's your name?

PHORMIO: My name is Phormio, and, by Heaven, I'm a friend of your family, and especially of your son, Phaedria.

NAUSISTRATA: Phormio, upon my soul, I'll be glad to help you, in both word and deed, any way I can, I surely will.

PHORMIO (*bowing low*): That's very kind of you.

NAUSISTRATA: Indeed and you *certainly have* deserved it!

PHORMIO: Do you really want to make me happy today, and at the same time make your husband's eyes fairly ache?

NAUSISTRATA: I'd love to.

PHORMIO: Then invite me in to dinner.

NAUSISTRATA: Of course, I certainly will. Come on.

PHORMIO: All right, let's go in right away.

NAUSISTRATA: Very good, but where's Phaedria, our judge?

PHORMIO (*starting off*): I'll see that he gets here right away.

THE ENTIRE TROUPE (*to the audience*): Good-bye, and give us your applause!

TERENCE

THE BROTHERS (ADELPHOE)

TRANSLATED BY WILLIAM ABBOTT OLDFATHER

CHARACTERS IN THE PLAY

MICIO, *an elderly bachelor, brother of Demea, father by adoption of his nephew, Aeschinus*

DEMEA, *older brother of Micio, father of Aeschinus and Ctesipho.*

SANNIO, *partly a slave dealer, and partly the manager of a bawdy house*

AECHINUS, *the elder son of Demea, adopted by his uncle Micio*

CTESIPHO, *the younger son of Demea*

SYRUS, *the ranking slave of Micio's household*

GETA, *slave of Sostrata, "Honest John"*

SOSTRATA, *mother of Pamphila*

CANTHARA, *a slave and old woman, 'Boozefighter"*

PAMPHILA, *young daughter of Sostrata, beloved of Aeschinus, "Altogether Lovable"*

HEGIO, *an honest old friend of the family of Sostrata, "Leader"*

THE BROTHERS

(*The scene is Athens, and the entire action takes place in the street outside the adjoining houses of* MICIO *and* SOSTRATA. *It is very early in the morning. A dapper little gentleman walks out of his front door and looks anxiously up and down an empty street.*)

MICIO: Damn it all! My boy Aeschinus isn't back yet from last night's party; nor any of the servants sent to meet him.—Well, there's a lot of truth in the old saying: "If you're away any place, or late coming home, you're far better off doing what your *wife* thinks you're up to, when she's all upset, than what fond parents imagine." If you don't get home as soon as *she* expects you, your *wife* thinks you're in love, or that someone's in love with *you*, or that you're drinking and amusing yourself, the only one that's having a good time, while *she's* at home neglected.

But the fond parents! Just look at me! All the things I'm thinking about, just because my boy's not back home yet! Yes, and worrying too! He may have caught the flu, or fallen down somewhere, or broken a leg, or something. The idea of any man deliberately creating for himself something that's dearer to him than even *he himself!*

Yes, and he isn't even my own son. He's only my brother's boy.

That brother! He's absolutely different from me, and always has been, ever since we were children. I have followed this easy-going, pleasant life in town, with lots of leisure, and, what some, no doubt, think is the luckiest feature of all, I've never got married. *He* is the diametrical opposite; lives out on the farm, pursuing a life of thrifty and rugged individualism; got married;

157

had two boys. I adopted the older one; brought him up from infancy, and kept him; loved him as though he were my very own. He's my chief joy, the only thing that I really love in the world. And I do my very best to have him feel the same way toward me. I give him things, I overlook things, I don't insist on my legal rights—in a word, what other boys do behind their fathers' backs—the sort of thing that young bloods will always be up to—I have accustomed *my* boy not to keep from me. And I'll tell you why. The fellow who's set about it, and has the gall to lie, and to cheat his own father, will have just so much more gall in treating other people the same way. I think it's much better to attach boys to you by appealing to their sense of honor and their instincts as gentlemen, than by intimidating them.

All this doesn't suit my brother; it doesn't please *him* the least bit. He often comes in shouting, "What *are* you up to, Micio? Why are you ruining this young fellow for us? Why does he have a love affair? Why does he drink? Why do you spend all that money on such things, and dress him so extravagantly? You are an utter fool!" But he himself is altogether too rigid, far beyond anything that fair and square dealing requires. And besides, he's 'way off, in my opinion, if he thinks that the authority which is established by force is firmer than that which is built up on affection.

This is the way *I* have it figured out, and I'm convinced that I'm right. The young man who does his duty under the threat of punishment is scared just as long as he thinks there is some danger of what he's done being found out. If he has reason to believe that he's going to get by with it, he goes right back to his natural inclinations. But the young man that you can attach to yourself by kindliness, always acts sincerely. He is eager to do as well as he has been done by; he'll be exactly the same sort of fellow, whether *you* are around or not. This is what a father ought to be about: helping his son to form the habit of doing right on his own initiative, rather than because he's afraid of some serious consequences. This is just the difference between a father and a slave-driver. The man who doesn't understand *that,* had better admit that he doesn't know how to manage boys.

But isn't this the very fellow I've been talking about? It certainly is. He's all glum about something or other. No doubt he'll start one of his regular rows.—Delighted to see you safe and sound this morning, Demea!

[ACT ONE: SCENE 2]

DEMEA: Uh! Lucky I met you; I was looking for you.

MICIO: Well, what are you feeling bad about?

DEMEA: When you and I have a boy like Aeschinus, do you ask *me* what *I* am feeling bad about?

MICIO (*aside, to the audience*): Didn't I tell you so? (*Calmly, to his brother*) What's he done?

DEMEA: "What's he done?" No sense of shame! No fear of anybody! Feels that no law is binding upon *him*! Why, to say nothing about anything that's happened before, look at what he's gone and done this time!

MICIO: Well, what's that?

DEMEA: He's smashed up a front door and broken into somebody else's house; just about beat the head of the household and all the servants to death; carried off a girl he was in love with. Everybody is denouncing it as a frightful outrage! (*As* MICIO *never bats an eyelash*) Why, Micio, how *many* people spoke to me about it as I was coming in this morning! It's the talk of the whole town! (*As* MICIO *still maintains an irritating imperturbability*) Oh, well, if I *have* to make an odious comparison, can't he see how his brother works on the farm, and lives out there a thrifty and sober life? *He* never did anything like that. And when I'm talking *about him*, Micio, I'm talking *at you*. *You* are allowing him to go to the dogs.

MICIO (*infuriatingly calm*): There's nothing in the world so unfair as a man who has no experience of life; he thinks nothing is done right except what he's doing himself.

DEMEA: And so what?

MICIO: Why, your judgment, Demea, on this matter is utterly at fault. It is *not* an outrage—I'm speaking seriously—for a young fellow to have a girl friend, or to drink. (*As* DEMEA *throws up his hands*) No, it isn't! Nor even to smash in somebody's front door. Of course, you and I didn't do that, and you know why. *We* couldn't afford it. Do you want to make a virtue *now* out of our poverty *then?* That's not fair. If we had been able to meet the expense, we'd have done precisely the same thing ourselves. And so right now, if you were a normal human being, you would be allowing that boy of yours to behave in much the same way, while he still has a little license because of his youth; rather than when he has waited and waited, and finally chucked you out of the front door, have him go and do exactly the same thing, and that at a time of life when it is no longer excusable.

DEMEA: Immortal Jupiter! Man, you'll drive me crazy! It isn't a scandal for a young man to behave this way?

MICIO: Oh, listen! Don't deafen me so many times on the same subject. You gave me your son to adopt. He became *my* son. If he gets into any bad scrapes, Demea, I'm the one that suffers. I make up the deficit in his allowance. He dines expensively; he drinks; he smells of perfume—*I'm* the one that's paying for it. He has a little romance; I'll meet the expenses as long as I find it convenient. When I don't find it convenient any longer, his girl may give him the gate. He has smashed in a front door, has he? *I'll* pay the repair bill. He has torn some clothes? They'll be patched. And, thank the gods, I still have the wherewithal, and up till now I haven't found it troublesome. Here's my last word: Either cut this all out, or let's appeal to any arbitrator you please. I'll prove that *you* are more in the wrong about this whole business than I am.

DEMEA: Good Lord! Learn how to *be* a father from those who really know!

MICIO: *You* are a father merely by a physical act. *I* am a father by virtue of using my brains.

DEMEA: Did you ever accomplish anything with your brains?

MICIO: Oh, well, if you insist on being abusive, I'll simply go back into the house.

DEMEA: So that's the way you are going to treat me, is it?

MICIO: And do you really expect me to listen to the same thing so *many* times?

DEMEA: But *I'm* worrying about it!

MICIO: So am I. But, Demea, let's go fifty-fifty on this business of worrying. You worry about one boy, and I'll worry about the other. (*And now* MICIO *uses his trump card, appealing to his brother's fundamental sense of fair play.*) Because, if *you* are going to worry about *both* of them, it's pretty much the same as if you asked me to return the boy you once let me have.

DEMEA: Oh, come now, Micio! You *can't* mean that!

MICIO: Yes, that's exactly the way I feel about it.

DEMEA: Very well, if that's what you really *like* to do, let him waste his money, let him ruin his prospects, let him go to the dogs,—it's nothing to me! Now if I ever say another word—

MICIO: Are you getting all wrought up again, Demea?

DEMEA: Oh, don't you believe that I'm telling the truth? *I'm* not asking back the boy I gave you, am I? I'm simply feeling bad. *I'm* no mere stranger. If I interfere . . . (*and then, as* MICIO, *with a gesture of despair, starts to walk away*) Oh, very well then, I'll stop. You suggest that I worry about one of them; *I'm doing just that*; and, thank the gods! he's the kind of son *I* want him to be! This boy of yours will find it out some day. I don't want to say anything harsher about him than that. (*And off he strides, muttering to himself.*)

MICIO (*left alone, uneasily*): There's *something* in what he has to say, even though it isn't the whole truth. This business has got *me* worried, too, but I didn't want to let on to *him* that I wasn't entirely happy about it. That's the kind of fellow he is. Even though I try to be ingratiating, am tactful about opposing him and heading him off, still, he hardly takes it like a human being. But if I should egg him on, or even help him, when he has one of these fits of fury, I'd be as crazy as he was. (*A pause*)

And yet Aeschinus hasn't treated me quite right this time. What wild woman is there in town that he hasn't fallen in love with? Is there one of them that he hasn't made presents to? And just a few days ago (no doubt he was about fed up on all of them) he said he wanted to get married. I had hopes that his youthful spirits had stopped frothing off at the top. I was delighted. Now he's at it all over again! Oh, well, I want to see what the whole business is about, and have a talk with the boy himself, if he's downtown. (*With this remark,* MICIO *walks off.*)

[ACT TWO: SCENE 1]

(*A moment or so later, the young man in question appears, leading a scared soubrette by the hand, both accompanied by a powerful slave armed with a club, and followed at a short distance by the badly battered-up, but furious and threatening legal owner of the girl.)*

SANNIO: Friends and fellow-citizens! I beseech you! Come to the rescue of the pitiful and the innocent! Aid the helpless!

AESCHINUS *(to the frightened slave-girl)*: Take it easy! Now, stand right there. What are you looking over your shoulder for? There's not a particle of danger. He'll never touch you, as long as I am around.

SANNIO: Indeed I *will* touch her, despite all of you!

AESCHINUS: Scoundrel though he is, he'll not do anything that will bring him a second dressing down today.

SANNIO: Aeschinus, listen to me. I don't want you to claim you didn't know the kind of person I was. I'm a one-man-gang keeper of a bawdy-house! [1]

AESCHINUS *(icily, and quite undisturbed)*: I know it.

SANNIO *(instantly shifting to a wheedling note, when he sees his bluff is called)*: But, at that, the most honest one that ever was. *(As AESCHINUS maintains a contemptuous and stony silence.)* As for any excuse you expect to make later on, that you're sorry this injury was done to me, *(with an expressive gesture)* I'll not give *that much* for it! *(As AESCHINUS still remains unmoved)* Take it from me! I'm going to get my full legal rights; and you'll *never* make good in *words* the damage you've done me in *fact*. I know the way you young fellows talk: "Sorry it happened; I'll take oath you didn't deserve it," when I've been treated in an outrageous manner.

AESCHINUS *(to PARMENO)*: Hurry on ahead and open the front door.

SANNIO: But aren't you paying *any* attention to what I say?

AESCHINUS *(to the girl, as the door is opened)*: Go on indoors now.

SANNIO: Indeed and I won't let her.

AESCHINUS *(sharply)*: Step up there, Parmeno; you were too far away. Stand *right by* this fellow. There, that's just what I

---

[1] "The word *leno* [keeper of a bawdy-house] is to be uttered in a blood-curdling tone," reports an ancient commentator, no doubt on the basis of some stage tradition.

want. Now don't let *your* eyes wander off anywhere from *mine,* so that the instant I give the signal your fist will be sinking right into his jaw.

SANNIO: I'd just like to see him try that. (*Laying hold of the girl*)

AESCHINUS: Hey, there! Watch out! Let go of that woman!

SANNIO (*as* PARMENO *delivers a tremendous wallop*): Oh! Outrage!

AESCHINUS: He'll do it again, if you're not careful.

SANNIO (*as* PARMENO *does hit him again*): Ouch! Oh grief!

AESCHINUS (*laughing*): *That* time I didn't give a signal; but if you *must* make a mistake, then better too much than too little.

SANNIO (*nursing his jaw*): What's the racket here? Are you the dictator in these parts, Aeschinus?

AESCHINUS: If I *were*, I'd see that *you* were treated the way you deserve.

SANNIO: What business do you have with me?

AESCHINUS: None at all.

SANNIO: Well, say, do you know who and what I am?

AESCHINUS: I haven't the least desire to.

SANNIO: Did I ever touch anything of yours?

AESCHINUS: If *you had* touched anything, it would have been just too bad.

SANNIO: How did *you* acquire a better right than I have to my slave-girl that I paid my own money for? Answer me that!

AESCHINUS: It will be better for you not to raise a row here in front of the house. For if you insist on making a nuisance of yourself, you will be dragged indoors in a jiffy, and there they'll dress you down with rawhide till you're a dead man.

SANNIO: Rawhide on a free man?

AESCHINUS: Exactly.

SANNIO: You dirty dog! And is *this* what they call a free country, where everybody gets a square deal?

AESCHINUS: If you're through raving, pimp, please listen now.

SANNIO: Who's been raving? *I*, or *you* against me?

AESCHINUS: Aw! Forget it! And settle down to business.

SANNIO: What business? What am I to settle down to?

AESCHINUS: Do you want me now to make you a straight business proposition?

SANNIO: I sure do, provided you give me a fair break.

AESCHINUS (*sarcastically*): Phooey! A *pimp* doesn't want me to give him a bad break!

SANNIO: I know I keep a bawdy-house; I'm a general center of infection for all young fellows, a crook, and a pestilence. And yet I never did *you* any harm.

AESCHINUS: Yes, by Heaven, that's your solitary negative virtue. (*Pausing*)

SANNIO: Well, please get back, Aeschinus, to what you were starting to talk about a moment ago.

AESCHINUS: You bought that girl (and bad luck to you, too, in the whole business!) for four thousand. I'll give you just what you paid for her.

SANNIO: Well, but suppose I don't *want* to sell her, are you going to force me to?

AESCHINUS: Not at all;—

SANNIO: And indeed that's just what I was afraid of.

AESCHINUS (*continuing, without any attention to* SANNIO's *interruption*): And I don't think she ought to be up for sale anyway. She's a free woman; and what's more, I hereby claim her scot free on a charge of illegal enslavement. And now the next move is up to you; either take the money, or else think up something to tell the judge. Turn that over in your mind till I come back, you pimp! (*Walks into the house.*)

SANNIO: Good Lord in heaven! I'll never be surprised again at people going crazy from mistreatment. He dragged me out of the house, and beat me up; despite all I could do he carried off my slave-girl; busted more than five hundred fisticuffs upon the miserable person of yours truly. (*A pause*) And now, as a reward for all that dirty deal, he wants me to turn the girl over to him at no more than what I paid for her. (*Another pause; then, ironically*) Why, of course, one good deed deserves another! That's only a fair request! (*Pausing again*) All right, I'm perfectly willing to accept it, if only he'll *pay* the money. But that's plain wishful thinking! Whenever I agree to sell her for that, immediately he'll produce witnesses to swear that the deal was closed. As for the money, that's only a pleasant dream: "Soon; come back tomorrow." (*Once more a pause*) I can put up with that, too, if only he *will* pay, even though it *is* a holdup. (*Still no one comes out of the door so anxiously watched.*) Well, *this* much is a fact anyway: Once you've started in *my* profession, you've got to take abuse from the young fellows, and like it, too. (*Desperately, after one final pause*) But nobody is going to give *me* anything; it's utterly useless for me to make all these calculations.

[ACT TWO: SCENE 2]

(SYRUS *enters, still speaking to* AESCHINUS, *as he comes out of the house.*)

SYRUS: Enough said already; I'll have a talk with him; I'll make him *eager* to take it and ready to admit that he has been treated fine.—(*Gaily*) Well, well, Sannio, what's this I hear about your having a little set-to with the boss?

SANNIO: I never saw such a one-sided match as that one of ours this morning; we're both of us winded, he by landing all the punches, and I by taking them.

SYRUS (*cheerfully*): All your own fault.

SANNIO: What should I have done?

SYRUS: Ah, you should have humored the young gentleman.

SANNIO: How *could* I have humored him any better? I just kept leading with my chin.

SYRUS: Come, come! I'm going to tell you something now. (*Impressively*) There *are times* when it is extremely profitable not to be too particular about a mere sum of money. Pooh! Were *you* afraid that, if you yielded up the least speck of your full legal rights, and humored the young gentleman, you nit-wit,— were you *really afraid* that you wouldn't *profit* by the transaction?

SANNIO: *I* am *not* in the market for blue sky with spot cash.

SYRUS: Well, you'll never make your fortune, then. Get out! Sannio, *you* don't know how to entice people.

SANNIO: No doubt your way is better, but hitherto I have never been so smart that I wouldn't rather take the bird in the hand.

SYRUS: Oh, I know what *you're* thinking about. As if four

thousand were either here or there, provided only you could do him a favor. (*Then, looking at him shrewdly, out of the corner of his eye*) Besides, I'm told you are taking a trip to Cyprus.

SANNIO (*greatly excited*): What's that?

SYRUS: Yes, you've bought up a lot of merchandise here in Athens to take to the fair there, and already hired your ship. There's no doubt about it. You're all on edge about the business. (*Pausing, and then ostentatiously starting to walk back into the house again*) Oh, well, when you *get back* from Cyprus, I hope you will find leisure *then* to attend to this little business of ours.

SANNIO (*terribly wrought up*): I'm not going to take a step out of town in any direction. (*Aside*) Damnation! I'm ruined! *That's* what those fellows were counting on when they started this thing!

SYRUS (*aside*): He's flabbergasted, all right! I threw a monkey-wrench into his plans that time.

SANNIO (*still aside, walking excitedly up and down*): The skunks! What do you know about that! He's got the drop on me! I've bought a lot of women, and a good deal of other merchandise, that I'm taking to Cyprus. If I don't get to the fair there, I've lost everything. But now if I leave this case unsettled, or try to take it up again when I get back, nothing doing. It'll be cold stuff. "You're only showing up *now*, are you? Why did you stand for it? Where have you been all this time?" It would be much better to lose the girl outright than either to stay here long enough to settle the case, or start an action after I get back.

SYRUS (*walking up to him insolently*): Well, have you finished counting up all the chickens you're going to hatch?

SANNIO: Is this a decent thing for him to do? A gentleman like Aeschinus starting something like that! Trying to take away my slave-girl by force and fraud!

SYRUS (*aside*): He's getting softened up. (*Then to* SANNIO) Here's my last offer. Take it or leave it. Rather than run the risk, Sannio, of keeping or losing the entire sum, let's go fifty-fifty. The young gentleman will dig up a couple of thousand some-where or other.

SANNIO: Ouch! Am I going to run the risk now of losing some of the original investment? Hasn't he any sense of shame? He has loosened every tooth I have; my whole head is just one black and blue bump from his slugging. Is he going to cheat me, too? I'll *never* go *anywhere!*

SYRUS: As you please; it's all right with *us.* There's nothing more I can do for you, is there, before I go back into the house?

SANNIO: Oh, don't do that! Good Lord! *Please,* Syrus! No matter what's happened, rather than go to court, let my own be returned to me, Syrus; at *least* what I paid for her. I know you haven't enjoyed my intimate friendship up till now. (*And then, as* SYRUS *sidles up to him with his hand open behind his back,* SANNIO *slips something into it and adds*) I'll guarantee that you'll admit I remember and repay a favor.

SYRUS (*distinctly changed*): I'll do the best I can for you. But hello, there's Ctesipho coming. He's all smiles about his girl.

SANNIO (*anxiously*): But what about my proposition?

SYRUS: Oh, wait a little while!

[ACT TWO: SCENE 3]

(*Enter* CTESIPHO, *from the farm.*)

CTESIPHO: If *anybody* does you a good turn, right when you need it, you've reason enough to be happy. But, when all's said and done, if the person who really *ought* to help you actually comes across, then that *is* something! Oh, brother, brother! How wonderful you are! This much is certain: I'll never be able to say anything so eloquent but what your virtues will surpass it. And so, here's the one point where I think that I have it over everyone else: No one has a brother that's more of a prince in all first-class qualities.

SYRUS: Why, Ctesipho!

CTESIPHO: Why, Syrus! Where's Aeschinus?

SYRUS: There, inside. He's waiting for you in the house.

CTESIPHO: Ah! (*Clasping his hands*)

SYRUS: What do you mean?

CTESIPHO: "What do I mean?" Why, Syrus, I'm just now beginning to *live,* and I owe it all to him. Dear soul! He never gave a thought to anything that concerned *him,* when it was a question of *my* happiness. All the severe criticism, the bad reputation, my trouble, and my misbehavior, he took upon himself. You can't beat *that*! But, say, what's the noise at your front door? (*Starting to run, coward that he is*)

SYRUS (*catching his coat-tail*): Hold on! Hold on! It's Aeschinus himself coming out.

[ACT TWO: SCENE 4]

(*Reenter* AESCHINUS.)

AESCHINUS: Where's that blasphemer?

SANNIO (*aside, recognizing his own description*): He's looking for *me*. Has he brought anything out with him? I'm ruined! I don't see a thing.

AESCHINUS (*to* CTESIPHO): Ah there! Lucky we met. I've been looking for you. Well, Ctesipho, what's doing? Everything's safe and sound; only *do* drop that gloomy look of yours.

CTESIPHO: So help me Heaven, I sure will, and it's just because I have a brother like you. My own dear Aeschinus! My own dear brother! Ah! I'm ashamed to say anything else nice to your face, for fear you'll think I'm talking this way just to be polite, and not because I'm honestly grateful.

AESCHINUS: Oh, come on, you simpleton! As if *we* didn't understand each other, Ctesipho! What makes *me* feel bad is that we were so late in finding out about it, and matters had almost reached such a pass, that all of us together couldn't have done anything to help, no matter how much we wanted to.

CTESIPHO (*almost with a finger in his mouth*): I was ashamed.

AESCHINUS: Oh, nonsense! That's plain stupid, not a case of tender conscience at all. For a trivial little thing like this to think of leaving home?! It's disgraceful even to speak about it! Heaven forbid!

CTESIPHO: But I made a bad slip.

AESCHINUS (*with an impatient gesture, turning away*): Well, and what answer is Sannio ready to give us?

SYRUS: He's perfectly tame by now.

AESCHINUS: I'm going downtown to pay him off. But you run on in and cheer up your girl, Ctesipho.

SANNIO: Get a move on, Syrus!

SYRUS (*maliciously*): Oh yes, let's go, for Sannio here is all in a hurry to start for Cyprus.

SANNIO: Not so much as you wish; fact is, I've nothing to do, and I'm staying here in town.

SYRUS: Oh, *he'll* pay you; don't you worry about that.

SANNIO: But see to it that he pays me *every penny*.

SYRUS: He will, every penny; just keep your mouth shut and trot along after us this way.

SANNIO: All right.

(*A pause, and as the stage is almost empty,* CTESIPHO, *before going into the house, shouts*)

CTESIPHO: Hey there! Hey there! Syrus!

SYRUS: What's the matter now?

CTESIPHO: Please, for Heaven's sake, pay off that dirty bum just as soon as you can. I'm afraid he'll get angry again, somehow or other father will get wind of it all, and then I *will* be sunk for good.

SYRUS: *That* will never happen; take it easy. For the next few minutes entertain yourself in the house with that girl. Have the blankets and cushions spread on the sofas for us, and get everything else ready. As soon as this piece of business has been attended to, I'll come back to the house with the delicatessen.

CTESIPHO: Please do! Since this has come off so well, let's make a regular holiday of it.

[ACT THREE: SCENE I]

(*An elderly lady,* SOSTRATA, *of the lower middle-class, together with an old nurse,* CANTHARA, *steps out into the street from the house next door to* MICIO'S.)

SOSTRATA: Oh, mercy on me! My dear nurse! What *is* going to happen now!

CANTHARA: "What's going to happen?" you say. Why, everything's going to come out all right, I guess. Her pains, my dear, are only just beginning. Are you getting scared already, as though you'd never attended a delivery, and had never had a baby yourself?

SOSTRATA: Dear oh me! I haven't anybody; we're all alone in the world. And besides, Geta isn't here either; there's no one to send after the midwife, and no one to call Aeschinus.

CANTHARA: For the land's sake! *He*, at least, will be here any minute. *He* never lets a day go by without making several calls.

SOSTRATA: Yes, indeed, he's the only help I have in all my trouble.

CANTHARA: Under the circumstances, Mistress, it couldn't have been better than it is, once the rape was committed, at least as far as the young man is concerned. *Such* a fine fellow, *such* a noble disposition and kind heart, from *such* a splendid family!

SOSTRATA: Goodness me! It's just as you say. The gods keep him safe for us! That's all my prayer!

[ACT THREE: SCENE 2]

(*Enter* GETA, *on the extreme left, blazing with righteous indignation; he fails to notice the two old women who have moved some distance away from their own front door by this time, and cannot quite catch at first all that he is saying.*)

GETA: The curse has come upon us! What a jam we're in! Even if everyone together tried to give us all the good advice there is, and save the situation, they couldn't get anywhere at all with it. (*And then, with a charming touch of naive loyalty, for* GETA *is really a lovable old fellow, he goes on.*) It's come down on *my* head, and the head of my mistress, and my mistress's daughter. Oh, grief! Oh, dear! Oh, dear! (*Mixing his metaphors slightly.*) There are so many things building walls about us, I can't get my head above the surface. Violence, poverty, wickedness, loneliness, disgrace! Such a world! O villainy! O wicked people! O damned scoundrel!

CANTHARA: Dear me, what's got Geta so scared and in such a hurry?

GETA: No sense of honor, no sworn oath, no kind heart to hold him back or change his purpose; not even the fact that she was just about to be confined that poor girl that he so outrageously and brutally assaulted.

SOSTRATA: I can't quite make out what he's talking about.

CANTHARA: Come on, Sostrata, please let's get up a little closer.

GETA: Ugh! Damn it all! I'm hardly in my right mind. I'm all burned up. There's nothing that I would rather have than that whole household put in front of me, so that I could disgorge all my fury on them while I'm still sore about it. I'd be perfectly satisfied if only I could treat them the way I want to. To start with, that old man who's the father of this abomination, I'd just *choke him* to death! And then Syrus who put him up to it. Whooee! How I would grind him up into sausagemeat! First I'd grab him around the waist, heave him up in the air, bash his head on the ground, and spatter his brains all over the street! As for the young man himself, first I'd gouge out his eyes, and then I'd throw him over a cliff. The rest of 'em I'd hurry, and hunt, and harry, and bang, and slam around! (*Finally, catching his breath after this tirade, which has been accompanied by vivid and vigorous pantomime, he adds*) But why don't I hurry up and tell the mistress about this trouble? (*Starting for the door of* SOSTRATA's *house*)

SOSTRATA: Let's call him back. Geta, I say.

GETA: Ugh, leave me alone; I don't care who you are.

SOSTRATA: It's me, Sostrata.

GETA: Where *is* she? You're just the person I'm looking for.

SOSTRATA: Yes, and *I'm* waiting to see *you*, too. It's awfully lucky I found you.

GETA: Mistress! (*Overcome.*)

SOSTRATA: What is it? What makes you tremble so?

GETA: Ah! Alas!

CANTHARA: What's all the rush about, my dear Geta? Catch your breath.

GETA: We're absolutely—

SOSTRATA: And what do you mean "absolutely"?

GETA: Sunk. It's all over now.

SOSTRATA: Tell me, please do, what it's all about.

GETA: Right now—

SOSTRATA: What's "right now," Geta?

GETA: Aeschinus—

SOSTRATA: Oh, *what* about him?

GETA: He's gone back on our family.

SOSTRATA: What's that? It will be the death of me! Why *did* he do it?

GETA: He has fallen in love with another girl.

SOSTRATA: Oh! Poor me!

GETA: And he's making no bones about it. In broad daylight he went and carried her off himself from the keeper of the bawdy-house.

SOSTRATA: Are you sure about it?

GETA: Absolutely. I saw it with my own eyes.

SOSTRATA: Dear me! Dear me! *What* can you believe? *Whom* can you believe? Our Aeschinus! The very life of all of us, our only help! Who used to swear that he couldn't live a single day without my daughter! Who used to tell us that he was going to take the little baby, and put him in his father's arms, and then pray that he might be allowed to take my daughter as his lawful, wedded wife!

GETA: Well, Mistress, just stop crying, and, instead of that, think what's going to be the best thing to do next. Shall we stand for it, or tell somebody?

CANTHARA: Good grief! My dear man! Have you lost your mind? Do you think this is the kind of thing we ought to start talking about?

GETA: As for myself, I don't like the idea. To begin with, what he's up and done proves that he has completely gone back on us. Now, if we start to tell this story, I'm absolutely certain he'll deny everything, and so your own reputation will be compromised, and your daughter's very life will be in danger. And besides, no matter how much he may admit the truth of what we say, now that he's fallen in love with another girl, it would never do for him to marry Pamphila here. And so, any way you look at it, we just *must* keep quiet.

SOSTRATA: Ah! Never in all the world! I'll *never* behave like that!

GETA: What are you going to do?

SOSTRATA: I'm going to tell everybody.

CANTHARA: Ah! Ah! My dear Sostrata, be careful about what you are starting to do!

SOSTRATA: Things simply *can't* be in any worse position than they are now. To start with, Pamphila hasn't any dowry; and then, what *was* her second dowry, has been lost. She can't be married as a virgin now. There's only one thing left. If he tries to deny it all, I have as my evidence the engagement ring that he sent her. And, finally, since I have a perfectly clear conscience, and know that I'm innocent, that we've never taken any money, nor done anything else that was unworthy of either my daughter or myself, Geta, *I'm* going to try to *do* something.

GETA: Oh, very well! I admit that you're right.

SOSTRATA (*to* GETA): Now you run off as fast as you can to cousin Hegio, and tell him the whole story, exactly the way it happened. For he was the very dearest friend of our Simulus and has done everything he could for us.

GETA: Yes, by Heaven, for there's nobody else that will even look at us.

SOSTRATA: And you, my dear Canthara, run and bring the midwife; there mustn't be any delay when we need her.

[ACT THREE: SCENE 3]

(*The stage is vacant for a moment, and then the honest farmer,* DEMEA, *comes rushing in, much more excited even than he was before.*)

DEMEA: Absolutely ruined! I've just been told that my boy Ctesipho was in cahoots with Aeschinus in carrying off that girl. There's only one thing needed to make my cup of sorrows full, and that's the possibility of bringing to some bad end the one son of mine who still amounts to something. But where can I find him? I suppose they've taken him off to some low dive. That profligate put him up to it, I'm sure. But, look, here's Syrus coming. I can find out from *him*. And yet, so help me Hercules! he's one of the gang himself. If he gets an idea that I'm looking for the boy, that dirty bum will never tell me anything. (*In a naively futile attempt to deceive a rascal like* SYRUS) Well, I won't let him know what I'm after.

(*Enter* SYRUS *from the market place, attended by a servant, both of them loaded down with all manner of fancy delicacies for a big party that they are going to give in the house.* SYRUS *catches sight of* DEMEA *and makes the most of this opportunity to josh the old stickler for the proprieties. Pretending at first, of course, not to have seen him,* SYRUS *begins to talk in a loud voice with the intention of being overheard.*)

SYRUS: I just saw the old man downtown, and told him the whole story, from beginning to end. I never saw anyone so happy.

DEMEA (*aside*): Immortal Jupiter! That fellow's asininity!

SYRUS: He congratulated the boy and he thanked me sincerely for having had the bright idea in the first place.

DEMEA (*still aside*): I feel that I am just going to burst!

SYRUS: He came across with the money right on the spot. In addition to that, he gave me a hundred for the party, and I've gone and spent it to the best of my *taste*.

DEMEA (*to the audience, but intentionally loud enough to be overheard this time*): Uh huh! If you want anything attended to *properly*, just turn it over to this fellow!

SYRUS: Well, well, there, Demea! I hadn't seen you before. What's doing?

DEMEA: "What's doing?" you say? I can't begin to express my amazement at the style of living in your household.

SYRUS: So help me Heaven, it *is* preposterous; to be frank, it's just plain *silly*, too. (*And then, shouting into the house*) Ah, there, Dromo! Clean the *rest* of those fish, but let that great big lobster flop around in the water a little while longer. When I get back *I'll* attend to *him*. (*With a jerk of his thumb towards* DEMEA)

DEMEA: Such scandals!

SYRUS: No, I can't say that I approve of it myself. I often raise my voice and call out (*with deliberate ambiguity*) Stephanio! Get that salt fish soaked carefully.

DEMEA: The gods help us! Has my brother set his *heart* on behaving like this? Does he think it's *praiseworthy* to ruin my son? Oh, wretched man that I am! I can just see the day coming when this young fellow will go bankrupt and run away from home somewhere to join the army.

SYRUS: Ah, Demea, now *that's* what *I* call sagacity, not merely to see what's right in front of your feet, but to be able to foretell the future!

DEMEA (*a little suspiciously*): Say, is that chorus-girl in the house?

SYRUS: Yes, right in there.

DEMEA: Whooee! Is my brother going to *keep* her in his house?

SYRUS: I suppose so, he's just that crazy.

DEMEA: Such carryings on!

SYRUS: It really *is* silly leniency on the part of his father, and a demoralizing laxness.

DEMEA: I'm thoroughly ashamed of my brother, and disgusted with him, too.

SYRUS: There *is* a lot of difference, Demea, between you and your brother. Understand, I am not saying that just because I am talking to *you*. In fact, there's a *world* of difference. *You*, every inch of you, are simon-pure sagacity; he's a mere trifler. *You* wouldn't let *your* boy behave like that, would you?

DEMEA: "Let my boy"—! Wouldn't I smell it out six whole months before he even *started* anything!

SYRUS: No need of telling me how smart you are.

DEMEA: I only hope, that he will always continue to behave just exactly the way he's doing now! (*The irony of the situation is that* CTESIPHO, *at this very moment, is just inside the door, drinking and making love to his disreputable girl friend.*)

SYRUS: That's right. (*Ironically*) You know how it is: Everybody's son turns out exactly the way his father wants him to.

DEMEA (*with affected nonchalance*): Well, what about him? Have you seen him today?

SYRUS: Your boy? (*Aside*) I'll get the old man out into the country. (*To* DEMEA) Oh, I've no doubt he's already working hard at some job or other out on the farm.

DEMEA: Are you sure of it?

SYRUS: What? When I myself escorted him to the edge of town?

DEMEA: That's fine. I was afraid he might be hanging around here.

SYRUS: Yes, and he was *hopping* mad.

DEMEA: You don't say!

SYRUS: Oh, he met his brother downtown, and bawled him out right in public about that chorus-girl.

DEMEA: Honest?

SYRUS: You bet! He didn't pull his punches. Just as the money was being paid out at the bank, up pops Ctesipho to everybody's surprise. He began to shout, "Oh, Aeschinus! The *idea* of your behaving in this scandalous fashion! To think that you would be doing things that are a disgrace to the family!"

DEMEA: Oh, I could just cry for joy!

SYRUS: "You're not merely losing all this money; you're ruining your character!"

DEMEA: God save the boy! That's all I pray for! (*Wiping his eyes*) He's exactly like what the men of our family have always been.

SYRUS: Oh, no doubt!

DEMEA: Syrus, he's just full of good, sensible ideas like that.

SYRUS: Yes, yes, to be sure! He's had somebody at home to teach him such things.

DEMEA (*a little modestly*): Well, of course, I do the best I can. I never let anything get by me. I form his habits; in a word, I teach him to look into the lives of men as though he were looking into a mirror, and from others to take an example for himself. I say: "Now, *that's* the thing to *do*."

SYRUS: Absolutely right.

DEMEA: "But *this* is something to *avoid*."

SYRUS: Sagacious!

DEMEA: "This thing is praiseworthy."

SYRUS: That's the ticket!

DEMEA: "But this other, again, is regarded as disreputable."

SYRUS: Absolutely perfect!

DEMEA: And besides (*warming up to a discourse on general morality*)—

SYRUS (*having listened long enough, and now beginning to mock the old puritan*): Oh, the Devil! I honestly haven't time to listen to the rest of the lecture right now, for I've got some fancy fish that I've just picked out. I simply *mustn't* let them get spoiled. Because, you should understand, Demea, it's *just* as much a *disgrace* for us to let good fish get spoiled, as it is for *you not* to do what you were talking about a moment ago. (*And then, mimick-ing* DEMEA, *he adds*) And to the best of *my* ability, too, I lay down the law to the rest of the servants in the house, exactly the way you do: "This is too salty." "This has been scorched." "This hasn't been washed clean." "That's right; now remember and do it *just* that way the next time." I give them the most careful advice I can, up to the very limit of my ability—and *taste*. In a word, Demea, I bid them look into the *pans,* as though they were looking into a mirror, and I tell them what they ought to be doing. I realize that all this behavior of ours is simply silly, but what would you have *me do*? Considering the kind of fellow your brother is, you've just got to humor him. Anything more that you'd like done for you, before I go on in?

DEMEA (*sullenly recognizing that he is being razzed*): All I'd like for *you* people would be the gift of better sense!

SYRUS: Leaving for the country, are you?

DEMEA: Yes, and by the shortest route.

SYRUS: Well, of course; what could you really accomplish here, where no one would pay any attention, even if you *should* give a piece of good advice? (*Going indoors with a leer*)

DEMEA: Indeed I *will* leave this place, as long as the boy, after whom I came here, has gone back to the farm. He's the one *I'm* taking care of; *he* is *my* concern. Since my brother feels that way about it, let *him* look after the other one.

But isn't that Hegio, my old friend? If my eyes don't deceive me, by Heaven, that's the man! (*With a glow of satisfaction*) Ah! He's been my very best friend ever since we were children together. Good Lord! There surely is a most plentiful lack, these days, of citizens like him, men of that fine old honor and loyalty! Hell will freeze over before *he* ever does his country any wrong! How happy I am when I see that there are still a few survivors of that breed! Why, already life seems worth living again! I'll wait and meet the old scout here, say hello, and pass the time of day with him.

[ACT THREE: SCENE 4]

(*Enter* HEGIO *and* GETA *in earnest conversation.*)

HEGIO: Immortal gods, Geta! It's an utter outrage! Are you sure of the facts?

GETA: That's just exactly what's happened!

HEGIO: To think that such an ungentlemanly deed was done by a member of so fine a family! Ah! Aeschinus! Good Lord! *That* wasn't the least bit like your father!

DEMEA (*aside*): You see? He's heard about this chorus-girl; *that's* what's hurting him now, and he isn't even a member of the family, either. The boy's *father*, of course, doesn't give a damn! Oh, dear me! If only Micio were around here somewhere close by and could be hearing this!

HEGIO: Unless they're prepared to do the square thing for people in their position, they'll not get away with it like that.

GETA: All our hope, Hegio, is centered in you. You're all we have, our patron, our father. Our old man entrusted us to your care on his death-bed. If *you* abandon us, we are ruined.

HEGIO: Don't so much as mention the word! *I'll* not abandon you; in common decency it would be quite impossible.

DEMEA (*walking up briskly*): I'm going to speak to him. My most cordial greetings to you, Hegio!

HEGIO: Ah, you're just the man I was looking for. And greetings to you, Demea.

DEMEA: Well, what's up?

HEGIO: Your older son, Aeschinus, that you allowed your brother to adopt, has gone and done something that no respectable and gentlemanly person would do.

DEMEA: Indeed, and what's that?

HEGIO: You knew our mutual friend Simulus, who grew up with us, didn't you?

DEMEA: Of course.

HEGIO: Aeschinus has raped his young daughter.

DEMEA: What?!

HEGIO: Wait a minute, Demea; you haven't yet heard the worst of it.

DEMEA: But can anything be worse?

HEGIO: Yes, it can. For in a way it is possible to understand something like that. It was night; a crime of passion; he'd been drinking; and he was young. Things like that *happen* to mere human beings. Well, when he came to, and *realized* what he had done, of his own initiative he went to the girl's mother, with tears in his eyes, praying, beseeching, pledging, swearing that he would marry the girl. They forgave him; said nothing about it; believed him. The girl got pregnant. All that was nine full months ago. And now this fellow that we took for an honorable gentleman, God save the mark! has gone and got him a chorus-girl to live with, and has left Pamphila flat.

DEMEA (*looking hard at him*): Are you absolutely certain about all these statements you're making?

HEGIO: The girl's mother's right here, the girl herself, the facts themselves; besides that, here's Geta, too, as slaves go, anything but vicious and lazy; he earns the living for them, and all alone supports the entire family. Take him into court, handcuff him, and get at the facts in the case.

GETA: Yes, by God! You can go even farther, and put me on the rack, Demea, if I haven't been telling the truth! Why, when all's said and done, he'll not deny it himself. Just bring him face to face with *me*.

DEMEA (*aside, completely upset and walking up and down in extreme agitation*): I'm ashamed, and I don't quite know either what to do, or what answer to give Hegio.

PAMPHILA (*overheard from inside the house*): Oh dear! Oh dear! I'm torn to pieces with pain. Juno Lucina, help me! Save me, I beseech thee!

HEGIO: Ah! It can't be that she's in labor right now, can it?

GETA: No doubt of it at all, Hegio.

HEGIO: Look, Demea, the girl is appealing to you people to show your good faith. Let her receive of your own free will what you'll be compelled to give her anyway. I pray the gods that you'll behave the way I'm suggesting, for with *your* family it's a straight case of noblesse oblige. *That's* what I'd prefer, first of all. (*Aggressively*) But, I'd have you understand, Demea, that if *you* feel differently about that matter, I'm going to stand by that girl and my dead friend down to the very last. He was my cousin; we were brought up together from early boyhood; we were always together in war and in peace; we've kept smiling, through a life of severe poverty, side by side. And so I'm going to fight, go right into action, do my damndest, and, if necessary and as a last resort, give up my life, before I abandon these women. What's your answer to that?

DEMEA (*deeply affected and confused*): I'll talk it over with my brother, Hegio.

HEGIO: But, Demea, here's something else for you to think over very seriously: Exactly as you and your family are in easy circumstances, extremely influential, wealthy, blessed by fortune, and prominent, to precisely that same extent you ought to do the square thing out of the kindness of your heart, if you want people to regard you as truly reputable citizens.

DEMEA: Come back a little later; everything that's right and proper will be done.

HEGIO: That's just what we expected of you. Geta, show me in now to Sostrata. (*Exeunt* HEGIO *and* GETA.)

DEMEA: *I* told him so! If only this is the end of the matter! But his utterly loose-end way of doing things will surely wind up in some terrible misfortune one of these days.—I'll go and hunt up my brother, and pour it all out on him. (*Exit* DEMEA.)

[ACT THREE: SCENE 5]

(*Reenter* HEGIO.)

HEGIO: Take it easy, Sostrata, and cheer her up all you can. I'll have an interview with Micio, if he's downtown, and tell him the whole story from first to last. If he's ready to do his duty, let him get busy; but if he feels otherwise about the matter, then he can tell me so; I want to know just as soon as possible what I'm to do next.

[ACT FOUR: SCENE 1]

(CTESIPHO *and* SYRUS *step out of* MICIO's *front door.*)

CTESIPHO: Honest now, has my father really gone back to the farm?

SYRUS: Oh yes, long ago.

CTESIPHO: Please tell me the truth.

SYRUS: He's at the farmhouse already. At this very moment, I've no doubt, he's working at some chore or other.

CTESIPHO: I sure hope so! Without permanently ruining his health, I wish he'd get so tired that for the next three days he'll be absolutely unable to get out of bed.

SYRUS: Me too! And better even than that, if possible!

CTESIPHO (*quite naively*): Yes, yes, just so. For I'm desperately eager to spend the whole of this day in bliss, just as I've started it; and the only reason I hate that farm so bitterly is because it's so close to town. If it had only been farther out in the country, it would have been dark before he could make it back here again. But, as it is, when he doesn't see me out there, he'll dash right back here, I'm absolutely certain. Then he'll ask where I've been: "I haven't laid eyes on you all day long." What am I going to say then?

SYRUS (*contemptuously*): Doesn't *anything* come to mind?

CTESIPHO: Never a thing.

SYRUS: What a boob! Haven't you and your father a client, a friend, an out of town guest?

CTESIPHO: Yes, but then what?

SYRUS: Say that you've been helping them out.

CTESIPHO: When I wasn't? That's not possible.

SYRUS: Oh yes it is!

CTESIPHO: Well, perhaps that will do for the daytime. But if I spend the *night* here, Syrus, what excuse can I offer then?

SYRUS (*disgusted*): Ugh! How I wish people were in the habit of performing services for their "friends" [2] at night, too! (*With a slight gesture towards the house where his girl is staying*) But you can take it easy; I'm dead on to the old man's disposition. When he's fairly burning up with rage, I can make him as gentle as a lamb.

CTESIPHO: How do you manage it?

SYRUS: He just loves to listen to your praises. I make you out a regular angel, while he listens. I recite your virtues.

CTESIPHO: My virtues?

SYRUS: Yes, yours. Why, in no time at all, tears of joy start falling from his eyes, as if he were a child. Hey there! Look out, will you!

---

[2] The word chosen is applicable to girl-friends as well as other kinds.

CTESIPHO: What in the world's the matter?

SYRUS: The wolf! Just as we were talking about him!

CTESIPHO: Is it father?

SYRUS: And nobody else!

CTESIPHO: Syrus, what *am* I to do?

SYRUS: Just run back into the house; *I'll* attend to all this.

CTESIPHO (*through the half-open door*): If he asks any question, remember, you haven't seen me anywhere. Did you hear me?

SYRUS: Oh, can't you shut up?

[ACT FOUR: SCENE 2]

(*Enter* DEMEA.)

DEMEA: I sure am unlucky. To begin with, I can't find my brother anywhere in the world. And then, while I was looking for him, I caught sight of a hired hand from the farm. He tells me my boy is not out in the country. And now I don't know *what* I'm going to do.

CTESIPHO (*through a crack*): Syrus.

SYRUS: What is it?

CTESIPHO: Is he looking for me?

SYRUS: You'd better believe he is!

CTESIPHO: I'm ruined, then.

SYRUS: Nonsense. Cheer up.

DEMEA: Damn it all! What's the meaning of this whole run of bad luck? I can't make head or tail of it, unless I'm to believe that I was born for nothing else, but only to have trouble. *I'm* the first to get wind of our misfortunes; *I'm* the first to find out everything; and, finally, *I'm* the first to bring in the bad news. If anything goes wrong, *I'm* the only one that's put out about it.

SYRUS (*aside*): He makes me laugh! Think of him saying *he's* the first to learn about things. Why, *he's* the *only* one who doesn't know anything at all!

DEMEA: I'm coming back now to see if my brother could have possibly returned to the house.

CTESIPHO (*through the partly open door*): Syrus, please! Don't let him just dash right in here!

SYRUS: *Won't* you shut up? *I'm* going to attend to that.

CTESIPHO (*in a complete funk*): By Jupiter, I'm *never* going to trust *that* to *you;* I'm going to lock myself up in some closet or other with my girl; *that's* the safest thing to do.

SYRUS: As you please. And yet I'll drive him away, just the same. (*Moving out into the middle of the street*)

DEMEA: But there's that confounded scoundrel Syrus.

SYRUS (*pretending to be talking aside, but really intending* DEMEA *to overhear him*): Good Lord! Nobody that wants to survive can keep on living *here,* if this is the way they're going to behave. I certainly would like to know how many bosses I have over me! What a miserable mess!

DEMEA (*aside*): What's he drivelling about? What's he up to now? (*To* SYRUS) What do you say, good sir? Is my brother in?

SYRUS: What the hell do you say "good sir" to *me* for? *I'm* down and out.

DEMEA: What's gone wrong with *you?*

SYRUS: You ask, eh? Ctesipho has just been slugging poor me and that chorus-girl till we're damn near dead.

DEMEA (*brightening up*): Ha! What's that you say?

SYRUS: There you are; just see how he busted my lip.

DEMEA: What was it all about?

SYRUS: He said *I* was the one that put Aeschinus up to buying the girl.

DEMEA (*suspiciously*): But didn't you tell me, a little while ago, you had escorted him out of town on his way back to the farm?

SYRUS: Sure thing; but he came back later, crazy mad; spared nothing. Such impudence, to beat up an old man! Why, when he was no bigger than *that,* I used to carry him around in my own arms!

DEMEA: Three cheers for you, Ctesipho! You're a chip off the old block! Well, well! It was a manly deed!

SYRUS: You applaud him, do you? I'm telling *you* something now. He'll keep his hands off *me* from this time on, if he's got any sense.

DEMEA: Gallant action!

SYRUS: Yes, awfully gallant, to beat up a poor female, and me, too, a puny slave who didn't dare hit back! Whee! *Super*-gallant!

DEMEA: He couldn't have done better. He realized, just as I

did, that you were the ringleader in this business.—But is my brother at home?

SYRUS: I know where he is, but I'm never going to tell *you*.

DEMEA: Ha! What's that you say?

SYRUS: That's just what I said.

DEMEA (*raising his long, heavy cane*): I'll knock your block off, if you don't.

SYRUS: Oh, well! I don't know the man's *name*, but I *do* know where he lives.

DEMEA: Then tell me where *that* is.

SYRUS: Do you remember where the colonnade by the meat-market is, over on *this* side?

DEMEA: Of course.

SYRUS: Go right on past, straight up the avenue, in *this* direction. When you get there, you'll find a ramp leading down hill; beat it down that. Afterwards there's a little chapel on *this* side. Near by is an alley-way.

DEMEA: What alley-way is that?

SYRUS: The one where there's a big wild-fig tree, too.

DEMEA: I know that.

SYRUS: Go on through it.

DEMEA: Wait a minute! That's a blind alley.

SYRUS: Gosh, you're right! Say! You'd think I was a goggling imbecile, wouldn't you? That was all wrong. Well, let's get back to the colonnade again. Now, I've got it! This route is much shorter, and you're far less likely to get lost. Do you know the house of this rich fellow Cratinus?

DEMEA: Yes.

SYRUS: After you pass that, go straight down the avenue, *this* way, to the left. When you get to the temple of Diana, turn right. Before you reach the city gate, just beside the watering-trough, there's a bakery, and right straight across the street from it, a carpenter's shop. That's where he is.

DEMEA: What's he doing there?

SYRUS: He's let out a contract for making some outdoor benches with legs of ilex-oak.

DEMEA: On which you people will sit and guzzle! A fine idea, no doubt of it! But why not hurry off to find him? (*Starting away briskly*)

SYRUS: Yes, beat it! I'll give you all the exercise *you* need today, you old stack of bones!—Aeschinus is disgustingly late. The dinner is getting spoiled; and Ctesipho is head over heels in love. So I guess I'll look out for myself. I'm going to go back in, and when anything looks particularly good I'll slice me off a sample, taking a sip at the punch-bowl, too, from time to time, and so manage to drag out the day. (*Goes back into the house.*)

[ACT FOUR: SCENE 3]

(*As* SYRUS *leaves,* MICIO *and* HEGIO *enter, coming from downtown.*)

MICIO: Really, Hegio, I can't see a *thing* in all this that deserves such words of praise. I'm merely doing my duty. The injury that our household did I am simply making good. (*Slyly, to tease him a little*) Unless, perhaps, you thought I was one of those people who feel that they themselves are being hurt, if you call attention to the harm they've done, and immediately turn around and start to blame *you*. Are you thanking me, simply because I haven't acted *that* way?

HEGIO (*embarrassed*): Oh no! Not at all! I never supposed you were any different from what you are. But, please, Micio, come in with me to see the girl's mother, and tell *her yourself* precisely what you have just told me: Namely, that, all this suspicious behavior was wholly on his brother's account, and that the chorus-girl is all his brother's.

MICIO: If you think that the courteous thing to do, or if it's really necessary, let's go.

HEGIO (*still extremely deferential*): That's awfully good of you; for in this way you'll be cheering up the girl, who is pretty low in her mind from pain and worry, and at the same time you'll be doing your full duty as a gentleman. But, if you feel otherwise about it, I'll go repeat to them myself what you've told me.

MICIO: Oh no, I'll go with you.

HEGIO: That's extremely kind of you. When things aren't going their way, people somehow or other are apt to get more touchy; they are all the more ready to take everything as an insult. Because they are helpless they always feel that people are making them the goat. And so it will help a lot towards a reconciliation, if you yourself explain everything to her personally.

MICIO: That's both right and true.

HEGIO: Follow me, then, inside the house.

MICIO: Yes, gladly. (*Exeunt* HEGIO *and* MICIO.)

[ACT FOUR: SCENE 4]

(AESCHINUS *enters, greatly distressed.*)

AESCHINUS (*beginning in lyric measures, as a sign of his agitation*): I'm anguished at heart! To think that such an enormous misfortune has come upon me so suddenly! I don't know what to do with myself nor how to act. My knees are weak with terror; my heart numb with fear; I can't get any sensible idea to stick in my head.

Ah me! How *am* I going to get out of this mess? They're so extremely suspicious about me now, and naturally, too. Sostrata thinks I've bought this chorus-girl for myself. Old Canthara made that plain enough to me. She'd been sent after the midwife, as luck would have it; I saw her, and rushed up to ask how Pamphila was, whether labor was near, and if that was why they were calling in the midwife. She screamed at me, "Get out! Get out, now, Aeschinus! You've played fast and loose with us long enough as it is! We're all fed up with your double-crossing!" "Ha!" said I, "what's the meaning of all this? if you please." "Good-bye," says she, "and keep the girl you love best!" It came to me then, all of a sudden, that they had their doubts about me; but I held in just the same. I wasn't going to tell *that* old gossip anything about my brother, and have the whole story get out.

And now, what *am* I going to do? Shall I tell them the chorus-girl is my brother's? But *that's* something which mustn't get out *anywhere*. Even so, supposing the story doesn't actually spread somehow or other. What I'm *really* afraid of is they won't believe what I tell them. There's such a mass of circumstantial evidence. *I* was the one that carried her off; *I* was the one that paid the money; it was *my* house she was taken to.

And it's absolutely my own fault, too; I admit that. To think that I never told the whole story to father, no matter how disreputable it was! I could have got his permission to marry her.

Well, so far I've been loafing on the job. But from this time on, Aeschinus, heads up! Now here's the first thing to do: Go to see the women and clear myself. I'll walk up to their front door. (*Trembling, and starting back again*) It's all off! I always get the shivers when I start to knock at that door. (*Finally coming up close*) Hello! Hello! It's me, Aeschinus! *Some* one of you hurry up and open the door!—Somebody or other is coming out. I'll just slip around here to one side.

[ACT FOUR: SCENE 5]

(MICIO *steps out, still talking to persons on the inside.*)

MICIO: Now you people do just as I said, Sostrata; I'll hunt up Aeschinus, and tell him the whole story.—But who's been knocking at the front door?

AESCHINUS (*aside*): Gosh! That's father! It's all over now!

MICIO (*catching sight of him*): Aeschinus!

AESCHINUS (*aside, afraid to answer*): What business has *he* had over here?

MICIO: Aeschinus, did you knock at this door? (*Aside*) He can't answer. Why not kid him a little bit? It wouldn't be such a bad idea, because he wasn't willing to tell me himself a word about this affair. (*Aloud, to* AESCHINUS) Aren't you going to answer my question?

AESCHINUS (*greatly confused*): I guess—er, I didn't knock at *that* door,—er, er,—as far as I can remember.

MICIO: So? I wondered what business *you* could have over here? (*Aside*) He blushed that time. Everything is all right now.

AESCHINUS: But father, *you* please tell *me*, what business have *you* got over there?

MICIO (*talks slowly and with infuriating nonchalance, two or three times pretending to forget that he is even telling a story at all, and accordingly has to be prodded by the jittery young man*): Oh, no business of my *own* at all, but there was a friend downtown a little while ago who brought me along with him to perform a little legal service in his behalf.

AESCHINUS: What about?

MICIO: Why, I'll tell you. There are some women living here

next door, in pretty modest circumstances. I suppose you wouldn't know anything about them; in fact, I'm sure you don't. They haven't been living here very long. (*He pauses.*)

AESCHINUS: Well, what next?

MICIO: Oh, yes! Well, there's some girl or other living over here with her mother. (MICIO *stops again.*)

AESCHINUS: All right, go on!

MICIO: To be sure! Well, the girl's father is dead. Now this friend of mine is the next of kin, and the law requires him to marry the orphan girl.

AESCHINUS (*tremendously wrought up, aside*): That's my death-sentence!

MICIO: Beg pardon, what did you say?

AESCHINUS: Nothing. It's all right. Go on.

MICIO: And now this friend of mine has come to take the girl away with him. He lives in Miletus.

AESCHINUS: What! To take the girl along with him?

MICIO: Yes, that's what I said.

AESCHINUS: All the way to Miletus?

MICIO: That's right.

AESCHINUS (*aside, with his hand clapped to his forehead*): I'm not feeling very well. (*To his father again*) But what about the women? What do they say?

MICIO: Well, what would you suppose? The merest nonsense. The mother's cooked up a story about a baby being born to the girl by some other man, but she won't tell us his name. She says the other fellow has first claim on the girl, and that she ought not to be allowed to marry this cousin.

AESCHINUS (*excitedly, grasping at any straw of hope*): What? What? Doesn't that seem to you to be a *perfectly* reasonable proposition?

MICIO (*coldly*): No.

AESCHINUS: What? You don't mean to say, "No"! Why, father, is that man to take her away from here?

MICIO: And why shouldn't he take her away from here?

AESCHINUS: Why, you've acted unsympathetically, father, and without any human kindness;—and, er, really, father, if I have to be frank about it, not quite like a gentleman.

MICIO: And how do you make that out?

AESCHINUS: Can you ask such a question? How do you suppose that poor fellow is going to feel, who—er, er, made the girl's acquaintance first? Poor devil, possibly he's *still* desperately in love with her. How will *he* take it, when right in front of his very eyes he will see her torn away, dragged out of his sight? Why, it's an outrage, father!

MICIO: How do you get that way? Who made the betrothal? Who gave her in marriage? Whom did she marry, and when? Who gave his consent for the whole affair? Why did he marry a strange girl?

AESCHINUS: But did you want a grown-up girl like her just to *sit* around the house and wait until a cousin should turn up from somewhere or other? Why, my dear father, *that's* the sort of thing you ought to have said, *that's* the line you should have takcn.

MICIO: Preposterous! Would you want me to argue against the interests of the man whom I came here to support? But anyway, Aeschinus, what's all this to you and me? What have *we* to do with those women? Come on, let's go on into the house. (*A pause, as* AESCHINUS *breaks down*) What's the matter? What are you crying about?

AESCHINUS: Father! Please! Listen!

MICIO: Aeschinus, I've heard the whole story; I know it all. I love you. That's what makes me worry so much about you.

AESCHINUS (*sobbing*): My dear father, as long as you live I sincerely hope to deserve your love, and I'm just as sincerely sorry and ashamed that I ever did a thing like this, and I simply can't look you in the face.

MICIO: So help me Heaven, of course you are! I know you've got the instincts of a gentleman, but I am afraid you've been a little too reckless. What kind of community did you think you were living in? You've gone and assaulted a young girl that you hadn't any right even to touch. In the first place, that's a grave offense. Grave, of course, but it's the sort of thing that *will* happen among human beings. Others have often done it, and they were good men too.

But, after you'd done that, say, I'm asking you, did you stop and think? Did you try to provide for what might happen to you, or how it was going to happen? If you were too much ashamed of yourself to tell me, how was I going to find out?

And now, while you have been shilly-shallying, nine months have gone by. As far as *you* had anything to do with it, you've betrayed yourself, that poor girl, and your baby, too. What? Did you suppose that the gods would fix this all up, while you were snoozing? Did you fancy that somehow or other, without your turning a finger, she'd just be transported to your bridal chamber? I'd hate to have you make such a fool of yourself in anything else. (*And then, taking pity upon the completely humiliated and crestfallen young man*) Cheer up, you're going to marry her.

AESCHINUS: What!

MICIO: Cheer up, I say.

AESCHINUS: Father, please! You're not kidding me, are you?

MICIO: I kid you? Why should I?

AESCHINUS: I don't know; I am just so desperately *eager* to believe what you say, that I'm all the more afraid it isn't true.

MICIO: Oh, go on into the house, and offer up a prayer to bring your wife over. (*As* AESCHINUS *stands stock still, even yet not believing his ears*) Get going!

AESCHINUS: What, bring her over right now, as my wife?

MICIO: Right now!

AESCHINUS: Right now?

MICIO: Yes, just as "right now" as you can!

AESCHINUS: Father, may all the gods hate me, if I don't love you more than I love my own eyes!

MICIO: What? More than you love *her*?

AESCHINUS: Well, just as much!

MICIO: Awfully kind of you!

AESCHINUS (*still incredulous*): But say, what about that cousin of hers from Miletus?

MICIO: Oh, he's disappeared, set sail. What are you loafing around for?

AESCHINUS: Father, you go into the house. It's much better for *you* to pray to the gods. I'm absolutely certain they're much more likely to listen to *you*, because you're a *much* better man than I am.

MICIO: All right, I'll go in and get things started; but do as I told you, if you have any sense. (*Exit.*)

AESCHINUS (*left alone, looking lovingly toward the front door which has just closed, and then turning to the audience*): And

what do you know about that! Is *that* like being a father? Or is
this like being a son? Why, if he'd been my own dearest brother,
how *could* he have treated me any more kindly? Doesn't he deserve
to be loved? Oughtn't I carry his image in my very heart? I'll
tell the world! But his kindness makes me just that much the
more worried. I'm afraid that without realizing it, some time
I'll go and do something he wouldn't want me to do. Well,
forewarned, forearmed! But why don't I go into the house and
quit delaying the wedding ceremony? (*Exit into* PAMPHILA'S
house.)

[ACT FOUR: SCENE 6]

(DEMEA *gets back all tired out from trying to find a place that
doesn't exist.*)

DEMEA: I'm all in from trudging around. May mighty Jupiter
damn you, Syrus, and all your directions! I've dragged all over the
town, to the gate, to the watering-trough, where didn't I go?
There wasn't any carpenter's shop there, and not a soul said he'd
seen my brother. Now I've made up my mind to sit down right
in front of the house and wait until he gets back home.

[ACT FOUR: SCENE 7]

(MICIO *opening the door of his own house, and, as usual,
finishing up a conversation with the people indoors, as he steps
out.*)

MICIO: I'll go over and tell them there's no occasion for delay
as far as we are concerned.
DEMEA: There's the man himself. I've been looking for you,
Micio, quite a long time.
MICIO: Well, what is it now?
DEMEA: I've got news of some other monstrous scandals of that
fine young fellow of ours.
MICIO: There you go again!
DEMEA: Brand new ones; criminal offenses!
MICIO: You don't say so!

DEMEA: *You* don't know the sort of person *he is.*

MICIO: Oh, yes, I do.

DEMEA: Oh, you idiot! You've got the silly idea that I am talking about that chorus-girl. *This* time he has gone and committed an outrage against a girl that's an Athenian citizen.

MICIO: I know all about that.

DEMEA: What! You know it and stand for it?

MICIO: Why not stand for it?

DEMEA: Tell me, aren't you screaming, aren't you raving?

MICIO: No; although I'd like to.

DEMEA: A baby's been born!

MICIO: God bless him!

DEMEA: The girl hasn't a penny.

MICIO: So I've heard.

DEMEA: He's got to marry her now without any dowry.

MICIO: Of course.

DEMEA: What are you going to do next?

MICIO: Going to do what the case suggests. Move the girl over into our house.

DEMEA: But, O Jupiter! Is that the way people ought to behave?

MICIO: What more do you want me to do?

DEMEA: "Do?" Why, if you don't honestly feel bad about it, it's only behaving like a human being to *pretend* that you do!

MICIO: Oh no! I've just betrothed the girl to Aeschinus; everything's fixed up; they're going to get married; I've relieved everybody's worries and *that's* what *I* call "behaving like a human being."

DEMEA: But, Micio, do you *like* this whole business?

MICIO: Why, no; not if I could *change* it; but since I *can't,* I'm simply taking it in my stride. The life of human beings is just like shooting dice. If you don't get the throw you'd like best, then you've got to use your brains and make good on what *does* come your way.

DEMEA: You and your "making good"! Yes, and those "brains" of yours have cost you four thousand for this chorus-girl, who's got to be thrown out of the house somewhere or other. If you can't sell her, you've got to give her away.

MICIO: Oh, no I don't, and I'm not at all eager to sell her.

DEMEA: What are you going to do with her?

MICIO: She's going to stay in the house.

DEMEA: The gods help us! An ordinary street-walker and a respectable married woman living together under the same roof!

MICIO: Why not?

DEMEA: Do you think you're in your right mind?

MICIO: I rather fancy I am.

DEMEA: Lord help me! I believe I see the method in your madness. You've gone and got somebody to sing duets with you.

MICIO: And why shouldn't I?

DEMEA: Yes, and the young bride will be taking the same kind of lessons.

MICIO: Of course!

DEMEA: And you'll get in between them, all join hands, and trip the light fantastic!

MICIO: That's perfect!

DEMEA: "Perfect"?!

MICIO: Yes, Demea, and you'll take a turn around the floor with us yourself, if we need you.

DEMEA: Alas, alack-a-day! *Aren't* you ashamed of this whole affair?

MICIO: Oh, forget it, Demea, all that bad temper of yours, and just make yourself cheerful and happy, as you ought to, on your son's wedding day. I'm going to have a talk with the people in the house next door; I'll be back in a minute.

DEMEA: Oh, Jupiter! Such a life! Such a way of carrying on! Such lunacy! There's a wife coming into the family, without a cent of dowry; a chorus-girl already inside; the household extravagant; the young man ruined with luxury; the old man raving, staving mad. If the Goddess of Salvation herself *wanted* to save this household there would be absolutely nothing she could do about it!

[ACT FIVE: SCENE I]

(*While* DEMEA *is still standing in the street, overwhelmed with angry frustration,* SYRUS *comes rolling out of the front door, feeling a little high.*)

SYRUS: Gosh, Syrus, old boy! You've made it pretty soft for yourself; you've got away with your job pretty slick. Go to! I'm full up with all the stuff in the house, and I thought I'd just take the air out of doors a little while. (*Reeling along*)

DEMEA: Look at that, will you! There's a fine specimen of their style of living!

SYRUS (*so tipsy he mistakes* DEMEA *for* MICIO): Hello there! Here's our old man. What's doing? What are you so mad about?

DEMEA: *You* damned scoundrel!

SYRUS: Oh, so? It's *you* spouting here, is it? You old well of wisdom!

DEMEA: If you were *my* slave—

SYRUS: You'd be a rich man, Demea, and you'd have nothing but gilt-edged investments.

DEMEA (*disregarding the interruption*): I'd make a terrifying example out of you!

SYRUS: And why, now? What have *I* done?

DEMEA: *You* ask such a question? Why, right in the midst of all this mess, and in a monstrous crime, before things have even got settled yet, you've gone and got drunk, just as though you had done something to be proud of, you damned scoundrel!

SYRUS (*not really fit for a serious quarrel*): Gee, I'm sorry I came out!

[ACT FIVE: SCENE 2]

(*Enter* DROMO *from* MICIO's *house*.)

DROMO: Hey there, Syrus! Ctesipho wants you to come back in.

SYRUS: Beat it, you! (*Kicking him back through the door*)

DEMEA: What was he saying about Ctesipho?

SYRUS: Nothing.

DEMEA: So ho! You low life! Is Ctesipho in there?

SYRUS: No.

DEMEA: Why did he mention his name, then?

SYRUS: Oh, there's another Ctesipho, a little runt of a penny-ante parasite. Possibly you know him?

DEMEA: I soon will. (*Starting energetically for the door*)

SYRUS (*trying to detain him*): What are you up to? Where are you going?

DEMEA: Let go of me!

SYRUS: Don't! I say!

DEMEA: Keep your hands off me, you dirty bum! (*Waving his long, heavy cane*) Or do you want me to splatter your brains all over the street? (*Breaking loose and dashing into the house*)

SYRUS: He's gone! Damn it! No very pleasant companion at a cocktail party, especially for Ctesipho! What am I going to do now? Don't know, except I guess I'll sneak off into a corner somewhere, until this row gets settled, and sleep off this edge. That's what I'll do!

[ACT FIVE: SCENE 3]

(SYRUS *reels away off stage. Enter* MICIO *from* SOSTRATA'S *house, still talking back through the door.*)

MICIO: We're all ready, on our side of the line, Sostrata, just as I have assured you. Whenever you wish—(*sounds of a scuffle in* MICIO'S *house, dishes upset, a girl screaming, general hullabaloo, and then a crash at the inside of the door.*) Who in the world bashed into my front door like that?

(*Out rushes* DEMEA.)

DEMEA: Oh, hell! What to do? What to start? What to cry? What complaint to raise? Oh, Heaven! Oh, Earth! Oh, seas of Neptune!

MICIO: There you are! He's found it all out. And that's what he is yapping about now. There's a brawl in the offing. To the rescue!

DEMEA: Here he is, the common ruination of our two boys.

MICIO: Oh, come to your senses some time, and cool off that hot head of yours!

DEMEA (*with a great effort*): I *have* cooled it off; I *have* come to my senses. I won't say a single hard word. Let's just take a look at the record. We agreed (and, fortunately, *you* said it first) that you wouldn't bother your head about my boy, and I shouldn't bother mine about yours, didn't you? Answer me!

MICIO: I did; there's no doubt about *that*.

DEMEA: Why is he now drinking in your house? Why do you take in my boy? Why do you go out and buy a girl for him, Micio? How is it any less fair for *me* to have rights with *you*, than it is for *you* to have rights with *me*? *I'm* not doing anything about *your* boy; *don't you* do anything about *mine*.

MICIO: That's not a fair proposition.

DEMEA: It isn't?

MICIO: No; it's an old saying that friends have everything in common.

DEMEA: Very smart! That's your line of talk now, is it?

MICIO: Listen to me for just a few moments, Demea, if you can stand the strain. In the first place, if the thought of all that the boys are spending is what's burning you up, please look at it this way. Some years ago you started to bring up two boys; you thought you were going to have enough property to take care of both of them right. At that time, of course, you thought that I was going to get married, too. Just keep on thinking the same way. Save all you can, make all you can, don't spend any more than you have to; leave them the very largest estate possible. You can have all the glory along that line you want. In the meantime, let the boys have the use of my estate, which you never expected them to get. Nothing will be lost from the sum total. Whatever income there is from this quarter, count that as just pure velvet. Now, Demea, if you're willing to think and feel sincerely about the matter in *this* way, you'll be sparing yourself, and myself, and the boys, too, a lot of grief.

DEMEA: I'm not concerned about the matter of money; the *habits* the two boys have formed—

MICIO: Just a moment! I know all that; I was just getting around to this point next. There are a lot of little signs about people, Demea, that enable you to make a shrewd guess as to how they are going to turn out eventually. Even when two persons are doing exactly the same thing, you can frequently say: "It won't hurt this fellow to do it, but it's not a good idea for the other." That's not because *what* they are doing is different, but because the *persons* who are doing it are different.[3] Now I see just those

---

[3] This passage even an ancient commentator found "extremely obscure in both substance and expression."

little signs in these boys of ours, and I'm confident that they're going to turn out the way we want them to. I can tell that they have taste and tact; they have intelligence; they know where and when to show respect and reverence; they love each other. Anybody can see that they have the temper and disposition of gentlemen. Any day you want to, you can bring them right back to your side.

But possibly you are afraid that they are a little too careless with their money. Oh, my dear brother Demea! About everything else we get wiser as we grow older. There's only one moral blemish that old age brings to man. All of us old fellows pay a great deal more attention to *money* than we ought to. Advancing years will take care of this little difficulty perfectly well.

DEMEA: But I'm afraid, Micio, that all this fine-sounding rationalization of yours, and all this imperturbable tranquillity, will finally be the ruin of us all.

MICIO: Not another word! That's not what's going to happen. Forget it! Turn yourself over to me today. Rub those wrinkles out of your forehead.

DEMEA: Very well, I'll *have* to behave as the situation seems to demand. But tomorrow morning I'm going to leave town, and go back to the farm, with my son, at the first crack of dawn.

MICIO: I'd get up while it was still dark, if I were you. Only be cheerful today!

DEMEA: And I'm going to take that chorus-girl along with me out to the farm.

MICIO: Now there's a master stroke. That way you'll have your son absolutely anchored to the place. Only be sure you *keep* the girl there.

DEMEA: I'll attend to *that,* all right! And I'll see that she gets all covered with ashes, and smoke, and flour, from cooking, and grinding at the mill; more than that, I'll make her go out at high noon and pick up kindling for the fire. I'll have her burned as black as a piece of charcoal.

MICIO: That's fine. Now, it seems to me, you're showing some sense; and I'd compel my son to keep on living with her, even if he wanted to change his mind.

DEMEA: Laughing at me, are you? You *are* a lucky fellow to have such a disposition. As for me, I can feel—

MICIO: Oh, have you broken loose again?

DEMEA: All right, all right! I'll stop.

MICIO: Come on into the house; let's catch the proper wedding spirit, and make this a real holiday.

(*The two old men walk into the house arm in arm. Wedding music is heard. Sounds within the house take on a cheerful character.*)

[ACT FIVE: SCENE 4]

(*In a few minutes* DEMEA *returns, at least partially converted.*)

DEMEA: Nobody ever draws up his plans for life so well but what the facts, and the years, and experience always introduce some modification, and show where he was wrong. You find you didn't *really* know what you thought you knew, and the things that you believed simply *had* to be done, you turn down when you come to put them into actual practice.

Now that's what's happened to me just now. This hard-boiled, rugged life that I have always lived before, I'm giving up on what's just about the last lap. And *why* am I doing *that*? Ample evidence has shown me that there is nothing finer for a human being than good nature and a pleasant disposition. Anybody can tell that this is true by simply comparing my brother and me. *He* has always lived in luxury, and at dinner parties; he's good-natured, easy-going, never hurts anybody's feelings, has a smile for everyone. *He* has lived for himself; he spends his money on himself; everybody speaks well of him; they all love him. But me! I'm that "hayseed," "hard," "sour," "stingy," "crabbed," "tightwad"! I went and got married. Oh, what a hard time I had then! Two boys were born; more trouble.

And now look at this: All the while I've been doing my damndest to make everything I possibly could for them, I've been wasting the time I had for actual living; I've lost the best years of my life in making money, and now, when it is practically all over, *this* is the return I get from my boys for all my trouble: their dislike. On the other hand, my brother, without taking any of the trouble, now has all the fun there is in being a father. The

boys *love him*; they fight shy of me. They tell *him* everything
they are thinking about; they dote on him, both of them live at
his house, and leave me all alone. They *want him* to keep on
living; without any doubt, they're just waiting for *me* to die.
And so the boys that *I* have brought up, with infinite trouble
on my part, *he* has come to possess, by spending scarcely anything. *I* get all the trouble, *he* has all the good time. (*And then
in a startling sudden act of conversion*) Go to! Go to! From now
on let's try the opposite tack. Let's see whether I can talk sweetly
and act handsomely, now that my brother has issued the chal-
lenge. I, too, want to be loved, and treated affectionately, by
my own flesh and blood. If the only way I can bring that about
is by paying the bills, and turning into a yes-man, very good,
I won't be outdone! No doubt we'll all go broke, but what's that
to *me*? I'm the oldest, anyway.

[ACT FIVE: SCENE 5]

(*Enter* SYRUS, *more or less in his right mind again.*)

SYRUS: Ah, there, Demea! Your brother asks you not to go too
far away from the house.
DEMEA: And who's the gentleman? Why, it's my good friend,
Syrus. (*Putting a hand on his shoulder*) How *do* you do? How's
everything? How are you making out?
SYRUS (*quite flabbergasted*): All right, I guess.
DEMEA: That's fine! (*Aside*) For the first time in my life right
now I added those three expressions that I never felt like using
before: "My good friend"; "How's everything?"; and "How are
you making out?" (*To* SYRUS) You've shown that although you
are a slave, still you've a fine sense of honor, and I should love
to do you a good turn.
SYRUS (*suspiciously*): Much obliged.
DEMEA: Never mind, Syrus, it's the simple truth, and you'll
realize it yourself pretty soon.

[ACT FIVE: SCENE 6]

(*Enter* GETA, *still talking to his mistress,* SOSTRATA, *indoors.*)

GETA: All right, mistress, I'll go over next door and find out how soon they'll be calling for the girl. But there's Demea. Good day, sir!

DEMEA: Ah, and what's *your* name? (*with a friendly gesture*)

GETA: Geta.

DEMEA: Geta, according to my judgment you're a man of extraordinary merit. In my eyes the slave that looks out for his master meets every requirement that can reasonably be expected of him; and that's what I've observed you doing, Geta. For that reason, if ever the opportunity arises, I should love to do you a good turn. (*Aside*) I'm practising being pleasant, and it's going over big.

GETA: It's very kind of you indeed to think so well of me.

DEMEA (*aside*): Little by little I'm winning over the masses.

[ACT FIVE: SCENE 7]

(AESCHINUS *now comes out and joins the group.*)

AESCHINUS: All this fuss and feathers they're determined to make about the wedding will be the death of me yet. They're wasting the whole day in merely getting ready.

DEMEA: Well, how are you making it, Aeschinus? (*Walking up to him cordially*)

AESCHINUS (*startled*): What! My dear father! Were you here?

DEMEA: By Jove, you're right! Your *own true father*, in heart as well as in blood! Who loves you more dearly than these very eyes of his. But why don't you bring your wife right over home?

AESCHINUS: I'd love to; but the delay is caused by trying to get a flute-player, and a chorus to sing the wedding-march.

DEMEA: Oho! Would you care for a tip from an old bird like me?

AESCHINUS: What's that?

DEMEA: Aw! Cut it all out, the wedding-march, the mob-scene, the torches, and the musicians, and just give orders to tear down this sleazy wall in the garden right off. Move her over that way. Make one household of the two establishments. Bring her mother and the whole outfit over to our place.

AESCHINUS: Fine! Father, you're a perfect pal!

DEMEA (*aside*): Three cheers! They're calling me "a perfect pal" now! My brother's house will become a highway; he'll have to take on the whole gang of them; it'll cost him plenty. What's that to *me*? *I'm* "a perfect pal," *I'm* getting popular. (*Aloud*) Go on now and tell that big shot of a millionaire to come across with four thousand. Syrus, why don't you get a move on you and do it?

SYRUS (*completely dazed*): Me? Do what?

DEMEA (*to* SYRUS, *who thereupon hurries away*): Tear down that wall. (*To* GETA) Go next door and bring the women over to our place.

GETA: God bless you, Demea, for this solid proof that you honestly wish our family well! (*Exit.*)

DEMEA (*airily*): It's no more than they deserve. (*Turning to* AESCHINUS) And what do we hear from you?

AESCHINUS (*still unadjusted*): All right, I guess.

DEMEA: Why, it's *far* better to manage it all this way, than to have the poor young mother, now while she's still feeling weak, brought around to our place by way of the street.

AESCHINUS: My dear father, I never *heard* of anything more sensible.

DEMEA (*with a gesture of self-satisfaction*): That's me all over! But here's Micio coming out of the house.

[ACT FIVE: SCENE 8]

(*Enter* MICIO, *distinctly ruffled over the unexpectedly sweeping success of his own missionary efforts on* DEMEA.)

MICIO: *My brother* give any such orders? Where is he? Did *you* tell them to do that, Demea?

DEMEA: Sure, I told them to do that; and in this thing and in everything else I think we ought to make just one big household out of the two establishments. We ought to cherish them, help them, bind them to ourselves.

AESCHINUS: Please do it, father.

MICIO (*a little ungraciously*): Well, I'll not stop it, then.

DEMEA (*warming up*): Heavens, that's no more than our plain duty. (*And then, with a wink at* AESCHINUS) To begin with, this wife of Aeschinus has a mother.

MICIO: She has. What of it?

DEMEA: Respectable and ladylike.

MICIO: So they say.

DEMEA: Pretty well along in years.

MICIO: I'm *sure* of that.

DEMEA: It's been a long time since she could have any children of her own; besides, she hasn't anybody now to take care of her; she's left all alone in the world.

MICIO (*aside, puzzled*): What's he up to?

DEMEA (*slowly and very emphatically, with all the moral power at his command*): I think it's only right and proper for *you* to marry her; and for *you*, Aeschinus, to help bring that marriage about.

MICIO: Me? Get married?

DEMEA: Yes, you.

MICIO: Me?

DEMEA: Yes, I'm talking about *you*!

MICIO: Well, then, you're a fool!

DEMEA (*to* AESCHINUS): If you were half a man, he'd do it.

AESCHINUS: Come on, father.

MICIO (*quite out of temper*): What are you listening to him for, you young donkey?

DEMEA: It's no use, you can't do anything else.

MICIO: You've gone crazy!

AESCHINUS: Please do me a favor, my dear father.

MICIO: You're balmy! Get out of here!

DEMEA: Come on, do your son a favor.

MICIO: Are you really in your right mind? Do you want me, at sixty-five years of age, to become a bridegroom and marry a decrepit old woman? Is that what the two of you are putting me up to?

AESCHINUS (*delivering himself of a whopping extempore lie*): Come on, father, I *promised* them you'd marry her.

MICIO: *You promised* them! See here, boy, you'd better make presents out of your own pocket.

DEMEA: Oh, come on! What if he should ask you to do something harder than that?

MICIO: As if that weren't the hardest thing imaginable!

DEMEA: *Do* us a kind turn!

AESCHINUS: *Don't* be grouchy!

DEMEA: Come on, say yes!

(*Brother and son have* MICIO *by either arm.*)

MICIO: *Won't* you let go of me?

AESCHINUS: Not until I get you to promise.

MICIO: Why, this is assault and battery.

DEMEA: Come on, Micio, do the generous thing!

MICIO (*finally giving in*): Although this looks bad, silly, ridiculous, and utterly alien to my way of life, still, if you two want it so badly, all right.

AESCHINUS: That's sweet of you, father.

DEMEA: *Now* you really deserve my affection. But—

MICIO: But what?

DEMEA: I'll tell you, now that I've got this first thing I was after.

MICIO: What's still left to do?

DEMEA: Here's Hegio, the closest relative to your wife's family. He's become related to us now by marriage. He's having a tough time making a living. I think we ought to do something for *him*!

MICIO: Do what?

DEMEA: You've got a small piece of farmland, not far outside of town, that you're in the habit of renting; let's turn it over to *him*. Let *him* live on it.

MICIO: You call that a "small" thing!

DEMEA: Oh, well, even if it *is* a pretty good-sized farm, we ought to *do* it anyway. He's practically a father to Aeschinus here; he's a good fellow, a friend of ours; it's a wise thing to do. In short, Micio, I'm taking to heart that little sermon you preached to me a while ago. It was an admirable and sagacious sermon: "There's one fault that all of us old fellows suffer from; we pay a great deal more attention to money than we ought to." And so it's our real duty to wipe that blot off the scutcheon. This is a faithful saying, and we ought to follow it in practice.

AESCHINUS: My dear father, please!

MICIO: All right, I'll give that farm to Hegio, as long as Aeschinus wants me to.

AESCHINUS: I'm delighted.

DEMEA (*eyeing* MICIO *up and down, and with a sinister tone in his voice*): *Now* you are my *real* brother just as much in heart as

in blood. (*And then, ironically, aside*) Cutting his throat with his
own sword!

[ACT FIVE: SCENE 9]

(*Reenter* SYRUS.)

SYRUS. (*cheerily*): Your order's been obeyed, Demea.

DEMEA: You're a worthy fellow. And so, by jiminy! the way it
strikes *me*, I think Syrus ought to be made a free man.

MICIO: *That* fellow a free man? What for?

DEMEA: Oh, er—*lots* of reasons.

SYRUS: O, my dear Demea! Gosh Almighty, you're a good man!
I've done the very best I could to bring up those two sons of
yours, ever since they were little boys. I've taught them, advised
them, instructed them in everything I knew, to the limit of my
ability.

DEMEA (*dryly*): Yes, *that* much is obvious! And over and above
all this, you've taught them to select the delicatessen competently,
grab off a street-walker, and start their parties before sunset. It
isn't everybody that can render services like that!

SYRUS: You dear soul!

DEMEA (*still ironically*): Last and latest of all, he helped to
buy this chorus-girl; really *managed* the affair. He ought to get
something for *that*. The rest of the servants will be just so much
the more faithful. And, finally, Aeschinus wants you to do it.

MICIO: Do *you really* want it done?

AESCHINUS: I certainly do.

MICIO: Very well, if that's what you two wish. Ho, there!
Syrus, come over here to me. (*And then, with the symbolism
used in informal manumission, a box on the ear, and a push
forward, which, in view of* MICIO's *present mood of irritation,
must have sent* SYRUS *reeling across the street*) Be a free man!

SYRUS: Thank you! I'm grateful to everybody, but especially to
you, Demea.

DEMEA: Glad to hear it.

AESCHINUS: So am I.

SYRUS: No doubt. (*Wheedling*) If only my present happiness

could be made perfect! I'd *so* love to see my wife Phrygia freed along with me!

DEMEA: She *certainly is* a worthy woman.

SYRUS: Yes, indeed, and she was the very first person to nurse your grandson today.

DEMEA (*ironically*): Heavens, yes! In all seriousness; if she really *was* the very first, there's no *doubt* but she ought to be set free!

MICIO: For simply *that*?

DEMEA: Yes, for simply *that*. (*Reassuringly*) Never mind, *I'll* make up myself whatever *she's* worth to you.

SYRUS (*on his knees and kissing his hands*): May all the gods give you, Demea, *always, everything* your heart desires!

MICIO: Syrus, you've done pretty well by yourself today.

DEMEA: There's just one thing more, Micio, if you're ready to do your *full* duty. Advance Syrus here a small amount of capital to enable him to go into business. He'll pay it back before long.

MICIO: Not that much! (*With a contemptuous snap of his fingers*)

AESCHINUS: He's honest.

SYRUS: By God, I'll pay it back! Just give it to me!

AESCHINUS: Come on, father!

MICIO: I'll think about it later.

DEMEA (*to* SYRUS *and* AESCHINUS): He'll do it, all right.

SYRUS (*to* DEMEA): Oh, you dear, good man!

AESCHINUS (*to* DEMEA): Oh, my very dearest, beloved father!

MICIO: Well, what the hell! What's gone and changed your character so suddenly? What freak of fancy is this? What do you mean by all this sudden generosity?

DEMEA: *I'll* tell you. And I'm going to make it perfectly clear that the reason these boys think you so nice and pleasant is not because of anything in your real life, nor, as a matter of cold fact, because of anything that's right and good. But it all comes from humoring them, Micio, indulging them, coming across every time they ask you for anything.

And now, Aeschinus, if you boys hate me so just because I don't gratify you, in absolutely everything, all the time, right or wrong, then I'm through with the whole business. Blow your money in; buy anything you want; do anything you want!

But if, on occasions when, because of your youth and inexperience, you don't see quite clearly, when you get too eager for something, and when you fail to foresee all the consequences; if, I repeat, under such circumstances you want to have *me*, to help you control yourselves, set you straight, and, at the proper time, assist and support you—well, here I am, all ready to serve in that capacity!

AESCHINUS: Father, we just turn everything over to you; you know a great deal better what ought to be done than we do.—But what's to become of my brother?

DEMEA: I'll let it pass this time; he can keep the girl, but he's got to stop right there!

MICIO (*chirking up a little bit*): Now *that's* not such a bad idea, after all!

THE ENTIRE TROUPE: Please, your applause!

SENECA

THE MEDEA

TRANSLATED BY ELLA ISABEL HARRIS

CHARACTERS IN THE PLAY

MEDEA, *daughter of Aeetes, king of Colchis, benefactor and divorced wife of Jason*

CHORUS *of Corinthians*

NURSE *of Medea*

CREON, *king of Corinth and father of Creusa*

JASON, *son of Aeson, deposed king of Iolcus, leader of the Argonauts and now in exile from Iolcus*

MESSENGER

THE MEDEA

(SCENE: *Before the house of* MEDEA *and the palace of* CREON *at Corinth.*)

MEDEA (*alone*): Ye gods of marriage;
Lucina, guardian of the genial bed;
Pallas, who taught the tamer of the seas
To steer the Argo; stormy ocean's lord;
Titan, dividing bright day to the world;
And thou three-formed Hecate, who dost shed
Thy conscious splendor on the hidden rites!
Ye by whom Jason plighted me his troth;
And ye Medea rather should invoke:
Chaos of night eternal; realm opposed
To the celestial powers; abandoned souls;
King of the dusky realm; Persephone,
By better faith betrayed; you I invoke,
But with no happy voice. Approach, approach,
Avenging goddesses with snaky hair,
Holding in blood-stained hands your sulphurous torch!
Come now as horrible as when of yore
Ye stood beside my marriage-bed; bring death
To the new bride, and to the royal seed,
And Creon; worse for Jason I would ask—
Life! Let him roam in fear through unknown lands,
An exile, hated, poor, without a home;
A guest now too well known, let him, in vain,

Seek alien doors, and long for me, his wife!
And, yet a last revenge, let him beget
Sons like their father, daughters like their mother!
'Tis done; revenge is even now brought forth—
I have borne sons to Jason. I complain
Vainly, and cry aloud with useless words,
Why do I not attack mine enemies?
I will strike down the torches from their hands,
The light from heaven. Does the sun see this,
The author of our race, and still give light?
And, sitting in his chariot, does he still
Run through the accustomed spaces of the sky,
Nor turn again to seek his rising place,
And measure back the day? Give me the reins;
Father, let me in thy paternal car
Be borne aloft the winds, and let me curb
With glowing bridle those thy fiery steeds!
Burn Corinth; let the parted seas be joined!
This still remains—for me to carry up
The marriage torches to the bridal room,
And, after sacrificial prayers, to slay
The victims on their altars. Seek, my soul—
If thou still livest, or if aught endures
Of ancient vigor—seek to find revenge
Through thine own bowels; throw off woman's fears,
Intrench thyself in snowy Caucasus.
All impious deeds Phasis or Pontus saw,
Corinth shall see. Evils unknown and wild,
Hideous, frightful both to earth and heaven,
Disturb my soul,—wounds, and the scattered corpse,
And murder. I remember gentle deeds,
A maid did these; let heavier anguish come,
Since sterner crimes befit me now, a wife!
Gird thee with wrath, prepare thine utmost rage,
That fame of thy divorce may spread as far
As of thy marriage! Make no long delay.
How dost thou leave thy husband? As thou cam'st.
Homes crime built up, by crime must be dissolved.

ACT ONE: SCENE 2

(*Enter* CHORUS OF CORINTHIANS, *singing the marriage song of* JASON *and* CREUSA.)

CHORUS: Be present at the royal marriage feast,
Ye gods who sway the scepter of the deep,
And ye who hold dominion in the heavens;
With the glad people come, ye smiling gods!
First to the scepter-bearing thunderers
The white-backed bull shall stoop his lofty head;
The snowy heifer, knowing not the yoke,
Is due to fair Lucina; and to her
Who stays the bloody hand of Mars, and gives
To warring nations peace, who in her horn
Holds plenty, sacrifice a victim mild.
Thou who at lawful bridals dost preside,
Scattering darkness with thy happy torch,
Come hither with slow step and drunk with wine,
Binding thy temples with a rosy crown.
Thou star that bringest in the day and night,
Slow-rising on the lover, ardently
For thy clear shining maids and matrons long.
   In comeliness the virgin bride excels
The Athenian women and the strong-limbed maids
Of Sparta's unwalled town, who on the top
Of high Taÿgetus try youthful sports;
Or those who in the clear Aonian stream,
Or in Alpheus' sacred waters bathe.
The child of the wild thunder, he who tames
And fits the yoke to tigers, is less fair
Than the Ausonian prince. The glorious god
Who moves the tripod, Dian's brother mild;
The skilful boxer Pollux; Castor, too,
Must yield the palm to Jason. O ye gods
Who dwell in heaven, ever may the bride
Surpass all women, he excel all men!
   Before her beauty in the women's choir

The beauty of the other maids grows dim;
So with the sunrise pales the light of stars,
So when the moon with brightness not her own
Fills out her crescent horns, the Pleiads fade.
Her cheeks blush like white cloth 'neath Tyrian dyes,
Or as the shepherd sees the light of stars
Grow rosy with the dawn. O happy one,
Accustomed once to clasp unwillingly
A wife unloved and reckless, snatched away
From that dread Colchian marriage, take thy bride,
The Æolian virgin—'tis her father's will.

   Bright offspring of the thyrsus-bearing god,
The time has come to light the torch of pine;
With fingers dripping wine flash out the fires,
Sound the gay music of the marriage song,
Let the crowd pass their jests; 'tis only she
Who fled her home to wed a stranger guest,
Need steal away into the silent dark.

ACT TWO: SCENE 1

MEDEA, NURSE.

MEDEA: Alas, the wedding chorus strikes my ears;
Woe, woe to me! I could not hitherto
Believe—can hardly yet believe such wrong.
And this is Jason's deed? Of father, home,
And kingdom reft, can he desert me now,
Alone and in a foreign land? Can he
Despise my worth who saw the flames and seas
By my art conquered? thinks, perchance, all crime
Exhausted! Tossed by every wave of doubt,
I am distracted, seeking some revenge.
Had he a brother! Ah, he has a bride;
Through her be thrust the steel! Is this enough?
If Grecian or barbarian cities know
Crime that this hand knows not, that crime be done!
Thy sins return to mind exhorting thee:
The stolen treasure of a kingdom, too;

Thy little comrade, wicked maid, destroyed,
Torn limb from limb and scattered on the sea
An offering to his father; Pelias old
Killed in the boiling cauldron. I have shed
Blood basely, but not yet, not yet have shown
The power of wrath, unhappy love did all.
    Had Jason any choice, by foreign law
And foreign power constrained? He should have bared
His breast to feel the sword. O bitter grief,
Speak milder, milder words. Let Jason live;
Mine as he was, if this be possible,
But, if not mine, still let him live secure,
To spare me still the memory of my gift!
The fault is Creon's; he abuses power
To annul our marriage, sever strongest ties,
And tear the children from their mother's breast;
Let Creon pay the penalty he owes.
I'll heap his home in ashes, the dark flame
Shall reach Malea's dreaded cape, where ships
Find passage only after long delay.
    NURSE: Be silent, I implore thee, hide thy pain
Deep in thy bosom. He who silently
Bears grievous wounds, with patience, and a mind
Unshaken, may find vengeance. Hidden wrath
Finds strength, when open hatred loses hope
Of vengeance.
    MEDEA: Light is grief that hides itself,
And can take counsel. Great wrongs lie not hid
I am resolved on action.
    NURSE: Foster-child,
Restrain thy fury; hardly art thou safe
Though silent.
    MEDEA: Fortune tramples on the meek,
But fears the brave.
    NURSE: When courage is in place
It wins approval.
    MEDEA: It can never be
That courage should be out of place.
    NURSE: To thee,

In thy misfortune, hope points out no way.

MEDEA: The man who cannot hope should naught despair.

NURSE: Colchis is far away, thy husband lost;
Of all thy riches nothing now remains.

MEDEA: Medea now remains! Land, sea, sword, fire,
God and the thunderbolt, are found in me.

NURSE: The king is to be feared.

MEDEA: I claim a king
For father.

NURSE: Hast thou then no fear of arms?

MEDEA: I, who saw warriors spring from earth?

NURSE: Thou'lt die!

MEDEA: I wish it.

NURSE: Flee!

MEDEA: Nay, I repent of flight.

NURSE: Thou art a mother.

MEDEA: And thou seest by whom.

NURSE: Wilt thou not fly?

MEDEA: I fly, but first revenge.

NURSE: Vengeance may follow thee.

MEDEA: I may, perchance,
Find means to hinder it.

NURSE: Restrain thyself
And cease to threaten madly; it is well
That thou adjust thyself to fortune's change.

MEDEA: My riches, not my spirit, fortune takes.
The hinge creaks,—who is this? Creon himself,
Swelling with Grecian pride.

ACT TWO: SCENE 2

CREON *with Attendants,* MEDEA.

CREON: What, is Medea of the hated race
Of Colchian Æëtes, not yet gone?
Still she is plotting evil; well I know
Her guile, and well I know her cruel hand.
Whom does she spare, or whom let rest secure?
Verily I had thought to cut her off

With the swift sword, but Jason's prayers availed
To spare her life. She may go forth unharmed
If she will set our city free from fear.
Threatening and fierce, she seeks to speak with us;
Attendants, keep her off, bid her be still,
And let her learn at last, a king's commands
Must be obeyed. Go, haste, and take her hence.

MEDEA: What fault is punished by my banishment?

CREON: A woman innocent doth ask, "What fault?"

MEDEA: If thou wilt judge, examine; or if king, Command.

CREON: Unjust or just, a king must be
Obeyed.

MEDEA: An unjust king not long endures.

CREON: Go now! To Colchians complain!

MEDEA: I go;
Let him who brought me hither take me hence.

CREON: Thy words come late, my edict has gone forth.

MEDEA: The man who judges, one side still unheard,
Were hardly a just judge, though he judge justly.

CREON: Pelias for listening to thee died, but speak,
Let me give time to hear so fair a plea.

MEDEA: How hard it is to calm a wrathful soul,
How he who takes the scepter in proud hands
Deems his own will sufficient, I have learned;
Have learned it in my father's royal house.
For though the sport of fortune, suppliant,
Banished, alone, forsaken, on all sides
Distressed, my father was a noble king.
I am descended from the glorious sun.
What lands the Phasis in its winding course
Bathes, or the Euxine touches where the sea
Is freshened by the water from the lakes,
Or where armed maiden cohorts try their skill
Beside Thermodon, all these lands are held
Within my father's kingdom, where I dwelt
Noble and favored, and with princely power.
He whom kings seek, sought then to wed with me.
Swift, fickle fortune cast me headlong forth,
And gave me exile. Put thy trust in thrones—

Such trust as thou mayst put in what light chance
Flings here and there at will! Kings have one power,
A matchless honor time can never take:
To help the wretched, and to him who asks
To give a safe retreat. This I have brought
From Colchis, this at least I still can claim:
I saved the flower of Grecian chivalry,
Achaian chiefs, the offspring of the gods;
It is to me they owe their Orpheus
Whose singing melted rocks and drew the trees;
Castor and Pollux are my twofold gift;
Boreas' sons, and Lynceus whose sharp eye
Could pierce beyond the Euxine, are my gift,
And all the Argonauts. Of one alone,
The chief of chiefs, I do not speak; for him
Thou owest me naught; those have I saved for thee,
This one is mine. Rehearse, now, all my crime;
Accuse me; I confess; this is my fault—
I saved the Argo! Had I heard the voice
Of maiden modesty or filial love,
Greece and her leaders had regretted it,
And he, thy son-in-law, had fallen first
A victim to the fire-belching bull.
Let fortune trample on me as she will,
My hand has succored princes, I am glad!
Thou hast the recompense for all my crimes.
Condemn me, but give back the cause of crime.
Creon, I own my guilt—guilt known to thee
When first a suppliant I touched thy knees,
And asked with outstretched hands protecting aid.
Again I ask a refuge, some poor spot
For misery to hide in; grant a place
Withdrawn, a safe asylum in thy realm,
If I must leave the city.
    CREON: I am no prince who rules with cruel sway,
Or tramples on the wretched with proud foot.
Have I not shown this true by choosing him
To be my son-in-law who is a man
Exiled, without resource, in fear of foes?

One whom Acastus, king of Thessaly,
Seeks to destroy, that so he may avenge
A father weak with age, bowed down with years,
Whose limbs were torn asunder? That foul crime
His pious sisters impiously dared,
Tempted by thee; if thou wilt go away,
Jason can then maintain his innocence;
No guiltless blood has stained him, and his hands
Touched not the sword, are yet unstained by thee.
Foul instigator of all evil deeds,
With woman's wantonness in daring aught,
And man's courageous heart—and void of shame,
Go, purge our kingdom; take thy deadly herbs,
Free us from fear; dwelling in other lands
Afar, invoke the gods.

  MEDEA: Thou bidst me go?
Give back the ship and comrade of my flight.
Why bid me go alone? Not so I came.
If thou fear war, both should go forth, nor choice
Be made between two equally at fault:
That old man fell for Jason's sake; impute
To Jason flight, rapine, a brother slain,
And a deserted father; not all mine
The crimes to which a husband tempted me;
'Tis true I sinned, but never for myself.

  CREON: Thou shouldst be gone, why waste the time with
    words?

  MEDEA: I go, but going make one last request:
Let not a mother's guilt drag down her sons.

  CREON: Go, as a father I will succor them,
And with a father's care.

  MEDEA: By future hopes,
By the king's happy marriage, by the strength
Of thrones, which fickle fortune sometimes shakes,
I pray thee grant the exile some delay
That she, perchance about to die, may press
A last kiss on her children's lips.

  CREON: Thou seekst
Time to commit new crime.

MEDEA: In so brief time
What crime were possible?
CREON: No time too short
For him who would do ill.
MEDEA: Dost thou deny
To misery short space for tears?
CREON: Deep dread
Warns me against thy prayer; yet I will grant
One day in which thou mayst prepare for flight.
MEDEA: Too great the favor! Of the time allowed,
Something withdraw. I would depart in haste.
CREON: Before the coming day is ushered in
By Phœbus, leave the city or thou diest.
The bridal calls me, and I go to pay
My vows to Hymen.

ACT TWO: SCENE 3

CHORUS: He rashly ventured who was first to make
In his frail boat a pathway through the deep;
Who saw his native land behind him fade
In distance blue; who to the raging winds
Trusted his life, his slender keel between
The paths of life and death. Our fathers dwelt
In an unspotted age, and on the shore
Where each was born he lived in quietness,
Grew old upon his father's farm content;
With little rich, he knew no other wealth
Than his own land afforded. None knew yet
The changing constellations, nor could use
As guides the stars that paint the ether; none
Had learned to shun the rainy Hyades;
None had as yet to Goat, or Northern Wain
That follows slow by old Boötes driven,
Or Boreas, or Zephyr, given names.
Rash Tiphys was the first to tempt the deep
With spreading canvas; for the winds to write

New laws; to furl the sail; or spread it wide
When sailors longed to fly before the gale,
And the red topsail fluttered in the breeze.
The world so wisely severed by the seas
The pine of Thessaly united, bade
The ocean suffer scourgings at our hands,
And distant waters bring us unknown fears.
The ill-starred ship paid heavy penalty
When the two cliffs, the gateway of the sea,
Moved as though smitten by the thunderbolt,
And the imprisoned waters smote the stars.
Bold Tiphys paled, and from his trembling hand
Let fall the rudder; Orpheus' music died,
His lyre untouched; the Argo lost her voice.
When, belted by her girdle of wild dogs,
The maid of the Sicilian straits gave voice
From all her mouths, who feared not at her bark?
Who did not tremble at the witching song
With which the Sirens charmed the Ausonian sea?
The Thracian Orpheus' lyre had almost forced
Those hinderers of ships to follow him!
What was the journey's prize? The golden fleece,
Medea, fiercer than the raging flood,—
Worthy reward for those first mariners!
    The sea forgets its former wrath; submits
To the new laws; and not alone the ship
Minerva builded, manned by sons of kings,
Finds rowers; other ships may sail the deep.
Old metes are moved, new city walls spring up
On distant soil, and nothing now remains
As it has been in the much-traveled world.
The cold Araxes' stream the Indian drinks;
The Persian quaffs the Rhine; a time shall come
With the slow years, when ocean shall strike off
The chains from earth, and a great world shall then
Lie opened; Tiphys shall win other lands—
Another Tiphys—Thule cease to be
Earth's utmost bound.

ACT THREE: SCENE I

MEDEA, NURSE.

NURSE: Stay, foster-child, why fly so swiftly hence?
Restrain thy wrath! curb thy impetuous haste!
As a Bacchante, frantic with the god
And filled with rage divine, uncertain walks
The top of snowy Pindus or the peak
Of Nysa, so Medea wildly goes
Hither and thither; on her face the mark
Of frenzied rage, her visage flushed, her breast
Shaken by sobs. She cries aloud, her eyes
Are drowned in scalding tears; again she laughs;
All passions surge within her angry heart.
Where will she fling the burden of her soul?
She hesitates, she threatens, storms, complains,
Where falls her vengeance? where will break this wave
Of fury? Passion overflows! she plans
No easy crime, no ordinary deed.
Herself she will surpass; I mark old signs
Of raging; something terrible she plans,
Some deed inhuman, devilish, and wild.
Ye gods, avert the horrors I foresee!
MEDEA: Wretch, dost thou seek how far to show thy hate?
Imitate love! And must I then endure
Without revenge the royal marriage-torch?
Shall this day prove unfruitful, sought and gained
Only by earnest effort? While the earth
Hangs free within the heavens; while the vault
Of heaven sweeps round the earth with changeless change;
While the sands lie unnumbered; while the day
Follows the sun, the night brings up the stars;
Arcturus never wet in ocean's wave
Rolls round the pole; which rivers seaward flow,
My hate shall never cease to seek revenge.
Did ever fierceness of a ravening beast;
Or Scylla or Charybdis sucking down

The waters of the wild Ausonian
And the Sicilian sea; or Ætna fierce,
That holds imprisoned great Enceladus
Breathing forth flame, so glow as I with threats?
Not the swift rivers, nor the storm-tossed sea,
Nor wind-blown ocean, nor the force of flame
By storm-wind fanned, can imitate my wrath.
I will o'erthrow and bring to naught the world!
Did Jason fear the king? Thessalian war?
True love fears naught. Or was he forced to yield,
And gave consent unwillingly? But still
He might have sought his wife for one farewell.
This too he feared to do. He might have gained
From Creon some delay of banishment.
One day is granted for my two sons' sake!
I do not make complaint of too short time,
It is enough for much; this day shall see
What none shall ever hide. I will attack
The very gods, and shake the universe!
    NURSE: Lady, thy spirit so disturbed by ills
Restrain, and let thy storm-tossed soul find rest.
    MEDEA: Rest I can never find until I see
All dragged with me to ruin; all shall fall
When I do;—so to share one's woe is joy.
    NURSE: Think what thou hast to fear if thou persist;
No one can safely fight with princely power.

ACT THREE: SCENE 2

(*The* NURSE *withdraws; enter* JASON.)

JASON: The lot is ever hard; bitter is fate,
Equally bitter if it slay or spare;
God gives us remedies worse than our ills.
Would I keep faith with her I deem my wife
I must expect to die; would I shun death
I must forswear myself. Not fear of death
Has conquered honor, but love full of fear
Knowing the father's death involves the sons.

O holy Justice, if thou dwell in heaven,
I call on thee to witness that the sons
Vanquish their father! Say the mother's love
Is fierce and spurns the yoke, she still will deem
Her children of more worth than marriage joys.
I fain would go to her with prayers, and lo,
She starts at sight of me, her look grows wild,
Hatred she shows and grief.

MEDEA: Jason, I flee!
I flee, it is not new to change my home,
The cause of banishment alone is new;
I have been exiled hitherto for thee.
I go, as thou compellst me, from thy home,
But whither shall I go? Shall I, perhaps,
Seek Phasis, Colchis, and my father's realm
Whose soil is watered by a brother's blood?
What land dost thou command me seek? what sea
The Euxine's jaws through which I led that band
Of noble princes when I followed thee,
Adulterer, through the Symplegades?
Little Iolchos? Tempe? Thessaly?
Whatever way I opened up for thee
I closed against myself. Where shall I go?
Thou drivest into exile, but hast given
No place of banishment. I will go hence.
The king, Creusa's father, bids me go,
And I will do his bidding. Heap on me
Most dreadful punishment, it is my due.
With cruel penalties let the king's wrath
Pursue thy mistress, load my hands with chains,
And in a dungeon of eternal night
Imprison me—'tis less than I deserve!
Ungrateful one, recall the fiery bull;
The earth-born soldiers, who at my command
Slew one another; and the longed-for spoils
Of Phrixus' ram, whose watchful guardian,
The sleepless dragon, at my bidding slept;
The brother slain; the many, many crimes
In one crime gathered. Think how, led by me,

By me deceived, that old man's daughters dared
To slay their aged father, dead for aye!
By thy hearth's safety, by thy children's weal,
By the slain dragon, by these blood-stained hands
I never spared from doing aught for thee,
By thy past fears, and by the sea and sky
Witnesses of our marriage, pity me!
Happy thyself, make me some recompense!
Of all the ravished gold the Scythians brought
From far, as far as India's burning plains,
Wealth our wide palace hardly could contain,
So that we hung our groves with gold, I took
Nothing. My brother only bore I thence,
And him for thee I sacrificed. I left
My country, father, brother, maiden shame:
This was my marriage portion; give her own
To her who goes an exile.

    JASON: When angry Creon thought to have thee slain,
Urged by my prayers, he gave thee banishment.

    MEDEA: I looked for a reward; the gift I see
Is exile.

    JASON: While thou mayst fly, fly in haste!
The wrath of kings is ever hard to bear.

    MEDEA: Thou giv'st me such advice because thou lov'st
Creusa, wouldst divorce a hated wife!

    JASON: And does Medea taunt me with my loves?

    MEDEA: More—treacheries and murders.

    JASON: Canst thou charge
Such sins to me?

    MEDEA: All I have ever done.

    JASON: It only needs that I should share the guilt
Of these thy crimes!

    MEDEA: Thine are they, thine alone;
He is the criminal who reaps the fruit.
Though all should brand thy wife with infamy,
Thou shouldst defend and call her innocent:
She who has sinned for thee, toward thee hold pure.

    JASON: To me my life is an unwelcome gift
Of which I am ashamed.

MEDEA: Who is ashamed
To owe his life to me can lay it down.

JASON: For thy sons' sake control thy fiery heart.

MEDEA: I will have none of them, I cast them off,
Abjure them; shall Creusa to my sons
Give brothers?

JASON: To an exile's wretched sons
A mighty queen will give them.

MEDEA: Never come
That evil day that mingles a great race
With race unworthy,—Phœbus' glorious sons
With sons of Sisyphus.

JASON: What, cruel one,
Wouldst thou drag both to banishment? Away!

MEDEA: Creon has heard my prayer.

JASON: What can I do?

MEDEA: For me? Some crime perhaps.

JASON: Two wrathful kings
I fear.

MEDEA: Medea's wrath is still more fierce!
Let us essay our power, the victor's prize
Be Jason.

JASON: Passion-weary, I submit;
Thou too shouldst fear a lot so often tried.

MEDEA: Fortune has ever served me faithfully.

JASON: Acastus comes.

MEDEA: Creon's a nearer foe,
Flee thou from both. Medea does not ask
That thou shouldst arm thyself against the king,
Or soil thy hands with murder of thy kin;
Flee with me innocent.

JASON: Who will oppose
If double war ensue, and the two kings
Join forces?

MEDEA: Add to them the Colchian troops
And King Æëtes, Scythian hosts and Greeks,
Medea conquers all!

JASON: I greatly fear
A scepter's power.

MEDEA: Do not covet it.

JASON: We must cut short our converse, lest it breed
Suspicion.

MEDEA: Now from high Olympus send
Thy thunder, Jupiter; stretch forth thy hand,
Prepare thy lightning, from the riven clouds
Make the world tremble, nor with careful hand
Spare him or me; whichever of us dies
Dies guilty; thy avenging thunderbolt
Cannot mistake the victim.

JASON: Try to speak
More sanely; calm thyself. If aught can aid
Thy flight from Creon's house, thou needst but ask.

MEDEA: My soul is strong enough, and wont to scorn.
The wealth of kings; this boon alone I crave,
To take my children with me when I go;
Into their bosoms I would shed my tears,
New sons are thine.

JASON: Would I might grant thy prayer;
Paternal love forbids me, Creon's self
Could not compel me to it. They alone
Lighten the sorrow of a grief-parched soul.
For them I live, I sooner would resign
Breath, members, light.

MEDEA (*aside*):   'Tis well! He loves his sons,
This, then, the place where he may feel a wound!
(*To* JASON) Before I go, thou wilt, at least, permit
That I should give my sons a last farewell,
A last embrace? But one thing more I ask:
If in my grief I've poured forth threatening words,
Retain them not in mind; let memory hold
Only my softer speech, my words of wrath
Obliterate.

JASON: I have erased them all
From my remembrance. I would counsel thee
Be calm, act gently; calmness quiets pain. (*Exit* JASON.)

ACT THREE: SCENE 3

MEDEA, NURSE.

MEDEA: He's gone! And can it be he leaves me so,
Forgetting me and all my guilt? Forgot?
Nay, never shall Medea be forgot!
Up! Act! Call all thy power to aid thee now;
This fruit of crime is thine, to shun no crime!
Deceit is useless, so they fear my guile.
Strike where they do not dream thou canst be feared.
Medea, haste, be bold to undertake
The possible—yea, that which is not so!
Thou, faithful nurse, companion of my griefs
And varying fortunes, aid my wretched plans.
I have a robe, gift of the heavenly powers,
An ornament of a king's palace, given
By Phœbus to my father as a pledge
Of sonship; and a necklace of wrought gold;
And a bright diadem, inlaid with gems,
With which they used to bind my hair. These gifts,
Endued with poison by my magic arts,
My sons shall carry for me to the bride.
Pay vows to Hecate, bring the sacrifice.
Set up the altars. Let the mounting flame
Envelop all the house.

ACT THREE: SCENE 4

CHORUS: Fear not the power of flame, nor swelling gale,
Nor hurtling dart, nor cloudy wind that brings
The winter storms; fear not when Danube sweeps
Unchecked between his widely severed shores,
Nor when the Rhone hastes seaward, and the sun
Has broken up the snow upon the hills,
          And Hæmus flows in rivers.
A wife deserted, loving while she hates,
Fear greatly; blindly burns her anger's flame,

She cares not to be ruled, nor bears the curb,
Nor fears to die; she courts the hostile swords.
Ye gods, we ask your grace divine for him
Who safely crossed the seas; the ocean's lord
Is angry for his conquered kingdom's sake;
          Spare Jason, we entreat!
Th' impetuous youth who dared to drive the car
Of Phœbus, keeping not the wonted course,
Died in the heavenly fires himself had lit.
Few are the evils of the well-known way;
Seek the old paths your fathers safely trod,
The sacred federations of the world
          Keep still inviolate.
The men who dipped the oars of that brave ship;
Who plundered of their shade the sacred groves
Of Pelion; passed between the unstable cliffs;
Endured so many hardships on the deep;
And cast their anchor on a savage coast,
Passing again with ravished foreign gold,
Atoned with fearful death for dire wrong
          To Ocean's sacred laws.
The angry deep demanded punishment:
To an unskilful pilot Tiphys gave
The rudder. On a foreign coast he fell,
Far from his father's kingdom, and he lies
With nameless shades, under a lowly tomb.
Becalmed in her still harbor Aulis held
Th' impatient ships, remembering in wrath
          The king that she lost thence.
Sweet voiced Camena's son, who touched his lyre
So sweetly that the floods stood still, the winds
Were silent, and the birds forgot to sing,
And forests followed him, on Thracian fields
Lies dead, his head borne down by Hebrus' stream.
He touched again the Styx and Tartarus,
          But not again returns.
Alcides overthrew the north wind's sons;
He slew that son of Neptune who could take
Unnumbered forms; but after he had made

Peace over land and sea, and opened wide
The realm of Dis, lying on Œta's top
He gave his body to the cruel fire,
Destroyed by his wife's gift—the fatal robe
          Poisoned with Centaur's blood.
Ancæus fell a victim to the boar
Of Caledonia; Meleager slew
His mother's brother, perished by the hand
Of his own mother. They have merited
Their lot, but what the crime that he atoned
Whom great Alcides sought so long in vain,
The tender Hylas drawn beneath safe waves?
Go now, brave soldiers, boldly plow the main,
          But fear the gentle streams.
Idmon the serpents buried in the sands
Of Libya, though he knew the future well.
Mopsus, to others true, false to himself,
Fell far from Thebes; and if the seer spoke true,
Peleus must wander exiled from his realm;
And Nauplius, seeking injury to the Greeks
By his deceitful beacon fires, shall fall
Into the ocean; Palamedes, too,
Shall suffer, dying for his father's sin.
Oïleus, smitten by the thunderbolt,
Shall perish on the sea; Admetus' wife
To save her husband's life shall give her own.
He who commanded that the golden spoil
Be carried in the ships had traveled far,
But, plunged in seething cauldron, Pelias died
In narrow limits. 'Tis enough, ye gods;
          Ye have avenged the sea!

ACT FOUR: SCENE I

NURSE: I shrink with horror! Ruin threatens us!
How terribly her wrath inflames itself!
Her former force awakes, thus I have seen
Medea raging and attacking God,
Compelling heaven. Greater crime than then

She now prepares. No sooner had she sought
Wildly her fatal shrine than she put forth
Her every power, and what before she feared
She does; lets loose all ills, mysterious arts.
With her left hand the dismal sacrifice
Preparing, she invokes whatever ills
The Libyan sands with their fierce heat create,
Or frost-bound Taurus with perpetual snow
Encompasses. Drawn by her magic spell,
Come from their desert holes a scaly host.
The serpent drags his heavy length along,
Darts his forked tongue, and seeks his destined prey.
Hearing her incantation, he draws back
And knots his swelling body coiling it.—
"They are but feeble poisons earth brings forth,
And harmless darts," she says, "heaven's ills I seek.
Now is the time for deeper sorcery.
The dragon like a torrent shall descend,
Whose mighty folds the Great and Lesser Bear
Know well (the Great Bear o'er the Phrygians shines,
The Less o'er Tyre); Ophiuchus shall loose
His grasp, and poison flow. Come at my call,
Python, who dared to fight twin deities.
The Hydra once cut off by Hercules,
Accustomed from its wounds to gain fresh strength,
Shall come. Thou ever watchful Colchian one,
Be present with the rest—thou, who first slept
Lulled by my incantations." When the brood
Of serpents has been called she blends the juice
Of poisonous herbs; all Eryx' pathless heights
Bear, or the snow-capped top of Caucasus
Wet with Prometheus' blood, where winter reigns;
All that the rich Arabians use to tip
Their poisoned shafts, or the light Parthians,
Or warlike Medes; all Suebian witches cull
In the Hyrcanian forests in the north;
All poisons that the earth brings forth in spring
When birds are nesting; or when winter cold
Has torn away the beauty of the groves

And bound the world in icy manacles.
Whatever herb gives flower the cause of death,
Or juice of twisted root, her hands have culled.
These on Thessalian Athos grew, and those
On mighty Pindus; on Pangæus' height
She cut the tender leaves with bloody scythe.
These Tigris nurtured with its eddies deep,
The Danube those; Hydaspes rich in gems
Flowing with current warm through levels dry,
Bætis that gives its name to neighboring lands
And meets the western ocean languidly,
Have nurtured these. The knife cut those at dawn;
These other herbs at dead of night were reaped;
And these were plucked with the enchanted nail.
Death-dealing plants she chooses, wrings the blood
Of serpents, and she takes ill-omened birds,
The sad owl's heart, the quivering entrails cut
From the horned owl living—sorts all these.
In some the eager force of flame is found,
In some the bitter cold of sluggish ice;
To these she adds the venom of her words
As greatly to be feared. But lo, I hear
The sound of her mad footstep and her song.
Earth trembles when she hears.

ACT FOUR: SCENE 2

(MEDEA, *before the altar of Hecate.*)

MEDEA: Lo, I invoke you, all ye silent shades,
Infernal gods, blind Chaos, sunless home
Of shadowy Dis, and squalid caves of Death
Bound by the banks of Tartarus. Lost souls,
For this new bridal leave your wonted toil.
Stand still, thou whirling wheel, Ixion touch
Again firm ground; come, Tantalus, and drink
Unchecked the wave of the Pirenian fount.
Let heavier punishment on Creon wait:
Thou stone of Sisyphus, worn smooth, roll back;

And ye Danaïdes who strive in vain
To fill your leaking jars, I need your aid.
Come at my invocation, star of night,
Endued with form most horrible, nor threat
With single face, thou three-formed deity!
   For thee, according to my country's use,
With hair unfilleted and naked feet
I've trod the lonely groves; called forth the rain
From cloudless skies; have driven back the sea;
And forced the ocean to withdraw its waves.
Earth sees heaven's laws confused, the sun and stars
Shining together, and the two Bears wet
In the forbidden ocean. I have changed
The circle of the seasons:—at my word
Earth flourishes with summer; Ceres sees
A winter harvest; Phasis' rushing stream
Flows to its source; and Danube that divides
Into so many mouths restrains its flood
Of waters—hardly moving past its shores.
The winds are silent; but the waters speak,
The wild seas roar; the home of ancient groves
Loses its leafy shade; and day returns
At my command; the sun stands still in heaven.
My incantations move the Hyades.
It is thy hour, Dian.
   For thee my bloody hands have wrought this crown
Nine times by serpents girt; those knotted snakes
Rebellious Typhon bore, who made revolt
Against Jove's kingdom; Nessus gave this blood
When dying; Œta's funeral pyre provides
These ashes which have drunk the poisoned blood
Of dying Hercules; and here thou seest
Althea's vengeful brand, she sacrificed
A mother's to a sister's love. These quills
The Harpies left within some trackless cave,
Their refuge when they fled from Zetes' wrath;
And these were dropped by the Stymphalian birds
That felt the wound of arrows dipped in blood
Of the Lernæan Hydra.

The altars find a voice, the tripod moves,
Stirred by the favoring goddess. Her swift car
I see approach—not the full-orbed that rolls
All night through heaven; but as, with darkened light,
Her orb contracted, with wan face she moves
Through night's dark skies, vexed by Thessalian charms.
So, pale one, from thy torch shed murky light,
Affright the nations that they clash for thee
Corinthian cymbals. Here I pay to thee,
On altars made of turf and red with blood,
These solemn rites; have stolen from the tomb
This torch that gives its baleful funeral light;
To thee with bowed head I have made my prayer;
And in accordance with funereal use,
Have filleted my loosened hair, have plucked
This branch that grows beside the Stygian wave;
Like a wild Mænad, laying bare my breast,
With sacred knife I cut for thee my arm;
My blood is on the altars! Hand, learn well
To use the knife and shed blood dear to thee.
See, from the wound, the sacred stream flows forth,
Daughter of Perses, have I asked too oft
Thine aid? Recall no more my former prayers.
Today as always I invoke thine aid
For Jason only! Ah, endue this robe
With such a baleful power that the bride
May feel at its first touch consuming fire
Of serpent's poison in her inmost veins;
For fire flames hid in the bright gold, a gift
Prometheus gave and taught me how to store—
He now atones his daring theft from heaven
With tortured vitals. Mulciber has given
This flame, and I in sulphur nurtured it;
I brought a spark from the destroying fire
Of Phaethon; I have the flame breathed forth
By the Chimæra, and the fire I snatched
From Colchis' savage bull; and mixed with these
Medusa's venom. I have bade all keep

Their poison unrevealed; now, Hecate, add
The sting to poison, keep the seeds of flame
Hid in my gift; let them deceive the sight
Nor burn the touch; but let them penetrate
Her very heart and veins, melt all her limbs,
Consume her bones in smoke. Her burning hair
Shall glow more brightly than the nuptial torch!
My vows are heard, and Hecate thrice has barked,
And shaken fire from her gleaming brand.
    'Tis finished! Call my sons. My royal gifts,
Ye shall be borne by them to the new bride.
Go, go, my sons, a hapless mother's brood,
Placate with gifts and prayers your father's wife!
But come again with speed, that I may know
A last embrace!

ACT FOUR: SCENE 3

CHORUS: Where hastes the blood-stained Mænad, headlong
            driven
By angry love? What mischief plots her rage?
With wrath her face grows rigid; her proud head
She fiercely shakes, and dares defiantly
Threaten the king.
Who would believe her exiled from the realm?
Her cheeks glow crimson, pallor puts to flight
The red, no color lingers on her face;
Her steps are driven to and fro as when
A tigress rages, of her young bereft,
Beside the Ganges in the gloomy woods.
Medea knows not how to curb her love
Or hate. Now love and hate together rage.
When will she leave the fair Pelasgian fields,
The wicked Colchian one, and free from fear
Our king and kingdom? Drive with no slow rein
Thy car, Diana; let the sweet night hide
The sunlight. Hesperus, end the dreaded day.

ACT FIVE: SCENE 1

MESSENGER, CHORUS.

MESSENGER (*enters in haste*): All are destroyed, the royal
         empire falls,
Father and child lie in one funeral pyre.
    CHORUS: Destroyed by what deceit?
    MESSENGER: That which is wont
To ruin princes—gifts.
    CHORUS: Could these work harm?
    MESSENGER: I myself wonder, and can hardly deem
The wrong accomplished, though I know it done.
    CHORUS: How did it happen?
    MESSENGER: A destructive fire
Spreads everywhere as at command; even now
The city is in fear, the palace burned.
    CHORUS: Let water quench the flames.
    MESSENGER: It will not these,
As by a miracle floods feed the fire.
The more we fight it so much more it glows.

ACT FIVE: SCENE 2

MEDEA, NURSE.

NURSE: Up! up! Medea! Swiftly flee the land
Of Pelops; seek in haste a distant shore.
    MEDEA: Shall I fly? I? Were I already gone
I would return for this, that I might see
These new betrothals. Dost thou pause, my soul,
And shrink to follow up thy first success?
This joy's but the beginning of revenge.
Thou still dost love if thou art satisfied
To widow Jason. For this work prepare:
Honor begone and maiden modesty,—
It were a light revenge pure hands could yield.
Strengthen thy drooping spirit, stir up wrath,

Drain from thy heart its all of ancient force,
Thy deeds till now call love; awake, and act,
That they may see how light, how little worth,
All former crime—the prelude of revenge!
What was there great my novice hands could dare?
What was the madness of my girlhood days?
I am Medea now, through crime made strong.
Rejoice, because through thee thy brother died;
Rejoice, because through thee his limbs were torn;
Through thee thy father lost the golden fleece;
That, armed by thee, his daughters Pelias slew.
Find thou a way, revenge. No novice hand
Thou bring'st to crime; what wilt thou do; what dart
Let fly against thy treacherous enemy?
I know not what of crime my madness plots,
Nor yet dare I confess it to myself!
In folly I made haste—would that my foe
Had children by this other! Mine are his,
We'll say Creusa bore them! 'Tis enough;
Through them my heart at last finds just revenge;
My soul must be prepared for this last crime.
Ye who were once my children, mine no more,
Pay ye the forfeit for your father's crimes.
Awe strikes my spirit and benumbs my hand;
My heart beats wildly; vanished is my rage,
And mother love, returning, now drives out
The hatred of the wife. I shed their blood?
My children's blood? Give better counsel, rage!
Be far from thee this crime! What guilt is theirs?
Is Jason not their father?—guilt enough!
And, greater guilt, Medea calls them sons.
They are not sons of mine, so let them die!
Nay, rather let them perish since they are!
But they are innocent!—my brother was!
Waverest thou? Do tears make wet thy cheek?
Do wrath and love like adverse tides impel
Now here, now there? As when the winds wage war
And the wild waves against each other smite,
And warring tides run high, and ocean raves,

My heart is beaten, and love drives out wrath,
As wrath drives love. My anger dies in love.
Dear sons, sole solace of a storm-tossed house,
Come hither, lock your arms about my neck;
You may be safe for him, if safe for me!
But I am driven into exile, flight;
Torn from my bosom weeping, soon they'll go
Lamenting for my kisses—let them die
For father and for mother! Once again
Rage swells, hate burns; again the fury seeks
Th' unwilling hand—I follow where wrath leads.
Would that the children that made proud the heart
Of Niobe were mine, that I had borne
Twice seven sons! In bearing only two
I have been cursed! And yet it is enough
For father, brother, that I have borne two.—
Where does that horde of furies haste? whom seek?
For whom prepare their fires? or for whom
Brandish the infernal band the bloody torch?
The huge snake hisses writhing; as they lash
Their serpent scourges; with her hostile brand
Whom does Megæra seek? What dim-seen shade
Is that which hither brings its scattered limbs?
It is my brother, and he seeks revenge;
I grant it, thrust the torches in my eyes;
Kill, burn; the furies have me in their power!
Brother, command the avenging goddesses
To leave me, and the shades to seek their place
In the infernal regions without fear;
Here leave me to myself, and use this hand
That held the sword—your soul has found revenge.

(*Kills one of her sons.*)

What means this sudden noise? They come in arms
And seek to slay me. Having thus begun
My murders, I will go upon the roof,
Come, follow thou, I'll take the dead with me.

Strike now, my soul, nor longer hide thy power,
But show the world thy strength.

(*She goes out with the nurse and the living boy, and carries
with her the body of her dead son.*)

ACT FIVE: SCENE 3

(JASON *in the foreground,* MEDEA *with the children appears
upon the roof.*)

JASON: Ye faithful ones, who share
In the misfortunes of your harassed king,
Hasten to take the author of these deeds.
Come hither, hither, cohorts of brave men;
Bring up your weapons; overthrow the house.
MEDEA: I have recaptured now my crown and throne,
My brother and my father; Colchians hold
The golden fleece; my kingdom is won back;
My lost virginity returns to me!
O gods at last appeased! Glad nuptial day!
Go, finished is the crime. Not yet complete
Is vengeance, finish while thy hand is strong
To smite. Why stay, why hesitate, my soul?
Thou art able! All thine anger falls to nought!
I do repent of that which I have done!
What hast thou done, O miserable one?
What, miserable? Though I should repent,
'Tis done, great joy fills my unwilling heart,
And, lo, the joy increases. But one thing
Before was lacking—Jason did not see!
All that he has not seen I count as lost.
JASON: She threatens from the roof; let fire be brought,
That she may perish burned with her own flame.
MEDEA: Pile high the funeral pyre of thy sons,
And rear their tomb. To Creon and thy wife
I have already paid the honors due.
This son is dead, and this one too shall die,

And thou shalt see him perish.

JASON: By the gods,
By our sad flight together, and the bond
I have not willingly forsaken, spare
Our son! If there is any crime, 'tis mine;
Put me to death, strike down the guilty one.

MEDEA: There where thou askest mercy, and canst feel
The sting, I thrust the sword. Go, Jason, seek
Thy virgin bride; desert a mother's bed.

JASON: Let one suffice for vengeance.

MEDEA: Had it been
That one could satisfy my hands with blood,
I had slain none. Although I should slay two,
The number is too small for my revenge.

JASON: Then go, fill up the measure of thy crime,
I ask for nothing but that thou should'st make
A speedy end.

MEDEA: Now, grief, take slow revenge;
It is my day; haste not, let me enjoy.

(Kills the other child.)

JASON: Slay me, mine enemy!

MEDEA: Dost thou implore
My pity? It is well! I am avenged
O vengeance, no more offerings can I give,
Nothing is left to immolate to thee!
Look up, ungrateful Jason, recognize
Thy wife; so I am wont to flee. The way
Lies open through the skies; two dragons bend
Their necks, submissive to the yoke. I go
In my swift car through heaven. Take thy sons!

*(She casts down to him the bodies of her children, and is
borne away in a chariot drawn by dragons.)*

JASON: Go through the skies sublime, and in thy flight
Prove that where thou art borne there are no gods.

SENECA

THE PHAEDRA

TRANSLATED BY ELLA ISABEL HARRIS

CHARACTERS IN THE PLAY

SPIRIT *of the elder* TANTALUS, *father of Pelops*
MEGÆRA, *a divine Fury*
CHORUS *of men of Mycenæ*
ATREUS, *King of Mycenæ, son of Pelops*
ATTENDANT *of Atreus*
THYESTES, *brother of Atreus*
TANTALUS, *son of Thyestes* (*and two other sons of Thyestes*)
MESSENGER

THE PHAEDRA

(SCENE: *before the royal house of* THESEUS *at Athens.*)

HIPPOLYTUS (*and his Huntsmen*).

HIPPOLYTUS: Athenians, go gird the shadowy groves,
And ridges of the mountains; traverse swift
The places that 'neath rocky Parnes lie,
Where, swiftly flowing through Thessalian vales,
The river roars; ascend the hills that shine
White ever with Rhipean snow. Where stand
The tangled woods of lofty elder, go;
Go where fields stretch o'er which sweet Zephyr blows
With dewy breath that wakens vernal herbs,
Where flows Ilissus' narrow, sluggish stream
Through barren lands and with its niggard thread
Touches the sterile sands. Turn leftward, ye,
To where the wooded highlands open out
Toward Marathon, where nightly for their young
The does seek food; go ye where, breathed upon
By the soft south wind, harsh Acharnæ's cold
Is tempered; tread ye sweet Hymettus' cliffs:
Seek ye Achidnæ small; too long has lain
Immune the land where on the curved sea shore
Sunion presses. If a huntsman's pride
Is felt by any, Phlius calls to him—
There dwells that fear of husbandmen, the boar,
Dreaded, well known, already scarred with wounds.
Give to the dogs that silent track the game
Free rein, but hold the swift Molossian hounds

In leash, and let the savage Cretans pull
On the stout chains with straining necks. Bind fast,
With care, by firmest knots, the Spartan dogs;
Daring and eager for the chase are they.
The time draws near when through the hollow rocks
Shall sound their baying. While it is but dawn
And while the dewy earth still shows the tracks,
With nostrils wide, sagacious let them snuff
The air, and with their noses to the ground
Search for the quarry's scent. Let some make haste
To carry on their backs the nets, and some
To bear the noose; and let the feathered snare,
Red dyed, with empty terror fill the prey.
Thou shalt the light dart poise; in both hands, thou,
Direct the heavy spear; thou, lying hid,
Shalt with thy clamor drive the wild beasts forth,
And thou, now victor, with curved slaughtering knife
Lay bare the victim's heart. Be present now
To us thy comrades, goddess hero-souled,
To whom the secret parts of earth lie bared,
Whose darts unerring ever find their prey
Whether the quarry drink Araxes' stream
Or on the frozen Hister play. Thy hand
Has slain Gætulian lions, and the deer
Of Crete; and now with lighter hand the flight
Of the swift doe is stayed. The tiger yields
To thee, to thee the rough-haired bison yields
And the wild, broad-horned ox. Whatever finds
In solitary places pasture land,
Whate'er the needy Garamantian knows,
Whate'er the Arabs in their fertile groves,
Or the Sarmatian wanderers in waste plains,
Whate'er the Pyrenees' wild summit hides,
All that Hyrcania's wooded pastures know,
Diana, fear thy bow. When to the woods
A worshipper accepted takes thy grace,
The toils hold conquered game, no foot breaks through
The net, the groaning wagon bears the spoils,
The muzzles of the dogs are wet with blood,

And joyously the rustics seek again
Their huts. Thou art propitious, goddess, now!
The signal by the loud-mouthed dogs is given,
Lo, to the woods I'm called; the shortest way
I follow.

ACT ONE: SCENE 2

PHÆDRA, NURSE.

PHÆDRA: O mighty Crete, thou ruler of wide seas,
Whose ships unnumbered sail by every coast,
Through every sea which Nereus' prows divide,
Far as Phœnician soil, why driv'st thou me
To pass my youth in sorrow and in tears,
A hostage given to the hated race,
And wedded to a foe. Lo, far away,
My husband Theseus is a fugitive
And keeps such faith as he is wont to keep.
Through the dense shadows of the infernal lake
That knows no backward path bold Theseus swam,
Pirithous' friend, that he might carry thence,
As bride, the infernal monarch's ravished wife;
He goes, the friend of folly, unrestrained
By fear or shame; in lowest Acheron
The father of Hippolytus seeks out
Unlawful marriage and adultery.
Yet other, greater griefs than this weigh down
My sad heart, neither quiet night nor sleep
Frees me from care: my grief is fed and grows,
And glows within me as the vapor glows
In Etna's depths. The web of Pallas lies
Neglected, from my idle hands the flax
Has fall'n; no longer am I glad to pay
My votive offerings at the holy shrines,
Nor to be present with the Attic choir
Among the altars, and to wave the torch
In sacred, silent rites, nor to approach
With pious ceremony and chaste hands

Her who was guardian goddess of the earth
Declared. My only pleasure is to hunt
Wild beasts, and with my supple hands to hurl
The heavy dart. O whither dost thou tend,
My soul? Why dost thou madly love the woods?
I feel my wretched mother's fatal sin:
Our family has been wont within the woods
To sin for love. O mother, I am moved
With pity for thee: to a shocking crime
Stirred, thou didst boldly love the savage lord
Of the wild herd, that fierce adulterer,
Impatient of the yoke, of untamed bands
The leader—yet for something he felt love!
What god, what Dædalus will aid my fires?
Not if again he could return himself,
Potent in Attic arts, who safely hid
Our minotaur within the labyrinth,
Could any aid to my distress be given.
Venus, against the offspring of the sun
Most deeply angered, by our homage now
Avenging both herself and Mars, weighs down
The race of Phœbus with most shameful crime.
No daughter of unfaithful Minos' house
Is free from love—love ever joined with crime.
  NURSE: O wife of Theseus, Jove's illustrious child,
From thy chaste bosom swiftly thrust such sin,
O quench these fires, nor yield to cruel hope.
Whoever from the first contends against
And conquers love, is safe, but those who nurse
The evil with sweet blandishments too late
Refuse to bear the yoke themselves assumed.
And yet I am not ignorant, in truth,
How the proud spirit of the princess spurns—
Haughty and arrogant—a guiding hand.
I'll bear whatever outcome fate may bring;
Approaching freedom makes the aged brave.
To wish for honor nor to go astray
From the right path is best, yet near to this
Is shame that one has known the thought of sin.

Where goest thou, unhappy one? wouldst spread
Thy household's infamy? Wouldst thou surpass
Thy mother? Greater is thy crime than hers;
Thou must impute the minotaur to fate,
Thy crime is offspring of thine own self-will.
If thou, because thy husband sees no more
The light of upper day, shouldst deem thy sin
To be committed safely, without fear,
Thou errst. Though Theseus is in depths profound
Of Lethe hidden, though forevermore
He dwell in Stygian darkness, yet why deem
That he who gives the law to many lands
And rules the waters with his empery wide
Would let so base a crime go undivulged?
Wise is a father's care.—Yet shouldst thou think
That we by subtilty or guile might hide
Such evil from him, wherefore shouldst thou think
Thy mother's parent who pours forth his light
On all things, or the father of the gods
Who shakes the world when in his flashing hand
He waves the thunderbolt from Etna's forge
Will see it not? Dost thou indeed believe
That it is possible to do this deed
In sight of these thy ancestors, who see
All thou wouldst hide? Yet should some favoring god
Conceal the shameful union, grant to lust
Protection hitherto denied to crime,
What of the everpresent punishment,
The conscious terror of a guilty mind,
The heart that knows its fault and fears itself?
Some crimes are safe, no sinner feels secure.
Stifle the flames of guilty love, I pray,
Do not a sin which never yet was done
In barbarous lands, not on the level plains
Of wandering Getæ, nor the unfriendly heights
Of Taurus, nor in lonely Scythia,
Make thy mind chaste, drive out the horrid thought,
And mindful of thy mother, fear to try
Strange unions. Wouldst thou give one marriage bed

To son and father, in thy impious womb
Conceive a progeny so basely mixed?
Forth then, and with thy bestial fires o'erthrow
The laws of nature; why should monsters fail?
Why empty leave thy brother's labyrinth?
As often as a Cretan woman loves
Shall she not dare unwonted prodigies?
Shall nature not withdraw from her own laws?

PHÆDRA: I know that what thou callst to mind is true,
Love's fire compels me choose the worser part.
My soul hastes downward not unknowingly,
And seeking saner counsels, vainly turns
Backward. So when his heavy boat is driven
By adverse currents does the sailor use
In vain his labor, and his conquered ship
Yields to the racing current. What avail
Is reason? Madness has o'ercome and reigns;
The potent god within my breast holds sway.
The unbridled, winged one in all the world
Holds sway, he burns with unrelenting flames
Ev'n wounded Jove, the warlike Mars has felt
Those torches, and the artisan who makes
Jove's triple thunderbolts has felt them too,
He, who Mount Etna's ever blazing forge
Keeps busy, with this tiny spark grows hot;
Phœbus himself, who from his bow directs
Sure darts, is by the boy's more certain shafts
Transfixed; they fly alike to earth and heaven.

NURSE: Base lust, crime-maddened, feigns that love's a god,
Those who have wished great liberty have given
Falsely the name of deity to lust.
Yea, doubtless, Venus sends her son to roam
Through every land! He with his tender hand
Prepares his shameless darts! So great a realm
The least of all the gods can claim! Mad souls
Created empty fables and have feigned
Venus' divinity, the love god's bow.
Whoever too much joys in happy days
And languishes in luxury desires

Some unaccustomed pleasure, then comes lust,
Ill-omened comrade of the fortunate:
Accustomed feasts no longer satisfy,
Nor home well-ordered, nor cheap wine to drink.
Why does this plague, selecting dainty roofs,
So rarely seek the poorer dwelling-place?
Why is it holy love abideth still
In humble homes, that temperate passions sway
The saner multitude of common folk
To practise self-restraint and soberness?
Why do the rich and powerful desire
More than is lawful? Who already has
Too much desires that he cannot have.
Thou knowest what is fitting her who sits
Upon the throne; honor and fear the crown
Of him who will return.

PHÆDRA: Love's empery
In me, I think, is greatest and no more
I fear returns. He never more has seen
The convex upper world who enters once
The home of silence and perpetual night.

NURSE: Yet though Death bars his realm and though the gates
Are ever guarded by the Stygian dog,
Theseus e'er finds forbidden paths.

PHÆDRA: Perchance
Theseus will find indulgence for our love.

NURSE: He has been, even to a faithful wife,
Most harsh. Antiope the Amazon
Made proof of his hard hand. Yet couldst thou bend
Thine angered husband's will, canst thou control
Hippolytus' hard heart? The very name
Of woman he abhors and flies them all;
Harshly he vows his years to singleness,
Shuns marriage: such the Amazonian race!

PHÆDRA: It pleases me through woods and lofty hills
To follow him, when on the snowy top
He stays his steps, or mocks the cruel rocks
With his swift foot.

NURSE: And will he stay his steps

And, softened, give himself to thy caress?
Will he for rites of unchaste Venus give
His chastity? Perchance his hate of thee
Is but the reason why he so hates all.
He cannot be by any prayers o'ercome.

PHÆDRA: Wild is he but we know wild beasts are tamed
By love.

NURSE: He'll flee thee.

PHÆDRA: Though through seas he flee,
I'll follow him.

NURSE: Recall thy father's fate.

PHÆDRA: My mother's I'll recall.

NURSE: He hates thy kind.

PHÆDRA: I shall be free from rivals in his love.

NURSE: Thy husband will return—

PHÆDRA: Pirithous' friend?

NURSE: Thy father'll come.

PHÆDRA: For Ariadne's send.

NURSE: I pray thee by the silvery locks of age,
And by this heart o'erwearied with its cares
And by the breast which nursed thee, curb thy rage.
Call up thy strength; who wishes to be well
Is partly healed.

PHÆDRA: Shame has not wholly fled
From my chaste spirit; nurse, I yield to thee.
Let love that wishes not to be controlled
Be overcome. Thee will I not allow,
O honor, to be stained. One way remains
One only refuge from my misery;
My husband I will follow, hinder crime
By death.

NURSE: O daughter, moderate the rush
Of thoughts unbridled, curb thy passion's force.
Now that thou thinkest thou art worthy death,
I think thee worthy life.

PHÆDRA: Death is decreed;
I only wait to seek the kind of death.
Shall I destroy my life with twisted noose,
Or fall upon the sword? Or shall I leap

Headlong from Pallas' lofty citadel?
   NURSE: In my old age, shall I permit thee thus
To perish by a violent death? Restrain
Thy impulse mad.
   PHÆDRA: No reason can prevent
The death of one who has resolved to die,
Who ought to die, we therefore arm our hand
To vindicate our chastity.
   NURSE: Sole stay
Of wearied age, if thus hot passions press
Upon thy heart, think not of thy fair fame:
Fame seldom sides with truth; kindest it is
To those who merit least and to the good
Most harsh. That soul intractable and stern
We will attempt; my labor let it be
To meet the youth and bend his fierce, wild will.

ACT ONE: SCENE 3

CHORUS.

O goddess, daughter of the stormy seas,
Whom Cupids twain call mother, how thy boy,
Ungoverned, wanton, smiling, from sure bow
Lets fly his fiery shafts! the wound when given
Shows no wide scar, but hidden deep within
Devours the heart. That freakish boy can know
No peace; he scatters swiftly through the world
His arrows: all who see the rising sun,
Or toward the bounds of Hesperus may dwell,
Or underneath the cold Parrhasian Bear,
Or fervid Cancer—ever-wandering tribes,—
They know those fires. In youth he wakes fierce flames,
Recalls to wearied age its long cooled heat,
Inflames with unaccustomed fires the hearts
Of virgins, and compels the gods to leave
Their heaven and in disguise to dwell on earth.
Phœbus Apollo shepherded the sheep
Of Thessaly and put aside his lyre

And called the bulls with unaccustomed pipe.
How often has he taken milder forms,
Who moves the sky and clouds: once, like a bird,
White wings he moved, and with a sweeter voice
Than dying swan he sang; then with fierce front,
A wanton bull, he took upon his back
The sportive maid, like slow oars moved his hoofs,
Breasted the deep, and through his brother's waves,
An unaccustomed realm, he took his way,
Made timid by the plunder rich he bore.
The shining goddess of the dark world burned
With love, forsook the night, her bright car gave
Into her brother's unfamiliar hand—
He learned to drive the chariot of the night
And turn a shorter circuit, while the wheels
Trembled beneath the heavier weight they bore;
Nor did the night retain its wonted length:
The day with tardy rising came to earth.
Alcmena's son, his quiver laid aside,
Put by the mighty lion's threatening spoil,
Suffered his fingers to be decked with gems,
Submitted to the comb his unkempt locks,
And bound his limbs about with shining gold,
While yellow sandals on his feet were tied,
And with the hand accustomed to the club
From the swift flying spindle drew the thread.
The Persians saw, saw too the men who dwell
In fertile Lydia's realm, the lion's skin
Put by, and on the shoulders that had borne
The skies the dainty Tyrian mantle laid.
Believe the wounded: sacred is love's fire
And all too potent. In whatever land
The deep surrounds, where'er the bright stars run
Their courses through the heavens, the cruel boy
There reigns: the Nereid's king has felt his dart
Within the depths of ocean, and the flame
No waters could extinguish; his hot fires
The winged ones knew well; the bull with love
Instinct will boldly for the whole herd war;

The timid stags will fight, if for their does
They fear; the swarthy Indian trembles then
At sight of the striped tiger; the fierce bear
Makes sharp his wounding tusks and all his mouth
Is foam; the Carthaginian lion then
Tosses his mane and gives a dreadful roar,
The sign of love conceived. When love compels,
The forests echo with the murmur harsh.
The monsters in the restless sea feel love
And the Lucanian bull; unto himself
Love arrogates all natures, nought is free,
And hatred perishes at Love's command;
Old angers are by passion's fires quelled.
What can I further say—love overcomes
The cruel stepdame!

ACT TWO: SCENE I

PHÆDRA, NURSE, CHORUS.

CHORUS: Say, nurse, what news thou bear'st; how does the
    queen?
How burn the cruel fires?
NURSE: No hope can soothe
Such troubles, and the fires can know no end;
Smothered, they still in secret grow more hot,
Conceal it how she will, her face betrays
Her passion; from her eyes the fire breaks forth,
Her pale cheeks hate the light, her troubled soul
Is pleased with nothing, and uncertain grief
Drives her from place to place. She totters now
With weak steps, and she seems about to die:
Scarce can her neck sustain her drooping head;
Now to repose she turns, but, sleep forgot,
In sad laments she wears away the night;
She bids me lay her down, then raise her up,
To loose her hair, to bind it up again;
Her dress she changes, ever with herself
Impatient. Not for food or health she cares;

Her strength is failing, with uncertain steps
She moves; no more her shining face is tinged
With health's rich red; her eyes, which used to show
Some sparks of Phœbus' torch, no longer shine
With light which proves her race and native land;
Her tears flow ever and with constant dew
Keep moist her cheeks, as when from Taurus' top
The melted snows flow down in warm, full streams.
    But see, the palace opens; she herself,
Reclining on her golden couch, rejects,
In her insanity, her wonted robe.
    PHÆDRA: The garments wrought of gold and purple, slaves,
Remove; bring not the red of tyrian conch,
The web the distant Eastern peoples weave
From fiber of the trees; my flowing robe—
Upgathered—let a girdle bind; take off
The necklace from my neck; the pearls, rich gift
Of Indian seas, shall not adorn my ears;
Free from Assyrian odors, let my hair
Hang loose; at random thus about my neck
And shoulders shall my unbound locks flow free,
And as I fly shall by the winds be blown;
The quiver in my left hand, in my right
The sharp Thessalian spear. Like her who left
The frozen seas and with her maiden hosts
From Tanais and Mæotis touched the soil
Of Athens—with loose hair and crescent shield
She came, in guise like hers I seek the woods.
    CHORUS: Cease thy laments: complaints will not avail
Thy sorrow; to the goddess of the woods,
The guardian god of virgins, make thy prayer.
    NURSE: Queen of the groves, who on the mountain tops
Lovest to dwell alone, we pray thee turn
To better omens thy unkindly threats.
O mighty goddess of the woods and vales,
Bright star of heaven, glory of the night,
Who with alternate shining dost relume
The world, O triformed Hecate, favoring shine
On this attempt; sway thou th' unbending mind

Of stern Hippolytus, that he may lend
A willing ear; Oh, soften his hard heart,
Teach him to love; Oh, charm his savage breast
To feel responsive fires, to Venus' laws
Submit his savage, harsh, and hostile soul.
Exert thy power; come thus with shining face,
Ride through the rifted clouds with crescent bright,
Be no Thessalian incantation strong
To draw thee from the starry sky of night
Through which thou ridest: let no shepheard take
Glory from thee. O goddess now invoked,
Be present, look with favor on our prayers.
Himself I see, who worships only thee;
Alone he comes. Why hesitate? Chance gives
Both time and place. Arts now must be employed.
Why do I fear? It is not light to dare
Crime's mandate. He who fears a queen's commands
Must banish thought of honor from his breast;
Poor servant of the royal will, indeed,
Is loyalty to duty.

ACT TWO: SCENE 2

HIPPOLYTUS, NURSE.

HIPPOLYTUS: O faithful nurse, why hither dost thou toil,
With aged, wearied steps; why bearest thou
This troubled face, this set and anxious brow?
Safe is my father, surely? Phædra safe?
Safe the two well-loved pledges of their love?
    NURSE: Put by thy fears; most prosperous is the realm,
By happy fortune blessed, thy family thrives.
But live thou gladlier in this fair estate,
For anxious am I in my care for thee,
Because thou dost so harshly rule thyself.
He may be pardoned who, by fate compelled,
Is wretched, but if any uncompelled
Gives himself up to trouble willingly,
Tortures himself—who knows not how to use

The goods of fortune well may forfeit them.
Rather be mindful of thy years, give rein
To thy free spirit, lift on high thy torch
On festal nights, let Bacchus lighten care;
Enjoy thy youth, it flies with nimble feet.
Thy bosom now is free, love smiles on youth,
Oh, let thy heart be glad; why dost thou keep
A widowed couch? Make cheerful thy sad youth,
Make haste, let loose the reins, life's richest days
Allow not to flow from thee unenjoyed.
God for each age provides its office fit,
And leads from step to step; a happy brow
Befits the young, austerity the old.
Why keep thyself in check and strangle thus
Thy rightful nature? To the husbandman
That grain gives increase that with pliant stem
Runs riot in the joyous fields, the tree
Cut or restrained by no unfriendly hand
Rises above the grove with lofty top;
So upright natures will the better gain
True glory, if unhampered liberty
Nourish the noble soul. Why dost thou pass
An austere youth, fair Venus all forgot,
Inhabiting the woods, fierce, ignorant
Of life? Dost deem this part alone to be
Assigned to men: that they should hardships bear,
Should learn in the swift race to drive the horse,
And wage, with streaming blood, most savage wars?
What various modes of death drag mortals down
And sweep away the throngs of men! the sea,
The sword, and treachery! But shouldst thou deem
That thou art safe from these—of our own will
We seek black Styx before our time when youth
Would pass its life in barren singleness.
These peoples that thou seest will endure
But one age, in themselves will come to nought.
The first great parent of the world took care,
When ravenous thus he saw the hand of fate,
That ever a new offspring should replace

The lost. Should Venus, who renews again
The race destroyed, withdraw from man's affairs,
The world were dark indeed, the sea would lie
Bereft of fish, the air would have no birds,
The woods no beasts, and all the ether be
A path for sun and winds alone. Make haste
To follow nature, the true lord of life;
Frequent the city, live among thy kind.
    HIPPOLYTUS: No other life there is more free from fault,
More full of liberty, which better keeps
The ancient customs, than the life of one
Who loves the woods and leaves the city walls;
No passion of the sordid soul inflames
Him who to mountain tops commits himself
Unstained; no voice of popular applause,
No common peoples false to honor's claims,
No deadly envy, no inconstant fame.
He serves no realm, nor, striving for a throne,
Pursues vain honor, perishable wealth;
Free both from fear and hope, black hungry spite
Attacks him not with his vile tooth, the crimes
Nourished among the folk who dwell in towns
He does not know, nor does he shrink afraid
At every sound, nor coin false words, nor seek
A home with columns numberless made rich,
Nor proudly hide his rafters 'neath much gold;
Blood in abundance does not overflow
His pious altars, nor a hundred bulls,
Sprinkled with sacred meal, their white necks bow
Beneath the sacrificial knife for him.
His are the lonely fields, and innocent
He roams beneath the open sky, he knows
Only to build the cunning trap for beasts,
When worn with labor, in Ilissus' stream
He finds refreshment; now he skirts the banks
Of swift Alphæus, now through thickets dense
Of the high groves he presses where flows down
Through silent ways, with pure and shining shoals,
Cold Lerna's stream, and where the querulous birds

Murmur, whence softly smitten by the winds
The mountain ash trees and the ancient beech
Tremble. He loves to lie upon the banks
Of winding rivers, or upon the sod
To find sweet sleep, whether abundant streams
Pour down swift floods or through fresh flowers flows
The slender brook and murmurs a sweet song.
Fruit gathered from the woods supplies his food,
And berries gathered from the thickets quench
His thirst. I wish not royal luxuries;
The proud man drinks from golden cup, the cause
Of anxious care; how sweet it is to drink
From hollowed hand the water of the spring!
A surer rest refreshes him who rests
On his hard bed secure: he does not seek,
Shameless, in secret corners, in the dark,
Intrigues, nor does he, fearful, hide himself
In hidden dwellings: but the light and air
He seeks; with heaven for his witness lives;
Lives like the men of old who with the gods
Mingled. No blind desire for gold was theirs,
No judge with boundary stones set off their lands,
Not yet were vessels, rashly confident,
Sailing the deep; only his own home seas
Each knew. They did not build about their towns
Vast walls and frequent towers, the warrior then
Knew not to use stern weapons, nor to break
Closed gates with warlike engines armed with stones;
Earth knew no master, nor was made a slave
To the yoked oxen, but the fields untilled
Brought forth their fruit, nor feared mankind's demands,
The woods gave natural wealth, the shadowy caves
Natural homes. Unholy thirst for gain,
And headlong wrath, and lust which fires the heart
Broke first this order; fierce desire to rule
Arose, the greater preyed upon the less,
And might made right. Man then with naked hands
Fought, and to weapons turned the stones and trees,
He was not armed with the light cornel spear

Pointed with iron, nor the sharp-edged sword,
Nor crested helmet; anger made such arms.
New arts by warlike Mars were learned, new ways
To kill, and blood polluted every land,
The sea was red with blood. Then everywhere
Was crime forever found, no evil deed
Was left untried; brother by brother's hand,
Parent by son's, was slain, the husband fell
By the wife's sword, and impious mothers killed
Their children. I pass over stepdame's wrath.
She is nowise less savage than the beasts.
But woman was the leader in all wrongs;
This bold artificer of crime beset
All hearts: so many cities are consumed,
So many peoples wage destructive war,
So many kingdoms ruined lie o'erthrown,
By reason of her vile adulteries.
Of others I am silent—Ægeus' wife
Medea shows how savage women are.
    NURSE: Why make all guilty of the crimes of one?
    HIPPOLYTUS: I hate, I fear, I loathe, I flee from all.
Say it is reason, nature, passions wild,
It pleases me to hate; sooner shall join
Water and flame, and vessels sooner find
In the uncertain Syrtes friendly depths,
Sooner from farthest confines of the west
Shall Tethys bring the day, and to the lambs
Shall wolves prove kindly, than I, overcome,
Turn friendly looks on woman.
    NURSE: Love has oft
About the stubborn cast his charms, and changed
Their hate to love. Look at thy mother's realm,
The Amazons felt Venus' yoke, thou prov'st
This truth—one son of Amazonian blood.
    HIPPOLYTUS: For mother lost, one consolation's mine—
I may hate womankind.
    NURSE: As cliffs resist
The waves, invincible on every side,
And hurl far back the waters that assail,

He spurns my words. But see, where Phædra comes
With headlong steps, impatient of delay.
Where leads her passion? What will fortune give?
Lifeless she falls; the color, as in death,
Deserts her face. O nursling, lift thy head,
Speak, see, Hippolytus embraces thee.

ACT TWO: SCENE 3

HIPPOLYTUS, PHÆDRA, NURSE.

PHÆDRA: Who gives me back my sorrow, brings again
My passion's heavy weight upon my soul?
How gladly would I put an end to life!
  HIPPOLYTUS: Why wish to flee the gift of life restored?
  PHÆDRA: Be bold, my soul, accomplish now thy will.
Though scorned, speak fearless words; who asks in fear
Teaches denial. Of my sin great part
Is done: it is too late for modesty;
I have loved basely. If I follow up
This my attempt, perchance the marriage torch
May hide my crime; success makes certain sins
Respectable. Lo, now begin, my soul!
I pray a little nearer bend thine ear,
Lest any of thy comrades should be nigh.
  HIPPOLYTUS: The place is free from any witnesses.
  PHÆDRA: My lips refuse a passage to my words:
'Tis a great pow'r that urges me to speak,
A greater holds me silent. O ye gods,
I call on you to witness: what I wish——
  HIPPOLYTUS: And one who wishes something cannot speak?
  PHÆDRA: Light cares find words, but heavy ones are dumb.
  HIPPOLYTUS: Mother, commit thy cares to me.
  PHÆDRA: The name
Of mother is an honorable name,
And all too powerful; a humbler one
Befits our love. Call me, Hippolytus,
Sister or slave, slave rather; I will bear
All servitude. If thou shouldst bid me go

Through deepest snows, Mount Pindus' frozen top
Would give me no annoy, or if through fire
And hostile battle lines, I would not shrink
From giving to the ready sword my breast.
Take back the scepter to my charge consigned,
Receive me as thy slave; it is not meet
A realm of cities by a woman's hand
Should be defended. Thou who flourishest
In the first bloom of youth, thy father's realm
Govern, O take thy suppliant to thy breast,
Pity the widow and protect the slave.

HIPPOLYTUS: This omen may the sovereign gods avert!
My father presently will come again.

PHÆDRA: The ruler of the realm whence none return
And of the silent Styx has made no way
Back to the upper air. Will he send back
The violator of his marriage couch?
Unless, perchance, now merciful to love,
He, too, inactive sits.

HIPPOLYTUS: The upright gods
Will truly give him back to earth. But while
God holds our wish ungranted, I will shield,
With duteous love, my brothers; care for thee
So that thou'lt no more feel thyself bereft
Of husband. I myself will fill for thee
My father's place.

PHÆDRA: O lover's trusting hope!
Deceitful love! Have I not said enough!
With prayers I will assail him. Pity me,
Hear my unspoken prayers; I long to speak,
Yet dare not.

HIPPOLYTUS: What is this that troubles thee?

PHÆDRA: What thou wouldst hardly think could overtake
A stepdame.

HIPPOLYTUS: Doubtful words thou utterest:
Speak openly.

PHÆDRA: My heart is all aflame
With love and madness, fiercest fires burn hot
Within my vitals, hidden in my veins,

As o'er the lofty roof the swift flame plays.

   HIPPOLYTUS: With wifely love for Theseus dost thou rage?

   PHÆDRA: Hippolytus, 'tis so: I love the form,
The face that Theseus in his boyhood bore,
When first his cheeks were darkened by a beard,
And he beheld the winding labyrinth
Where dwelt the Theban monster; by a thread
He found his path. How glorious was he then!
A fillet bound his locks, a modest blush
Reddened his tender cheeks, on his soft arms
Were iron muscles. Thy Diana's face,
Or my Apollo's had he, or thine own!
Lo! such he was when he made glad his foe,
Thus proudly did he hold his head; in thee
Shines forth his manly beauty unadorned
But greater; all thy father is in thee,
And yet some part of thy stern mother's look,
A Scythian sternness on thy Grecian face.
If thou with him had crossed the Cretan straits,
For thee my sister would have loosed the thread.
O sister, in whatever part of heaven
Thou shinest, I invoke thee in a cause
Both thine and mine; one house has snatched away
Two sisters, thee the father, me the son.
Lo! fallen at thy feet a suppliant lies,
Child of a kingly race. Unstained I was,
Pure, innocent—'tis thou hast wrought this change.
See, to entreaty I have sunk: this day
Must either end my sorrow or my life.
Have pity on my love.

   HIPPOLYTUS: O king of gods,
Dost thou so mildly hear, so mildly see
Such baseness? When will fly the thunderbolt
Sent from thy hand, if thou art now unmoved?
Oh! Let the firmament be rent apart,
The daylight be by sable clouds concealed,
The backward driven stars be turned aside
To run inverted courses. Thou bright sun,
Chief of the stars, canst thou behold the crimes

Of this thy offspring? Let thy light depart!
Fly to the shades! Ruler of gods and men,
Why is thy right hand idle, hurling not
Thy triple thunderbolt against the world?
Thunder upon me, pierce me with thy bolt,
And swiftly burn me with thy smiting fires.
Guilty I am, I have deserved to die,
For I have pleased my stepdame. Lo, was I
Worthy of incest deemed? Did I alone
Seem to thee facile subject for thy crimes?
Is this what my austerity deserved?
O thou in crime surpassing all thy kind,
More wicked than thy mother thou art found!
She stained herself with lust most infamous,
And though her crime was long a secret held,
The two-formed offspring brought at last to light
The mother's guilt—the child's ambiguous form
Betrayed her crime—of that womb thou art born.
O thrice, O four times happy call I those
Destroyed and given to a violent death,
By stepdame's hate and treachery o'ercome.
Father, I envy thee! This scourge is worse,
Worse than thy Colchian stepdame.

  PHÆDRA: I also recognize our family's fate,—
Fleeing we find it; yet I o'er myself
No more have power; I'll madly follow thee,
Through flames and seas, through rocks and raging streams;
Where'er thou turnst thy steps my love drives me.
Again, O proud one, at thy feet I fall.

  HIPPOLYTUS: Withdraw from my chaste body thy foul touch.
Ha, what is this? She falls upon my breast!
The sword shall slay her, she shall meet just death.
See, I bend backward by the twisted hair
With my left hand her shameless head; ne'er fell
Upon thy altars, goddess of the bow,
Blood shed in better cause.

  PHÆDRA: Thou giv'st me now
My wish, Hippolytus. Thou mak'st me sane.
Better is this than aught that I could wish.

I'm saved, with honor by thy hand I die!

HIPPOLYTUS: Live, yet go hence lest somehow, by thy prayers,
Thou shouldst avail—and let this sword, defiled
By thee, my chaste side leave. Could Tanais' stream,
Or the Mæotis, or the Euxine sea,
Cleanse me—e'en Neptune could not wash away,
With all the waters of the mighty deep,
So great impurity. O wilderness!
O forests!

ACT TWO: SCENE 4

PHÆDRA, NURSE.

NURSE: The fault is known; why rest inactive? Up,
Throw back on him the blame; sin must be hid
By sin. The safest way for one in fear
Is to attack. Since no one saw the crime,
Who shall be witness whether we first dared
Or suffered ill? Athenian women, haste!
Help, faithful band of slaves; Hippolytus,
The ravisher, pursues, attacks the queen;
He threatens death, and with the sword attacks
That virtuous one. Lo, headlong has he fled,
Affrighted, in his hasty flight has left
His sword; we hold the token of his crime.
First bring again to life the fainting form:
Leave as they are torn and loosened locks,
Proofs of the crime attempted; bear her forth
Into the city. Mistress, take thou heart;
Why shouldst thou wound thyself and shun all eyes?
Unchastity lies not in chance but thought.

ACT TWO: SCENE 5

CHORUS.

As swiftly as the hurricane he fled,
More swiftly than the hurricane that drives

The clouds before it, swifter than swift flame
That burns when meteors, driven by the winds,
Send forth long fires. On thee, Hippolytus,
Shall fame confer all beauty that aroused,
In ages past, man's wonder; lovelier shines
Thy form than, when her crescent orbs have poured
Their fires, Diana moves with glowing face
All night, full-orbed, in her swift car through heaven,
And lesser stars no longer show their face.
So Hesperus, the messenger of night,
At twilight shines, fresh bathed in ocean's waves;
So Lucifer drives darkness into flight.
Thou Thyrsus-bearing Liber, Indian born,
Whose unshorn locks shine with immortal youth,
Who fightest tigers with thy vineclad staff,
Who bindest with broad bands thy horned head,
Thou art not fairer than Hippolytus;
Nor shouldst thou think too highly of thy form,
For fame has blazoned through all lands his fame
Whom Phædra's sister did to Bromius
Prefer.
O beauty, doubtful gift to mortals given,
A fleeting good that but a moment stays,
With what swift feet thou flyest. Not so soon,
When noon glows hot and night a brief course runs,
Does burning summer's breath deprive the fields
Of all the comeliness of early spring.
As the pale flowers of the lily fall,
So falls the hair, the glory of the head;
The glow which brightens on the tender cheek
Is in a moment gone, and one day spoils
The body's grace. A transitory thing
Is beauty: who may in so frail a good
With wisdom trust? Oh! use it while thou mayst;
Time silently destroys thee, and each hour
Is worse than that which just has passed away.
Why shouldst thou seek the desert's loneliness
Beauty is no more safe in pathless ways.
Thee will the saucy bands of wanton nymphs,

Accustomed to imprison lovely youths
In streams, surround at midday in the wood;
And dryads, who upon the mountain tops
Follow some Pan, will in thy sleep assail;
Or from the starry heavens, beholding thee,
The moon, less old than old Arcadian folk,
Will lose her power to drive her shining car.
Lately she blushed, no sordid cloud obscured
Her shining face; but by her angry light
Disturbed, and fearing dark Thessalian charms,
We offered prayers—thou wast her trouble's cause,
And thou the cause of her unwonted stay;
Because the goddess of the night saw thee,
She checked her rapid course.
Did bitter winds blow less upon thy face,
Didst thou less oft expose it to the sun,
Whiter than Parian marble would it shine.
How pleasant is thine austere, manly face,
The sternness of thy brow! that glorious neck
Thou mayst with bright Apollo's well compare,
His hair about his shoulders flowing free,
Knowing no bond, adorns and covers him,
Thy hirsute front, thy shorter, uncombed locks,
Become thee. Thou mayst with the gods contend
In battles stern and conquer by thy strength,
For equal is thy strength with Hercules',
Broader thy breast than that of warlike Mars.
If it had pleased thee on a horse to ride,
Thou couldst have reined the Spartan Cyllarus
More easily than Castor. With thy hand
Make tense the bowstring, and with all thy strength
Direct the shaft: the Cretan, apt to learn
The art of shooting, not so far could send
The slender arrow; if in Parthian wise
Thou shootest skyward, not a dart descends
Without a bird; within the warm breast hid
It brings its prey from out the very clouds.
Seldom has man been beautiful and safe:
Look at the ages. May a kindlier god

Leave thee in safety, and thy beauty gain
The aspect of unbeautiful old age!
What will a woman's passion leave undared?
She plots 'gainst youth and innocence base crime.
Behold the sinner! she would find belief
By her torn locks, the glory of her hair
Is all dishevelled, and her cheeks are wet;
Her woman's cunning doth devise all frauds.
But who is this that comes with kingly form,
And lofty bearing? To Pirithous
How like his face, were not his cheeks so pale,
His unkept hair so rough about his brow.
Ah! Theseus comes, returned again to earth!

ACT THREE: SCENE I

THESEUS, NURSE.

  THESEUS: I have at last escaped the land where reigns,
Eternal darkness, where night holds the dead
In its vast prison. Hardly can my eyes
Endure the brightness of the hoped-for day.
Four times the plow, gift of Triptolemus,
Has cut Eleusis' soil, four times the Scales
Have measured day the equal of the night,
Since first the doubtful toils of unknown fate
Have led me twixt the ills of life and death—
To me, though dead, a part of life remained,
The sense of ills. Alcides was their end.
He when he carried off from Tartarus
Th' unwilling dog, brought me as well to earth.
My wearied body lacks its ancient strength,
My footsteps tremble—ah! how hard the task
It was to seek the far-off upper air
From lowest Phlegethon, to flee from death
And follow Hercules.
                    What sound is this
Of lamentation strikes upon my ears?
Ah, some one, tell me! Grief, and tears, and woe,

And sad lament, e'en at my very door
Assail me; truly, worthy auspices
For one who as a guest from Hades comes.

NURSE: Phædra maintains her firm resolve to die,
She spurns our prayers, and is resolved on death.

THESEUS: What cause is there for death? Why should she die,
Her husband come again to life?

NURSE: E'en this
Hastens her death.

THESEUS: I know not what may mean
The riddle of thy words. Speak openly.
What heavy sorrow weighs upon her mind?

NURSE: To none she tells it, she conceals her woe,
Determined that her ills shall die with her.
But haste, I pray thee, haste, for there is need.

THESEUS: Unbar the portals of my royal house.

ACT THREE: SCENE 2

PHÆDRA, NURSE, THESEUS.

THESEUS: O wife, dost welcome thus my late return?
Dost thus behold thy husband's longed-for face?
Let go the sword and take me to thy breast,
Tell me what makes thee seek to flee from life.

PHÆDRA: Alas, great Theseus, by thy scepter's might,
And by the inborn nature of thy sons,
And by thy coming from the shades again,
Yes, by thy ashes, suffer me to die.

THESEUS: What reason urges thee to die?

PHÆDRA: The fruit
Of death would perish if its cause were known.

THESEUS: None other than myself shall hear the cause.

PHÆDRA: A virtuous wife dreads but her husband's thoughts.

THESEUS: Speak, hide thy secret in my faithful breast.

PHÆDRA: That which thou wouldst not have another tell,
Tell not thyself.

THESEUS: Death shall not have the power
To touch thee.

PHÆDRA: Death can never fail to come
To him who wills it.
THESEUS: Tell me what the fault
Thou must by death atone.
PHÆDRA: The fault of life.
THESEUS: And art thou not affected by my tears?
PHÆDRA: The sweetest death is one by loved ones mourned.
THESEUS: Thou wilt keep silence? Then with blows and chains
Thy aged nurse shall be compelled to speak
What thou wouldst not. Now cast her into chains,
Let blows drag forth the secrets of her mind.
PHÆDRA: Cease, I myself will speak.
THESEUS: Why turn away
Thy mournful face, why cover with thy robe
The tears that wet so suddenly thy cheek?
PHÆDRA: O father of the gods, on thee I call
To witness, and on thee, bright light of heaven,
From whom our family springs; I strove to stand
Against his prayers, my spirit did not yield
Either to threats or steel. Yet to his force
My body yielded; this the stain my blood
Must wash away.
THESUS: Who was it, tell me who
Thus stained our honor?
PHÆDRA: Him thou least suspectest.
THESEUS: I earnestly entreat thee, tell me who.
PHÆDRA: The sword will tell thee, that th' adulterer left,
When by approaching tumult terrified,
He feared the gathering of the citizens.
THESEUS: Alas, what crime is this which I behold?
What awful thing is this I look upon?
The royal hilt of ivory, carved and bright,
The glory of Actæon's race! But he—
Where has he fled?
PHÆDRA: His fear and hasty flight
These slaves beheld.
THESEUS: O holy piety!
O ruler of the sky, and thou who holdest
The kingdom of the waters! Whence has come

This foul infection of my sinning son?
Did Greek soil nourish him, or was he reared
On Scythian Taurus, and by Colchis' stream?
The child repeats the father, and base blood
Bespeaks its primal source. This passion comes
From that armed race that hated ties of love
And, too long chaste, made common to the crowd
Their bodies. O vile people, to no laws
Of milder climes obedient! Even beasts
Shun sins of love and with unconscious awe
Obey the laws of nature. Where that face,
That feigned majesty and manner stern,
That seeking after old austerity,
That sad affected gravity of age?
O treacherous life, thou carriest hidden thoughts,
And hidest with fair form a sinful soul;
A modest bearing covers shamelessness,
Gentleness boldness, seeming goodness crime;
The false looks true, and harshness tender seems.
O dweller in the woods, wild, virgin, chaste,
Unconquered, hast thou kept thyself for me?
Wilt thou first try thy manhood with such crime,
In my own bed? Now to the gods above
Be praises that Antiope has fallen,
Struck by my hand; that when I sought the Styx
Thy mother was not left behind for thee.
O fugitive, seek unknown climes afar,
By ocean's plains shut off in earth's last bounds,
Be hid within the region 'neath our feet.
Shouldst thou have crossed the realms of bitter cold,
And deep within its farthest nook be lost,
Or, placed beyond hoar frost and winter snows,
Have left behind cold Boreas' bitter threats,
Thou yet shalt pay the penalty for crime;
Undaunted, fast upon thy flying steps,
Through every lurking place I'll follow thee.
Long, diverse, difficult, and pathless ways,
Aye, ways impossible shall we pass through;
Nothing shall hinder. Whence I have returned

Thou knowest. Whither arrows cannot go
I'll send my curse. Neptune has promised me
Three wishes by his favor gratified,
And has confirmed his promise with an oath
Sworn by the river Styx. My stern desire
Perform, O ruler of the restless seas!
Let not Hippolytus behold again
The day's fair light, but let the youth go down
Among the wrathful spirits of the dead—
Wrathful because of me. O father, bring
Thy son thy dreaded aid—I had not asked
Of thy divinity this gift supreme
But that such heavy evil pressed me sore.
Even within the depths of Tartarus,
Dread realm of Dis, and threatened by the wrath
Of the infernal king, I still withheld
This wish. Fulfil thy promise. Why delay?
Why, father, are thy waters silent still?
Black clouds with driving wind should hide the sky,
Snatch from the heavens the stars, upheave the deep,
Arouse the monsters of the sea, call forth
The swelling floods from Ocean's farthest bounds!

ACT THREE: SCENE 3

CHORUS.

O nature, mighty mother of the gods,
And thou of fiery Olympus king,
Who speedest through the flying firmament
The scattered constellations, and the stars'
Uncertain courses, and the heavens that turn
So swiftly, why continue with such care
To keep the pathway of the airy heights
That in its season winter's cold and snow
Lay bare the forests, that the leafy shade
Returns, that summer's constellation shines
And ripens with its fervid heat the grain,
That milder autumn comes? But since thou rul'st.

Since by thy power alone the balance weight
Of the vast universe revolves, why, then,
No longer careful of the race of men,
Careless to punish evil or reward
The good, dost thou desert Hippolytus?
Fortune by ways unordered rules man's life;
The worse she cherishes, and blindly flings
Her gifts, and base desire conquers law,
And fraud is king within the palace walls,
The populace rejoice to give the base
High office and to hate the very man
Whom they should honor. Rigid virtue finds
The recompense of evil, poverty
Follows the pure in heart, and strong in crime
Th' adulterer reigns. O reputation vain!
O empty honor! But with headlong steps
Why comes the messenger with tear-wet cheeks!

ACT FOUR: SCENE I

THESEUS, MESSENGER.

MESSENGER: O hard and bitter lot, grim servitude!
Why am I called by fate to bring such news?
THESEUS: Be brave to speak, e'en of the bitterest woes.
I have a heart not unprepared for grief.
MESSENGER: Alas, alas, Hippolytus is dead!
THESEUS: The father knew long since his son was dead.
Now dies the ravisher, but tell me how?
MESSENGER: When he, a fugitive, with troubled steps,
Had left the city, taking his swift course
With flying feet, he quickly yoked his steeds,
With bit and bridle curbed them; with himself
Revolving many things, he cursed his land
And oft invoked his father. With loose rein
He shook his lash, impetuous. Suddenly
The depths of ocean thundered, and its waves
Smote on the stars; no wind blew on the sea;
And nowhere were the quiet heavens stirred,

The tempest moved the placid deep alone.
No south wind e'er blew up Sicilia's straits
Like this, nor did the wild Ionian sea
E'er rise before the northwest wind like this,
When cliffs shake with the beating of the waves,
And the foam flashes white on Leucas' top.
The great deep rose in billows mountain high,
But not for ships was this disaster planned,
The earth was threatened; not with gentle roll
The waves swept onward, some strange thing the surge
Bore on its burdened bosom. What new world
Slowly upheaves its head? What island new
Rises among the Cyclades? While thus
Questioning we gazed, the whole wide ocean roared,
The cliffs on every side sent back the sound;
His head all dripping with the driving spray,
Belching the flood from out his cavernous jaws,
Foaming and vomiting the waters forth,
Through the great straits was dragged a monster vast;
The mound of waters, smitten, sank amazed,
Opened, and on the shores spewed out a beast
Most terrible. The deep with landward rush
Followed the monster—at the thought I quake!
Ah, that huge body, what a form it had!
A great bull with blue neck, it lifted up
On a green brow a lofty crest, its ears
Were shaggy, and of changing hue its eyes;
Such form the wild herd's lord on earth might have,
Or bull of ocean born. Its eyes shot flame,
Wondrously with the ocean blue they shone;
A thick mane grew upon its brawny neck,
With every breath it snorted; breast and throat
Were green with clinging moss, its monster sides
Were dotted with red lichens; backward thence
It showed a monstrous form, a scaly fish,
Vast, horrible, dragging huge length along;
Such are the fish that in the outer seas
Swallow swift ships or wreck them. The land shook,
The frightened herds fled madly through the fields,

The shepherd was not mindful of the lambs,
The wild beasts in the wooded pastures fled,
The huntsmen stood alarmed and faint with fear.
Hippolytus, alone untouched by fear,
With tight rein curbed his horses, checked their flight,
And with his well-known voice encouraged them.
A pathway wide bends through the parted hills
Into the fields, along the ocean strand;
That mound of flesh there armed him for the fight,
Lashed up his rage, and having taken heart
And stretched himself, he then essayed his strength;
He sped along, scarce touching in his flight
The surface of the ground, and stayed his course
Before the frightened horses. With fierce look
Thy son arose to meet its menaces,
Nor was he silent; with loud voice he cried:
"My courage is not mastered by this threat,
To conquer bulls has been my family's task."
The horses, disobedient to the rein
And turning from the way, dragged off the car;
Where'er blind terror drove them there they went;
They fled among the rocks, but he, thy son,
Guided the chariot as the pilot guides
His vessel in a storm, nor lets it turn
Aslant the wave, and by his skill escapes.
Now with tight rein he pulled upon the bit;
Now with the twisted lash he smote the steeds.
The fish, a constant comrade, followed him,
Devouring now the ground with equal pace,
Now lying in the way the car was turned,
And causing greatest fear on every side.
Nor farther was it possible to flee,
For the great horned monster of the deep
Lying in wait with open mouth assailed.
Then the excited horses, mad with fear,
Freed themselves from the guidance of the rein
And rearing struggled from the yoke to tear
Themselves. They hurled their burden to the ground,

Headlong he fell, entangled in the lines;
The more he fought against the tightening noose,
The more its knots were strengthened. What they'd done
The frightened horses felt, and, driverless,
Where fear impelled they rushed with the light car.
So through the air the horses of the sun,
Not recognizing their accustomed load
And angry that a false god brought the day,
Upon their devious course hurled Phaethon forth!
The field was red with blood, his wounded head
Rebounded from the cliffs, the brambles tore
His hair, hard rocks destroyed his lovely face,
His illstarred beauty marred by many wounds
Perished. Upon the wheels his dying limbs
Were whirled about; pierced through the midst at last
By a burnt stake, upon its point was fixed
His trunk, the car was stayed a little while
Held fast by its prone driver, and the steeds
At the disaster stayed their hasty course,
Then broke through all delays and tore away
Their master. Brambles cut the lifeless form,
Each stinging brier and sharp thorn took part
Of that torn trunk. The band of sorrowing slaves
Followed through all the field where, dragged along,
Hippolytus in bloody characters
Marked the long path, the howling dogs tracked out
Their master's members, but most loving care
Could not find all. Is this his noble form?
Illustrious sharer of his father's throne,
And certain heir, who like a star in heaven
Shone bright, he now was gathered from all sides
For the last honors, for his funeral pyre
Was brought together from the plain.
   THESEUS: O nature, all too potent, with what chains
Thou holdst the parent's heart! we cherish thee
Although against our will. I wished to slay
The guilty one and now I weep his loss.
   MESSENGER: What one has wished not always makes one glad.

THESEUS: This is, I think, the farthest reach of ill:
That chance should make me curse the thing I loved.
    MESSENGER: Why wet thy cheeks with tears for one thou hat'st?
THESEUS: Not that I lost but that I slew I weep.

ACT FOUR: SCENE 2

CHORUS.

How many chances rule the lot of man!
Fortune against the humble least is roused,
The god more lightly smites the little worth;
Obscurity finds peace and quietness,
The cottage offers undisturbed old age.
The pinnacles that tower toward the skies
Most feel the east wind and the south wind smite,
Endure the savage north wind's menaces,
The blowing of the rainy north-west wind;
The moist vale seldom feels the thunderbolt,
But lofty Caucasus, the Phrygian grove
Of mother Cybele, are often shaken
By thundering Jove's attack, for Jupiter,
Fearing their nearness to his heavenly heights,
Aims there his bolts. Beneath the humble roofs
Of lowly homes great tumults never come.
Fickle and restless is the hour's flight,
And faith with none does flying fortune keep.
Theseus, who left the gloomy shades of night,
And sees the starry skies, the sunny day,
Must sadly mourn his sorrowful return,
And find his native land more full of grief
Than dread Avernus.
Chaste Pallas, venerated by the Greeks,
Because thy Theseus sees the upper world
And has escaped the waters of the Styx,
Thou owest to thy robber uncle naught;
The tyrant finds hell's number still the same.
What voice from out the mourning palace sounds?
With weapon drawn why comes sad Phædra forth?

ACT FIVE: SCENE I

THESEUS, PHÆDRA.

THESEUS: What fury animates thee, and with grief?
Wherefore that sword, and why those sad laments?
Why beat thy bosom for such hated dead?
    PHÆDRA: Me, me, O cruel ruler of the seas,
Assail, and send the blue sea's awful shapes
To war on me—whate'er far Tethys bears
Within its inmost bosom, whatsoe'er
Ocean, embracing with its restless waves
The world, conceals within its farthest flood!
O Theseus, ever most unfeeling one,
Thou ne'er returnest safely to thy home.
Father and son must pay for thy return
By death; thou, ever guilty, dost destroy
Thy home with love or hate. Hippolytus,
Such as I made thee do I see thee now?
Did Sinis or Procrustes scatter thus
Thy members, or some savage Cretan bull,
Half man, half beast, refilling with its roar
The labyrinth of Dædalus, destroy
With its great horns? Oh! whither now is fled,
My star, the glory of thy brilliant eyes?
Dost thou lie lifeless? Come, one moment come,
And hear my words, 'tis nothing base I speak!
With my own hands I'll pay thee what I owe,
Into this sinful breast will thrust the sword,
Will by one deed take Phædra's life away,
And cleanse her from her sin, and follow thee
Madly through floods, through Tartarean lake,
Through Styx and fiery rivers. Let me die—
Let me placate the spirit of the dead:
Receive the lock of hair here cut for thee,
It was not lawful that our souls should wed,
But still, perchance, we may in fate be one.
Let me, if chaste, die for my husband's sake,

And if unchaste, die for the loved one's sake!
Shall I approach my husband's marriage bed
That am with such crime stained? This one sin lacked:
That I, as one unstained, should still enjoy
That bed as if it were my right. O death,
The only solace for the pains of love;
O death, last grace of injured chastity,
To thee I fly, take me to thy calm breast!
Hear me, Athena, let his father hear—
He than the cruel stepdame sterner found—
Falsely have I accused him of a crime
Which I myself in my mad heart conceived;
I spoke a lie. Thou, father, hast in vain
Sought punishment; of all incestuous crime
The youth is pure, unstained and innocent.
Recover now thy former spotless fame,
The sinful breast lies bare for justice' sword;
My blood is offered to a holy man.

(PHÆDRA *stabs herself with* HIPPOLYTUS' *sword and dies.*)

THESEUS: What thou should'st do,
O father, for thy son thus snatched away,
Learn from his stepdame. Seek the Acheron!
O jaws of pale Avernus and ye caves
Of Tænarus, ye waves of Lethe's stream
So welcome to the wretched, stagnant fens,
Hide ye the wretched one, with endless woes
O'erwhelm! Ye cruel monsters of the deep,
Great sea, and whatsoever Proteus hides
Within the farthest corner of his waves,
Be present now; into the whirling deeps
Drag me, so long rejoicing in such crimes.
O father, ever all too easily
Approving of my wrath, I am not meet
To suffer easy death—I who have strewn
My son's torn members in unheard-of ways
Through all the fields. Crime did I truly find
When, as the harsh avenger, I pursued

One falsely charged with crime. The seas and stars
And land of shadows by my crimes are filled;
No place remains, me the three kingdoms know.
Have I returned for this? Was upward way
Opened but that I might behold the dead,
That, widowed, childless, I might with the torch
Light the sad funeral pyres of wife and son?
Giver of light, Alcides, take thy gift
Back to the sable groves of shadowy Dis,
Restore me to the Manes whence I came.
Me miserable! Vainly I invoke
The death that I deserted. Bloody one,
Artificer of death, contrive thou now
And bring to light unheard-of means of death,
Inflict upon thyself just punishment.
Shall a great pine be bent until the top
Touches the earth, then, being freed again,
Upspringing, bear me with it to the stars?
Or shall I fling myself from Sciron's cliffs?
Yet heavier punishment than that I've seen,
Which Phlegethon compels the guilty souls
Prisoned within its circling waves of fire
To suffer: well I know the dwelling place,
The bitter penalties reserved for me.
Ye guilty souls give place and let the rock
That to the ancient son of Æolus
Gives ceaseless labor weigh these shoulders down,
Weary these hands; let rivers, flowing near
My thirsty lips, ever elude their touch.
Let the fierce vulture, leaving Tityus,
Hover about my liver and increase
My punishment. Mayst thou have rest at last,
Thou father of my friend Pirithous:
On the swift flying wheel that never stays
Its turning let my limbs be whirled about.
Earth, open! Dire chaos, take me back!
Take me! The pathway to the shades of hell
Is mine by better right; I follow him!
O thou who rul'st the spirits of the dead,

Fear not, for we who come to thee are chaste.
Receive me to thy everlasting home,
There will I stay. My prayers the gods hear not,
But had I asked their help in evil deeds,
How ready had they been!

   CHORUS: Eternity
Is thine, O Theseus, for lament; pay now
The honors due thy son, and quickly hide
In earth his scattered members so dispersed.

   THESEUS: O hither, hither bring the dear remains,
Give me the parts from many places brought.
Is this Hippolytus? The crime is mine,
'Twas I destroyed thee; and not I alone—
A father, daring crime, I called to aid
My father, I enjoy a father's gift!
How bitter is such loss to broken age!
Embrace whatever of thy son is left,
And clasp him to thy bosom, wretched one.

   CHORUS: O father, in their rightful order place
The mangled body's separated parts,
Restore the severed members to their place.
Lo, here the place the strong right hand should rest,
And here the left that learned to hold the reins;
I recognize the marks on his left side.
How great a part is absent from our tears!

   THESEUS: For this sad duty, trembling hands, be strong;
O cheeks be dry, and let abundant tears
Be stayed, the while I count my son's torn limbs,
And form his body. What is this I see,
Lacking in beauty, base, with many wounds?
What part of thee it may be I know not,
Yet part of thee it is. Here, here repose,
Not in thine own but in a vacant place.
Is this the face that like the bright stars shone?
His eyes that overcame his enemy?
Thus has his beauty fallen? Bitter fate!
O cruel kindness of the deity!
And is my son thus given back to me,
As I have wished? O son, in fragments borne

Forth to thy burial, from thy father take
These funeral rites; thee shall the fire burn.
Lay wide the house with dismal murder filled,
Let Mopsopia sound with loud lament.
Ye, to the royal funeral pyre bring flame,
And ye, seek out his body's scattered parts
Through all the fields. When she is buried,
(*turning to* PHÆDRA's *body*) Let earth lie heavy on her, let the soil
Weigh down her impious head!

SENECA

THE THYESTES

TRANSLATED BY ELLA ISABEL HARRIS

CHARACTERS IN THE PLAY

HIPPOLYTUS, *son of Theseus and Antiope, an Amazon*
PHÆDRA, *daughter of Minos, King of Crete, and wife of Theseus*
NURSE *of Phædra*
CHORUS *of Athenians*
THESEUS, *son of Neptune (or Aegeus), King of Athens and Troezen*
MESSENGER

THE THYESTES

(SCENE: *Before the palace of* ATREUS *at Mycenæ.*)

SPIRIT OF TANTALUS, MEGÆRA.

SPIRIT: Who drags me from my place among the shades,
Where with dry lips I seek the flying waves?
What hostile god again shows Tantalus
His hated palace? Has some worse thing come
Than thirst amid the waters or the pangs
Of ever-gnawing hunger? Must the stone,
The slippery burden borne by Sisyphus,
Weigh down my shoulders, or Ixion's wheel
Carry my limbs around in its swift course,
Or must I fear Tityus' punishment?
Stretched in a lofty cave he feeds dun birds
Upon his vitals which they tear away,
And night renews whatever day destroyed,
And thus he offers them full feast again.
Against what evil have I been reserved?
Stern judge of Hades, whosoe'er thou art
Who metest to the dead due penalties,
If something can be added more than pain,
Seek that at which the grim custodian
Of this dark prison must himself feel fear,
Something from which sad Acheron shall shrink,
Before whose horror I myself must fear;
For many sprung from me, who shall outsin
Their house, who, daring deeds undared by me,
Make me seem innocent, already come.

283

Whatever impious deed this realm may lack
My house will bring; while Pelops' line remains
Minos shall never be unoccupied.

MEGÆRA: Go, hated shade, and drive thy sin-stained home
To madness; let the sword try every crime,
And pass from hand to hand; nor let there be
Limit to rage and shame; let fury blind
Urge on their thoughts; let parents' hearts be hard
Through madness, long iniquity be heaped
Upon the children, let them never know
Leisure to hate old crimes, let new ones rise,
Many in one; let sin while punished grow;
From the proud brothers let the throne depart,
Then let it call the exiled home again.
Let the dark fortunes of a violent house
Among unstable kings be brought to naught.
Let evil fortune on the mighty fall,
The wretched come to power; let chance toss
The kingdom with an ever-changing tide
Where'er it will. Exiled because of crime,
When god would give them back their native land
Let them through crime reach home, and let them hate
Themselves as others hate them. Let them deem
No crime forbidden when their passions rage;
Let brother greatly fear his brother's hand,
Let parents fear their sons, and let the sons
Feel fear of parents, children wretched die,
More wretchedly be born; let wife rebel
Against her husband, wars pass over seas,
And every land be wet with blood poured forth;
Let lust, victorious, o'er great kings exult
And basest deeds be easy in thy house;
Let right and truth and justice be no more
'Twixt brothers. Let not heaven be immune—
Why shine the stars within the firmament
To be a source of beauty to the world?
Let night be different, day no more exist.
O'erthrow thy household gods, bring hatred, death,
Wild slaughter, with thy spirit fill the house,

Deck the high portals, let the gates be green
With laurel, fires for thy advent meet
Shall glow, crimes worse than Thracian shall be done.
Why idle lies the uncle's stern right hand?
Thyestes has not yet bewept his sons;
When will they be destroyed? Lo, even now
Upon the fire the brazen pot shall boil,
The members shall be broken into parts,
The father's hearth with children's blood be wet,
The feast shall be prepared. Thou wilt not come
Guest at a feast whose crime is new to thee:
Today we give thee freedom; satisfy
Thy hunger at those tables, end thy fast.
Blood mixed with wine shall in thy sight be drunk,
Food have I found that even thou wouldst shun.
Stay! Whither dost thou rush?

SPIRIT: To stagnant pools,
Rivers and waters ever slipping by,
To the fell trees that will not give me food.
Let me go hence to my dark prison-house,
Let me, if all too little seems my woe,
Seek other shores; within thy channels' midst
And by thy floods of fire hemmed about,
O Phlegethon, permit me to be left.
O ye who suffer by the fates' decree
Sharp penalties, O thou who, filled with fear,
Within the hallowed cave dost wait the fall
Of the impending mountain, thou who dreadst
The ravening lion's open jaws, the hand
Of cruel furies that encompass thee,
Thou who, half burned, dost feel their torch applied,
Hear ye the voice of Tantalus who knows:
Love ye your penalties! Ah, woe is me,
When shall I be allowed to flee to hell?

MEGÆRA: First into dread confusion throw thy house,
Bring with thee battle and the sword and love,
Strike thou the king's wild heart with frantic rage.

SPIRIT: 'Tis right that I should suffer punishment,
But not that I myself be punishment.

Like a death-dealing vapor must I go
Out of the riven earth, or like a plague
Most grievous to the people, or a pest
Widespread, I bring my children's children crime.
Great father of the gods, our father too—
However much our sonship cause thee shame—
Although my too loquacious tongue should pay
Due punishment for sin, yet will I speak:
Stain not, my kinsmen, holy hands with blood,
The altars with unholy sacrifice
Pollute not. I will stay and ward off crime.
(To MEGÆRA) Why dost thou terrify me with thy torch,
And fiercely threaten with thy writhing snakes?
Why dost thou stir the hunger in my reins?
My heart is burning with the fire of thirst,
My parched veins feel the flame.

MEGÆRA: Through all thy house
Scatter this fury; thus shall they, too, rage,
And, mad with anger, thirst by turns to drink
Each other's blood. Thy house thy coming feels
And trembles at thy execrable touch.
It is enough; depart to hell's dark caves
And to thy well-known river. Earth is sad
And burdened by thy presence. Backward forced,
Seest thou not the waters leave the streams,
How all the banks are dry, how fiery winds
Drive the few scattered clouds? The foliage pales,
And every branch is bare, the fruits are fled.
And where the Isthmus has been wont to sound
With the near waters, roaring on each side,
And cutting off the narrow strip of land,
Far from the shore is heard the sound remote.
Now Lerna's waters have been backward drawn,
Sacred Alpheus' stream is seen no more,
Cithæron's summit stands untouched with snow,
And Argos fears again its former thirst.
Lo, Titan's self is doubtful—shall he drive
His horses upward, bring again the day?
It will but rise to die.

ACT ONE: SCENE 2

CHORUS.

If any god still cherish love for Greece,
Argos, and Pisa for her chariots famed,
If any cherishes the Isthmian realm,
And the twin havens, and the parted seas,
If any love Taygetus' bright snows
That shine afar, which northern winter lays
Upon its highest summits and the breath
Of summer trade winds welcome to the sails
Melts, let him whom Alpheus' ice-cold stream
Touches, well known for his Olympic course,
Wield the calm influence of his heavenly power,
Nor suffer crimes in constant series come.
Let not a grandson, readier for that crime
E'en than his father's father, follow him,
Nor let the father's error please the sons.
Let thirsty Tantalus' base progeny,
Wearied at length, give up their fierce attempts;
Enough of crime! No more is right of worth,
And common wrongs of little moment seem;
The traitor Myrtilus betrayed his lord
And slew him—by such faith as he had shown
Himself dragged down, he gave the sea a name;
To ships on the Ægean never tale
Was better known. Met by the cruel sword,
Even while he ran to gain his father's kiss,
The little son was slain; he early fell
A victim to the hearth, by thy right hand,
O Tantalus, cut off that thou mightst spread
Such feasts before the gods. Eternal thirst
And endless famine followed on the feast;
Nor can a worthier punishment be found
For savage feast like that. With empty maw
Stands weary Tantalus, above his head
Hangs ready food, more swift to take its flight

Than Phineus' birds; on every side it hangs;
The tree beneath the burden of its fruit
Bending and trembling, shuns his open mouth;
He though so eager, brooking no delay,
Yet oft deceived, neglects to touch the tree,
And drops his head and presses close his lips,
And shuts his hunger in behind clenched teeth.
The ripe fruit taunts him from the languid boughs,
And whets his hunger till it urges him
To stretch again his hand oft stretched in vain.
Then the whole harvest of the bended boughs
Is lifted out of reach. Thirst rises then,
More hard to bear than hunger, when his blood
Is hot within him and his eyes aflame;
Wretched he stands striving to touch his lips
To the near waters, but the stream retreats,
Forsakes him when he strives to follow it,
And leaves him in dry sands; his eager lips
Drink but the dust.

ACT TWO: SCENE I

ATREUS, ATTENDANT.

ATREUS: O slothful, indolent, weak, unavenged
(This last I deem for tyrants greatest wrong
In great affairs), after so many crimes,
After thy brother's treachery to thee,
After the breaking of all laws of right,
Dost thou, O angry Atreus, waste the time
In idle lamentations? All the world
Should echo with the uproar of thy arms,
And either sea should bear thy ships of war;
The fields and cities should be bright with flame;
The flashing sword should everywhere be drawn;
All Greece shall with our horsemen's tread resound;
Woods shall not hide the foe nor towers built
Upon the highest summits of the hills;
Mycenæ's citizens shall leave the town

And sing the warsong; he shall die hard death
Who gives that hated head a hiding-place.
This palace even, noble Pelops' home,
Shall fall, if it must be, and bury me
If only on my brother too it fall.
Up, do a deed which none shall e'er approve,
But one whose fame none shall e'er cease to speak.
Some fierce and bloody crime must now be dared,
Such as my brother seeing shall wish his.
A wrong is not avenged but by worse wrong.
What deed can be so wild 'tis worse than his?
Does he lie humbled? Does he feel content
When fortune smiles, or tranquil when she frowns?
I know the tameless spirit of the man,
Not to be bent but broken, therefore seek
Revenge before he makes himself secure,
Renews his strength, lest he should fall on me
When I am unaware. Or kill, or die!
Crime is between us to be seized by one.
    ATTENDANT: Fearest thou not the people's hostile words?
    ATREUS: Herein is greatest good of royal power:
The populace not only must endure
Their master's deeds, but praise them.
    ATTENDANT: Fear shall make
Those hostile who were first compelled to praise;
But he who seeks the fame of true applause
Would rather by the heart than voice be praised.
    ATREUS: The lowly oft enjoy praise truly meant,
The mighty ne'er know aught but flattery.
The people oft must will what they would not.
    ATTENDANT: The king should wish for honesty and right;
Then there is none who does not wish with him.
    ATREUS: When he who rules must wish for right alone
He hardly rules, except on sufferance.
    ATTENDANT: When reverence is not, nor love of law,
Nor loyalty, integrity, nor truth,
The realm is insecure.
    ATREUS: Integrity,
Truth, loyalty, are private virtues; kings

Do as they will.

ATTENDANT: O deem it wrong to harm
A brother, even though he be most base.

ATREUS: No deed that is unlawful to be done
Against a brother but may lawfully
Be done against this man. What has he left
Untainted by his crime? Where has he spared
To do an impious deed? He took my wife
Adulterously, he took my realm by stealth,
The earnest of the realm he gained by fraud,
By fraud he brought confusion to my home.
There is in Pelops' stalls a noble sheep,
A magic ram, lord of the fruitful herd;
O'er all his body hangs the golden fleece.
In him each king sprung from the royal line
Of Tantalus his golden scepter holds,
Who has the ram possesses too the realm,
The fortunes of the palace follow him.
As fits a sacred thing, he feeds apart,
In a safe meadow which a wall surrounds
Hiding the pasture with its fateful stones.
The faithless one, daring a matchless crime,
Stole him away and with him took my wife,
Accomplice in his sin. From this has flowed
Every disaster; exiled and in fear
I've wandered through my realm; no place is safe
From brother's plots; my wife has been defiled,
The quiet of my realm has been disturbed,
My house is troubled, and the ties of blood
Are insecure, of nothing am I sure
Unless it be my brother's enmity.
Why hesitate? At length be strong to act.
Look upon Tantalus, on Pelops look;
To deeds like theirs these hands of mine are called.
Tell me, how shall I slay that cursed one?

ATTENDANT: Slain by the sword let him spew forth his soul.

ATREUS: Thou tellest the end of punishment, I wish
The punishment itself. Mild tyrants slay;
Death is a longed-for favor in my realm.

ATTENDANT: Hast thou no piety?

ATREUS: If e'er it dwelt
Within our home, let piety depart.
Let the grim company of Furies come,
Jarring Erinnys and Megæra dread
Shaking their torches twain. My breast burns not
With anger hot enough. I fain would feel
Worse horrors.

ATTENDANT: What new exile dost thou plot,
In thy mad rage?

ATREUS: No deed that keeps the bounds
Of former evils, I will leave no crime
Untried, and none is great enough for me.

ATTENDANT: The sword?

ATREUS: 'Tis poor.

ATTENDANT: Or fire?

ATREUS: 'Tis not enough.

ATTENDANT: What weapon then shall arm such hate as thine?

ATREUS: Thyestes' self.

ATTENDANT: This ill is worse than hate.

ATREUS: I own it. In my breast a tumult reigns;
It rages deep within, and I am urged
I know not whither, yet it urges me.
Earth from its lowest depths sends forth a groan,
It thunders though the daylight is serene,
The whole house shakes as though the house were rent,
The trembling Lares turn away their face.
This shall be done, this evil shall be done,
Which, gods, ye fear.

ATTENDANT: What is it thou wilt do?

ATREUS: I know not what great passion in my heart,
Wilder than I have known, beyond the bounds
Of human nature, rises, urges on
My slothful hands. I know not what it is,
'Tis something great. Yet be it what it may,
Make haste, my soul! Fit for Thyestes' hand
This crime would be; 'tis worthy Atreus, too,
And both shall do it. Tereus' house has seen
Such shocking feasts. I own the crime is great,

And yet it has been done; some greater crime
Let grief invent. Inspire thou my soul
O Daulian Procne, thou wast sister too;
Our cause is like, assist, impel my hand.
The father, hungrily, with joy shall tear
His children, and shall eat their very flesh;
'Tis well, it is enough. This punishment
Is so far pleasing. But where can he be?
And why is Atreus so long innocent?
Already all the sacrifice I see,
As in a picture, see the morsels placed
Within the father's mouth. Wherefore, my soul,
Art thou afraid? Why fail before the deed?
Forward! It must be done. Himself shall do
What is in such a deed the greater crime.

ATTENDANT: But captured by what wiles, will he consent
To put his feet within our toils? He deems
That all are hostile.

ATREUS: 'Twere not possible
To capture him but that he'd capture me.
He hopes to gain my kingdom; through this hope
He will make haste to meet the thunderbolts
Of threatening Jove, in this hope will endure
The swelling whirlpool's threats, and dare to go
Within the Lybian Syrtes' doubtful shoals,
To see again his brother, last and worst
Of evils deemed; this hope shall lead him on.

ATTENDANT: Who shall persuade him he may come in peace?
Whose word will he believe?

ATREUS: Malicious hope
Is credulous, yet I will give my sons
A message they shall to their uncle bear:
"The wandering exile, leaving chance abodes,
May for a kingdom change his misery,
May reign in Argos, sharer of my throne."
But if Thyestes sternly spurn my prayers,
His artless children, wearied by their woes
And easily persuaded, with their plea
Will overcome him; his old thirst for rule,

Beside sad poverty and heavy toil,
With weight of evil, will subdue his soul
However hard it be.

ATTENDANT: Time will have made
His sorrow light.

ATREUS: Thou errest; sense of ills
Increases daily. To endure distress
Is easy, but to bear it to the end
Is hard.

ATTENDANT: Choose others for thy messengers
In this dread plan.

ATREUS: Youth freely dares the worst.

ATTENDANT: What now thou teachest them in enmity
Against their uncle, they may later do
Against their father; evil deeds return
Full oft upon their author.

ATREUS: If they learned
The way of treachery and crime from none,
Possession of the throne would teach it them.
Art thou afraid their natures will grow base?
So were they born. That which thou callest wild
And cruel, and deemst hardly to be done,
Ruthless, nor showing honor for god's laws,
Perchance is even now against ourselves
Attempted.

ATTENDANT: Shall thy sons know what they do?

ATREUS: Discretion is not found with so few years.
They might perhaps discover all the guile;
Silence is learned through long and evil years.

ATTENDANT: The very ones through whom thou wouldst deceive
Another thou deceivest?

ATREUS: That themselves
May be exempt from crime or fault of mine;
Why should I mix my children in my sins?
My hatred shall unfold itself in me.
Yet say not so, thou doest ill, my soul;
If thine thou sparest, thou sparest also his.
My minister shall Agamemnon be,
And know my plan, and Menelaus too

Shall know his father's plans and further them.
Through this crime will I prove if they be mine;
If they refuse the contest nor consent
To my revenge, but call him uncle, then
I'll know he is their father. It shall be.
But oft a frightened look lays bare the heart,
Great plans may be unwillingly betrayed;
They shall not know how great affairs they aid.
Hide thou our undertaking.

ATTENDANT: Scarce were need
That I should be admonished; in my breast
Both fear and loyalty will keep it hid,
But loyalty the rather.

ACT TWO: SCENE 2

CHORUS.

The ancient race of royal Inachus
At last has laid aside fraternal threats.
What madness drove you, that by turns you shed
Each other's blood and sought to mount the throne
By crime? You know not, eager for high place,
What kingly station means. It is not wealth
That makes the king, nor robes of Tyrian dye,
'Tis not the crown upon the royal brow,
Nor gates made bright with gold; a king is he
Whose hard heart has forgotten fear and pain,
Whom impotent ambition does not move,
Nor the inconstant favor of the crowd,
Who covets nothing that the west affords,
Nor aught that Tagus' golden waves wash up
From its bright channels, nor the grain thrashed out
Upon the glowing Libyan threshing-floors,
Who neither fears the falling thunderbolt,
Nor Eurus stirring all the sea to wrath,
Nor windy Adriatic's swelling rage;
Who is not conquered by a soldier's lance,
Nor the drawn sword; who seated on safe heights,

Sees everything beneath him; who makes haste
Freely to meet his fate, nor grieves to die.
Let kings who vex the scattered Scythians come,
Who hold the Red Sea's shore, the pearl-filled sea,
Or who intrenched upon the Caspian range
To bold Sarmatians close the way, who breast
The Danube's waves, or those who dare pursue
And spoil the noble Seres where'er they dwell.
The mind a kingdom is; there is no need
Of horse, or weapon, or the coward dart
Which from afar the Parthian hurls and flees—
Or seems to flee, no need to overthrow
Cities with engines that hurl stones afar,
When one possesses in himself his realm.
Whoever will may on the slippery heights
Of empire stand, but I with sweet repose
Am satisfied, rejoice in gentle ease,
And, to my fellow citizens unknown,
My life shall flow in calm obscurity,
And when, untouched by storm, my days have passed,
Then will I die, a common citizen,
In good old age. Death seemeth hard to him
Who dies but too well known to all the world,
Yet knowing not himself.

ACT THREE: SCENE I

THYESTES, TANTALUS, *son of* Thyestes (*and two other sons*).

THYESTES: The longed-for dwelling of my native land
And, to the wretched exile greatest boon,
Rich Argos and a stretch of native soil,
And, if there yet be gods, my country's gods
I see at last; the Cyclopean towers,
Of greater beauty than the work of man;
The celebrated race-course of my youth
Where oft, well known, I drove my father's car
And carried off the palm. Argos will come
To meet me, and the people come in crowds,

Perchance my brother Atreus too will come!
Rather return to exile in the woods
And mountain pastures, live the life of brutes
Among them. This bright splendor of the realm
With its false glitter shall not blind my eyes.
Look on the giver, not the gift alone.
In fortunes which the world deemed hard I lived
Joyous and brave, now am I forced to fear,
My courage fails me, fain would I retreat,
Unwillingly I go.

TANTALUS: What see I here?
With hesitating step my father goes,
He seems uncertain, turns away his head.

THYESTES: Why doubt, my soul? or why so long revolve
Deliberations easy to conclude?
In most uncertain things dost thou confide
And in thy brother's realm, and stand in fear
Of ills already conquered and found mild?
Dost fly the troubles thou hast learned to bear?
Now to be wretched with the shades were joy,
Turn while thou yet hast time.

TANTALUS: Why turn away?
From thy loved country? Why deny thyself
So much of happiness? His wrath forgot,
Thy brother gives thee back the kingdom's half
And to the jarring members of his house
Brings peace, restores thee once more to thyself.

THYESTES: Thou askest why I fear; I do not know.
I see not aught to fear and yet I fear.
Fain would I go and yet with slothful feet
I waver and am borne unwillingly
Whither I would not; thus the ship propelled
By oar and sail is driven from its course
By the opposing tide.

TANTALUS: Whatever thwarts
Or hinders thee, o'ercome; see what rewards
Are waiting thy return. Thou mayst be king.

THYESTES: Since I can die.

TANTALUS: The very highest power—

THYESTES: Is naught, if thou hast come to wish for naught.

TANTALUS: Thy sons shall be thy heirs.

THYESTES: No realm can have
Two kings.

TANTALUS: Does one who might be happy choose
Unhappiness?

THYESTES: Believe me, with false name
Does power deceive; and vain it is to fear
Laborious fortunes. High in place, I feared,
Yea, feared the very sword upon my side.
How good it is to be the foe of none,
To lie upon the ground, in safety eat.
Crime enters not the cottage; without fear
May food be eaten at the humble board,
Poison is drunk from gold. I speak known truth—
Ill fortune is to be preferred to good.
The humble citizen fears not my house:
It is not on the mountain summit placed,
Its high roofs do not shine with ivory;
No watchman guards my sleep; we do not fish
With fleets, nor drive the ocean from its bed
With massive walls, nor feed vile gluttony
With tribute from all peoples; not for me
Are harvested the fields beyond the Getes
And Parthians; men do not honor me
With incense, nor are altars built for me
Instead of Jove; upon my palace roofs
No forests nod, no hot pools steam for me;
Day is not spent in sleep nor night in crime
And watching. Aye, none fears me and my home,
Although without a weapon, is secure.
Great peace attends on humble circumstance;
He has a kingdom who can be content
Without a kingdom.

TANTALUS: If a favoring god
Give thee a realm, it should not be refused,
Nor should it be desired. Thy brother begs
That thou wouldst rule.

THYESTES: He begs? Then I must fear.

He seeks some means whereby he may betray.

TANTALUS: Full often loyalty that was withdrawn
Is given back, and true affection gains
Redoubled strength.

THYESTES: And shall his brother love
Thyestes? Rather shall the ocean wet
The northern Bear, and the rapacious tides
Of the Sicilian waters stay their waves,
The harvest ripen in Ionian seas,
And black night give the earth the light of day;
Rather shall flame with water, life with death,
The winds with ocean join in faithful pact.

TANTALUS: What fraud dost thou still fear?

THYESTES: All. Where may end
My cause for fear? His hate is as his power.

TANTALUS: What power has he to harm thee?

THYESTES: For myself
I do not fear; my sons, for you I dread
My brother Atreus.

TANTALUS: Dost thou fear deceit?

THYESTES: It is too late to seek security
When one is in the very midst of ill.
Let us begone. This one thing I affirm:
I follow you, not lead.

TANTALUS: God will behold
With favor thy design; boldly advance.

ACT THREE: SCENE 2

ATREUS, THYESTES, TANTALUS, *son of Thyestes*
(*and two other sons*).

ATREUS (*aside*): At last the wild beast is within my toils:
Lo, I behold him with his hated brood.
My vengeance now is sure, into my hands
Thyestes has completely fall'n; my joy
Scarce can I temper, scarcely curb my wrath.
Thus when the cunning Umbrian hound is held
In leash, and tracks his prey, with lowered nose

Searching the ground, when from afar he scents
By slightest clue the bear, he silently
Explores the place, submitting to be held,
But when the prey is nearer, then he fights
To free himself, and with impatient voice
Calls the slow huntsman, straining at the leash.
When passion hopes for blood it will not own
Restraint; and yet my wrath must be restrained!
See how his heavy, unkempt hair conceals
His face, how loathsome lies his beard. Ah, well!
Faith shall be kept. (*To* THYESTES) To see my brother's face
How glad I am! All former wrath is past.
From this day loyalty to family ties
Shall be maintained, from this day let all hate
Be banished from our hearts.

    THYESTES (*aside*):   O wert thou not
Such as thou art, all could be put aside.
(*To* ATREUS.) Atreus, I own, I own that I have done
All thou believest; this day's loyalty
Makes me seem truly base: he sins indeed
Who sins against a brother good as thou.
Tears must wash out my guilt. See at thy feet
These hands are clasped in prayer that ne'er before
Entreated any. Let all anger cease,
Let swelling rage forever be dispelled;
Receive these children, pledges of my faith.

    ATREUS: No longer clasp my knees, nay, rather seek
My warm embrace. Ye, too, the props of age,
So young, my children, cling about my neck.
And thou, put off thy raiment mean and coarse;
Oh, spare my sight, put on these royal robes
Like mine, and gladly share thy brother's realm.
This greater glory shall at last be mine:
To my illustrious brother I give back
His heritage. One holds a throne by chance,
To give it up is noble.

    THYESTES: May the gods
Give thee, my brother, fair return for all
Thy benefits. Alas, my wretchedness

Forbids me to accept the royal crown,
My guilty hand shrinks from the scepter's weight;
Let me in lesser rank unnoted live.

ATREUS: This realm recovers its two kings.

THYESTES: I hold,
O brother, all of thine the same as mine.

ATREUS: Who would refuse the gifts that fortune gives?

THYESTES: He who has learned how swiftly they depart.

ATREUS: Wouldst thou refuse thy brother such renown?

THYESTES: Thy glory is fulfilled, but mine still waits:
Firm is my resolution to refuse
The kingdom.

ATREUS: I relinquish all my power
Unless thou hast thy part.

THYESTES: I take it then.
I'll wear the name of king, but law and arms
And I shall be thy slaves, for evermore.

ATREUS: Wear then upon thy head the royal crown.
I'll give the destined victim to the gods.

ACT THREE: SCENE 3

CHORUS.

Who would believe it? Atreus, fierce and wild,
Savage and tameless, shrank and was amazed
When he beheld his brother. Stronger bonds
Than nature's laws exist not. Wars may last
With foreign foes, but true love still will bind
Those whom it once has bound. When wrath, aroused
By some great quarrel, has disseevered friends
And called to arms, when the light cavalry
Advance with ringing bridles, here and there
Shines the swift sword which, seeking fresh-shed blood,
The raging war god wields with frequent blows;
But love and loyalty subdue the sword,
And in great peace unite unwilling hearts.
What god gave sudden peace from so great war?
Throughout Mycenæ rang the crash of arms

As though in civil strife, pale mothers held
Their children to their bosoms, and the wife
Feared for her steel-armed husband, when the sword,
Stained with the rust acquired in long peace,
Unwillingly obeyed his hand. One sped
To strengthen falling walls, to build again
The tottering towers, to make fast the gates
With iron bars; and on the battlements
The pale watch waked through all the anxious night.
The fear of war is worse than war itself.
But threatenings of the cruel sword have ceased,
The trumpet's deep-toned voice at last is stilled,
The braying of the strident horn is hushed,
And to the joyous city peace returns.
So when the northwest wind beats up the sea
And from the deep the swelling waves roll in,
Scylla from out her smitten caverns roars
And sailors in the havens fear the flood
That ravening Charybdis vomits forth,
And the fierce Cyclops, dwelling on the top
Of fiery Ætna, dreads his father's rage,
Lest whelmed beneath the waves, the fires that roar
Within his immemorial chimney's throat
Should be profaned, and poor Laertes thinks,
Since Ithaca is shaken, that his realm
May be submerged; then, if the winds subside,
More quiet than a pool the ocean lies,
Scattered on every side gay little skiffs
Stretch the fair canvas of their spreading sails
Upon the sea which, late, ships feared to cut;
And there where, shaken by the hurricane,
The Cyclades were fearful of the deep,
The fishes play. No fortune long endures:
Sorrows and pleasures each in turn depart,
But pleasure soonest; from the fairest heights
An hour may plunge one to the lowest depths;
He who upon his forehead wears a crown,
Who nods and Medians lay aside the sword,
Indians, too, near neighbors of the sun,

And Dacians that assail the Parthian horse,
He holds his scepter with an anxious hand,
Foresees the overthrow of all his joy,
And fears uncertain time and fickle chance.
Ye whom the ruler of the earth and sea
Has given power over life and death,
Be not so proud, a stronger threatens you
With whatsoever ills the weaker fears
From you; each realm is by a greater ruled.
Him whom the rising sun beholds in power
The setting sees laid low. Let none confide
Too much in happiness, let none despair
When he has fallen from his high estate,
For Clotho blends the evil with the good;
She turns about all fortunes on her wheel;
None may abide. Such favoring deities
No one has ever found that he may trust
Tomorrow; on his flying wheel a god
Spins our swift changing fortunes.

ACT FOUR: SCENE I

MESSENGER, CHORUS.

MESSENGER: Oh, who will bear me headlong through the air,
Like a swift wind, and hide me in thick cloud
That I no longer may behold such crime?
O house dishonored, whose base deeds disgrace
Pelops and Tantalus!
CHORUS: What news is thine?
MESSENGER: What region can it be that I behold?
Argos and Sparta to which fate assigned
Such loving brothers? Corinth or the shores
Of the two seas? The Danube that compels
The fierce Alani frequently to flee?
Hyrcania underneath eternal snows?
Is it the wandering Scythians' changing home?
What land is this that knows such monstrous deeds?
CHORUS: Speak and declare the ill whate'er it be.

MESSENGER: If I have courage, if cold fear relax
Its hold upon my members. Still I see
Th' accomplished slaughter. Bear me far from hence,
O driving whirlwind; whither day is borne
Bear me, torn hence!

CHORUS: Control thy fear, wrung heart,
What is the deed that makes thee quake with fear?
Speak and declare its author, I ask not
Who it may be, but which. Now quickly tell.

MESSENGER: Upon the heights a part of Pelops' house
Faces the south; the further side of this
Lifts itself upward like a mountain top
And overlooks the city; thence their kings
May hold the stubborn people 'neath their sway.
Here shines the great hall that might well contain
An army, varicolored columns bear
Its golden architraves; behind the room
Known to the vulgar, where the people come,
Stretch chambers rich and wide, and far within
Lies the arcana of the royal house,
The sacred penetralia; here no tree
Of brilliant foliage grows, and none is trimmed;
But yews and cypress and black ilex trees
Bend in the gloomy wood, an ancient oak
Rises above the grove and, eminent
Over the other trees, looks down on all
From its great height. Here the Tantalides
Are consecrated kings, and here they seek
Aid in uncertain or untoward events
Here hang their votive offerings, clear-toned trumps,
And broken chariots, wreckage of the sea,
And wheels that fell a prey to treachery,
And evidence of every crime the race
Has done. Here Pelops' Phrygian crown is hung,
Here the embroidered robe from barbarous foes
Won. In the shade trickles a sluggish rill
That in the black swamp lingers lazily,
Like the unsightly waters of black Styx
By which the gods make oath. 'Tis said that here

The gods of the infernal regions sigh
Through all the dark night, that the place resounds
With rattling chains, and spirits of the dead
Go wailing up and down. Here may be seen
All dreadful things: here wanders the great throng
Of spirits of the ancient dead sent forth
From antique tombs, and monsters fill the place
Greater than have been known, and oft the wood
With threefold baying echoes, oftentimes
The house is terrible with mighty forms.
Nor does the daylight put an end to fear,
Night is eternal in the grove, and here
The sanctity of the infernal world
Reigns in the midst of day. Here sure response
Is given those who seek the oracle;
From the adytum with a thundering noise
The fatal utterance finds a passage out,
And all the grot re-echoes the god's voice.
Here raging Atreus entered, dragging in
His brother's sons; the altars were adorned—
Ah, who can tell the tale? The noble youths
Have their hands bound behind them and their brows
Bound with the purple fillet; incense too
Is there, and wine to Bacchus consecrate,
And sacrificial knife, and salted meal;
All things are done in order, lest such crime
Should be accomplished without fitting rites.
    CHORUS: Whose hand took up the sword?
    MESSENGER: He is himself
The priest: He sang himself with boisterous lips
The sacrificial song, those given to death
He placed, he took the sword and wielded it;
Nothing was lacking to the sacrifice.
Earth trembled, all the grove bent down its head,
The palace nodded, doubtful where to fling
Its mighty weight, and from the left there shot
A star from heaven, drawing a black train.
The wine poured forth upon the fire was changed.
And flowed red blood; the royal diadem

Fell twice, yea thrice; within the temple walls
The ivory statues wept: all things were moved
At such a deed; himself alone unmoved,
Atreus stood firm and faced the threatening gods.
And now delay at last was put aside;
He stood before the altar, sidelong, fierce
In gaze. As by the Ganges, in the woods,
The hungry tiger stands between two bulls,
Uncertain which one first shall feel his teeth—
Eager for both, now here now there he turns
His eyes and in such doubt is hungry still—
So cruel Atreus gazes on the heads
Devoted sacrifices to his rage:
He hesitates which one shall first be slain,
And which be immolated afterward;
It matters not and yet he hesitates,
And in the order of his cruel crime
Takes pleasure.
    CHORUS: Which is first to feel the sword?
    MESSENGER: Lest he should seem to fail in loyalty
First place is given to his ancestor—
The one named Tantalus is first to fall.
    CHORUS: What courage showed the youth? How bore he death?
    MESSENGER: He stood unmoved, no useless prayers were heard.
That cruel one hid in the wound the sword,
Pressing it deep within the victim's neck,
Then drew it forth; the corpse was upright still:
It hesitated long which way to fall,
Then fell against the uncle. Atreus then,
Dragging before the altar Plisthenes,
Hurried him to his brother: with one blow
He cut away the head; the lifeless trunk
Fell prone and with a whispered sound the head
Rolled downward.
    CHORUS: Double murder thus complete,
What did he then? Spared he the other boy?
Or did he heap up crime on crime?
    MESSENGER: Alas!
As crested lion in Armenian woods

Attacks the herd, nor lays aside his wrath
Though sated, but with jaws that drip with blood
Follows the bulls, and satisfied with food
Threatens the calves but languidly; so threats
Atreus, so swells his wrath, and holding still
The sword with double murder wet, forgets
Whom he attacks; with direful hand he drives
Right through the body and the sword, received
Within the breast, passes straight through the back.
He falls and with his blood puts out the fires;
By double wound he dies.

CHORUS: O savage crime!

MESSENGER: Art horrified? If there the work had ceased,
It had been pious.

CHORUS: Could a greater crime
Or more atrocious be by nature borne?

MESSENGER: And dost thou think this was the end of crime?
'Twas its beginning.

CHORUS: What more could there be?
Perchance he threw the bodies to wild beasts
That they might tear them, kept from funeral fire?

MESSENGER: Would he had kept, would that no grave might
          hide
The dead, no fire burn them, would the birds
And savage beasts might feast on such sad food!
That which were torment else is wished for here.
Would father's eyes unburied sons might see!
O crime incredible to every age!
O crime which future ages shall deny!
The entrails taken from the living breast
Tremble, the lungs still breathe, the timid heart
Throbs, but he tears its fibre, ponders well
What it foretells and notes its still warm veins.
When he at last has satisfied himself
About the victims, of his brother's feast
He makes secure. The mangled forms he cuts,
And from the trunk he separates the arms
As far as the broad shoulders, savagely
Lays bare the joints and cleaves apart the bones;

The heads he spares and the right hands they gave
In such good faith. He puts the severed limbs
Upon the spits and roasts them by slow fire;
The other parts into the glowing pot
He throws to boil them. From the food the fire
Leaps back, is twice, yea thrice, replaced and forced
At last reluctantly to do its work.
The liver on the spit emits shrill cries,
I cannot tell whether the flesh or flame
Most deeply groaned. The troubled fire smoked,
The smoke itself, a dark and heavy cloud,
Rose not in air nor scattered readily;
The ugly cloud obscured the household gods.
O patient Phœbus, thou hast backward fled
And, breaking off the light of day at noon,
Submerged the day, but thou didst set too late.
The father mangles his own sons, and eats
Flesh of his flesh, with sin polluted lips;
His locks are wet and shine with glowing oil;
Heavy is he with wine; the morsels stick
Between his lips. Thyestes, this one good
Amid thy evil fortunes still remains:
Thou knowest it not. But this good too shall die.
Let Titan, turning backward on his path,
Lead back his chariot and with darkness hide
This foul new crime, let blackest night arise
At midday, yet the deed must come to light.
All will be manifest.

ACT FOUR: SCENE 2

CHORUS.

Oh, whither, father of the earth and sky,
Whose rising puts the glory of the night
To flight, oh, whither dost thou turn thy path,
That light has fled at midday? Phœbus, why
Hast thou withdrawn thy beams? The evening star,
The messenger of darkness, has not yet

Called forth the constellations of the night,
Not yet the westward turning course commands
To free thy horses that have done their work,
The trumpet has not yet its third call given,
The signal of declining day, new night.
The plowman is amazed at the swift fall
Of supper-time, his oxen by the plow
Are yet unwearied; from thy path in heaven
What drives thee, O Apollo? What the cause
That forces from their wonted way thy steeds?
Though conquered, do the giants strive again
In war, hell's prison being opened wide?
Or does Tityus in his wounded breast
Renew his ancient wrath? The mountains rent,
Does Titan's son, Typhœus, stretch again
His giant body? Is a pathway built
By Macedonian giants to the sky,
On Thracian Ossa is Mount Pelion piled?
The ancient order of the universe
Has perished! rise and setting will not be!
Eos, the dewy mother of the dawn,
Wont to the god of day to give the reins,
Sees with amaze her kingdom overthrown,
She knows not how to bathe the wearied steeds,
Nor dip the smoking horses in the sea.
The setting sun himself, amazed, beholds
Aurora, and commands the darkness rise
Ere night is ready, the bright stars rise not,
Nor do the heavens show the faintest light,
Nor does the morn dissolve the heavy shades.
Whate'er it be would it were only night!
Shaken with mighty fear my bosom quakes,
Lest all the world to ruin should be hurled,
And formless chaos cover gods and men,
And nature once again enfold and hide
The land and sea and starry firmament.
With the upspringing of its deathless torch
Bringing the seasons, never more shall come
The king of stars and give the waiting world

Changes of summer and of winter's cold;
No more shall Luna meet the sun's bright flame
And take away the terror of the night,
And running through a briefer circuit pass
His brother's car; into one gulf shall fall
The heaped-up throng of gods.
The zodiac, pathway of the sacred stars,
Which cuts the zones obliquely, shall behold
The falling stars and fall itself from heaven.
Aries, who comes again in early spring
And with warm zephyr swells the sails, shall fall
Headlong into the sea through which he bore
Timorous Helle; and the Bull, that wears
The Hyades upon its shining brow,
Shall with himself drag down the starry Twins
And Cancer's claws; the Lion, glowing hot,
That Hercules once conquered, shall again
Fall from the skies; and to the earth she left
The Virgin too shall fall, and the just Scales,
And with them drag the churlish Scorpion.
Old Chiron, who holds fixed the feathered dart
In the Thessalian bow, shall loose his shaft
From the snapped bowstring, and cold Capricorn
Who brings the winter's cold shall fall, and break
For thee, whoe'er thou art, thy water-jug,
Thou Water-bearer; with thee too shall fall
The Fishes, last of stars; and Charles's Wain,
That never yet has sunk below the sea,
Falling shall plunge beneath the ocean wave.
The slippery Dragon, that between the Bears
Winds like a winding river, shall descend;
And, with the Dragon joined, the Lesser Bear
So icy cold, and slow Boötes too,
Already tottering to his overthrow,
Shall fall from heaven with his heavy wain.
Out of so many do we seem alone
Worthy to be beneath the universe
Buried, when heaven itself is overthrown?
In our day has the end of all things come?

Created were we for a bitter fate,
Whether we've banished or destroyed the sun.
Let lamentation cease, depart base fear;
Eager for life is he who would not die
Even though with him all the world should fall.

ACT FIVE: SCENE 1

ATREUS.

ATREUS: High above all and equal to the stars
I move, my proud head touches heaven itself;
At last I hold the crown, at last I hold
My father's throne. Now I abandon you,
Ye gods, for I have touched the highest point
Of glory possible. It is enough.
Ev'n I am satisfied. Why satisfied?
No shame withholds me, day has been withdrawn;
Act while the sky is dark. Would I might keep
The gods from flight, and drag them back by force
That all might see the feast that gives revenge.
It is enough the father shall behold.
Though daylight be unwilling to abide,
Yet will I take from thee the dark that hides
Thy miseries; too long with merry look
Thou liest at thy feast: enough of wine,
Enough of food, Thyestes. There is need,
In this thy crowning ill, thou be not drunk
With wine. Slaves, open wide the temple doors,
And let the house of feasting open lie.
I long to see his color when he sees
His dead sons' heads, to hear his words that flow
With the first shock of sorrow, to behold
How, stricken dumb, he sits with rigid form.
This is the recompense of all my toil.
I do not wish to see his wretchedness
Save as it grows upon him. The wide hall
Is bright with many a torch; supine he lies
On gold and purple, his left hand supports

His head that is so heavy now with wine;
He vomits. Mightiest of the gods am I,
And king of kings! my wish has been excelled!
Full is he, in the silver cup he lifts
The wine. Spare not to drink, there still remains
Some of the victims' blood, the old wine's red
Conceals it; with this cup the feast shall end.
His children's blood mixed with the wine he drinks
He would have drunken mine. Lo, now he sings,
Sings festal songs, his mind is dimmed with wine.

ACT FIVE: SCENE 2

ATREUS, THYESTES.

THYESTES (*singing*): By long grief dulled, put by thy cares, my
              heart,
Let fear and sorrow fly and bitter need,
Companion of thy timorous banishment,
And shame, hard burden of afflicted souls.
Whence thou hast fallen profits more to know
Than whither; great is he who with firm step
Moves on the plain when fallen from the height;
He who, oppressed by sorrows numberless
And driven from his realm, with unbent neck
Carries his burdens, not degenerate
Or conquered, who stands firm beneath the weight
Of all his burdens, he is great indeed.
Now scatter all the clouds of bitter fate,
Put by all signs of thy unhappy days,
In happy fortunes show a happy face,
Forget the old Thyestes. Ah, this vice
Still follows misery: never to trust
In happy days; though better fortunes come,
Those who have borne afflictions find it hard
To joy in better days. What holds me back,
Forbids me celebrate the festal tide?
What cause of grief, arising causelessly,
Bids me to weep? What art thou that forbids

That I should crown my head with festal wreath?
It does forbid, forbid! Upon my head
The roses languish, and my hair that drips
With ointment rises as with sudden fear,
My face is wet with showers of tears that fall
Unwillingly, and groans break off my words.
Grief loves accustomed tears, the wretched feel
That they must weep. I would be glad to make
Most bitter lamentation, and to wail,
And rend this robe with Tyrian purple dyed.
My mind gives warning of some coming grief,
Presages future ills. The storm that smites
When all the sea is calm weighs heavily
Upon the sailor. Fool! What grief, what storm,
Dost thou conceive? Believe thy brother now.
Be what it may, thou fearest now too late,
Or causelessly. I do not wish to be
Unhappy, but vague terror smites my breast!
No cause is evident and yet my eyes
O'erflow with sudden tears. What can it be,
Or grief, or fear? Or has great pleasure tears? (*Song ends.*)

ACT FIVE: SCENE 3

ATREUS, THYESTES.

ATREUS: Brother, let us together celebrate
This festal day: this day it is which makes
My scepter firm, which binds the deathless pact
Of certain peace.
    THYESTES: Enough of food and wine!
This only could augment my happiness,
If with my own I might enjoy my bliss.
    ATREUS: Believe thy sons are here in thy embrace.
Here are they and shall be, no single part
Of thy loved offspring shall be lost to thee.
Ask and whate'er thou wishest I will give,
I'll satisfy the father with his sons;
Fear not, thou shalt be more than satisfied.
Now with my own thy young sons lengthen out

The joyous feast: they shall be sent for; drink
The wine, it is an heirloom of our house.
  THYESTES: I take my brother's gift. Wine shall be poured
First to our fathers' gods, then shall be drunk.
But what is this? My hands refuse to lift
The cup, its weight increases and holds down
My right hand, from my lips the wine retreats,
Around my mouth it flows and will not pass
Within my lips, and from the trembling earth
The tables leap, the fire scarce gives light,
The air is heavy and the light is dim
As between day and darkness. What is this?
The arch of heaven trembles more and more,
To the dense shadows ever thicker mist
Is added, night withdraws in blacker night,
The constellations flee. Whate'er it is,
I pray thee spare my sons, let all the storm
Break over my vile head. Give back my sons!
  ATREUS: Yea, I will give them back, and never more
Shalt thou be parted from them. (*Exit.*)

ACT FIVE: SCENE 4

THYESTES.

                              What distress
Seizes my reins? Why shake my inward parts?
I feel a burden that will forth, my breast
Groans with a groaning that is not my own.
Come, children, your unhappy father calls;
Come, might I see you all this woe would flee.
Whence come these voices?

ACT FIVE: SCENE 5

  ATREUS, THYESTES (*slave bearing a covered platter*).

  ATREUS: Father, spread wide thy arms, they come, they come
Dost thou indeed now recognize thy sons?

  (*Platter is uncovered.*)

THYESTES: I recognize my brother: Canst thou bear
Such deeds, O earth? O Styx, wilt thou not break
Thy banks and whelm in everlasting night
Both king and kingdom, bearing them away
By a dread path to chaos' awful void?
And, plucking down thy houses, fallest thou not,
O city of Mycenæ, to the ground?
We should already be with Tantalus!
Earth, ope thy prisons wide on every side;
If under Tartarus, below the place
Where dwell our kinsmen, rests a lower deep,
Within thy bosom let a chasm yawn
Thitherward, under all of Acheron
Hide us: let guilty souls roam o'er our heads
Let Phlegethon that bears its fiery sands
Down through its glowing channels, flow o'er me!
Yet earth unmoved lies but a heavy weight,
The gods have fled.
ATREUS: Take, rather, willingly
Those whom thou hast so long desired to see;
Thy brother does not hinder thee. Rejoice;
Kiss them, divide thy love between the three.
THYESTES: This is thy compact? This thy brother's faith?
Is this thy favor? Layst thou thus aside
Thy hate? I do not ask to see my sons
Unharmed; what wickedness and deathless hate
May give, a brother asks: grant to my sons
Burial; give them back, thou shalt behold
Straightway their burning. Lo, I ask thee naught,
The father will not have but lose his sons.
ATREUS: Thou hast whate'er remains, whate'er is lost.
THYESTES: And do they furnish food for savage birds?
Are they destroyed by monsters, fed to beasts?
ATREUS: Thyself hast banqueted upon thy sons,
An impious feast.
THYESTES: 'Tis this that shamed the gods!
This backward drove the daylight whence it came!
Me miserable! What cry shall I make,
What wailing? What words will suffice my woe?

I see the severed heads, the hands cut off,
Greedy and hungry, these I did not eat!
I feel their flesh within my bowels move;
Prisoned, the dread thing struggles, tries to flee,
But has no passage forth; give me the sword,
Brother, it has already drunk my blood:
The sword shall give a pathway to my sons.
It is denied? Then rending blows shall sound
Upon my breast. Unhappy one, refrain
Thy hand, oh, spare the dead! Whoe'er beheld
Such hideous crime? Not wandering tribes that dwell
On the unkindly Caucasus' rough cliffs,
Or fierce Procrustes, dread of Attica.
Behold, the father feasts upon his sons,
The sons lie heavy in him—is there found
No limit to thy base and impious deeds?
   ATREUS: Crime finds a limit when the crime is done,
Not when avenged. Even this is not enough.
Into thy mouth I should have poured the blood
Warm from the wounds; thou shouldst have drunk the blood
Of living sons. My hate betrayed itself
Through too much haste. I smote them with the sword,
I slew them at the altar, sacrificed
A votive offering to the household gods,
From the dead trunks I cut away the heads,
And into tiniest pieces tore the limbs;
Some in the boiling pot I plunged, and some
I bade should be before a slow flame placed;
I cut the flesh from the still living limbs,
I saw it roar upon the slender spit,
And with my own right hand I plied the fire.
All this the father might have better done:
All of my vengeance falls in nothingness!
He ate his sons with impious lips indeed,
Alas, nor he nor they knew what he did!
   THYESTES: Hear, O ye seas, stayed by inconstant shores;
Ye too, ye gods, wherever ye have fled,
Hear what a deed is done! Hear, gods of Hell,
Hear, Earth, and heavy Tartarean night

Dark with thick cloud! Oh, listen to my cry!
Thine am I, Hell, thou only seest my woe,
Thou also hast no star. I do not make
Presumptuous prayer, naught for myself I ask—
What could be given me? I make my prayer
For you, my sons. Thou ruler of the heavens,
Thou mighty king of the ethereal courts,
Cover the universe with horrid clouds,
Let winds contend on every side, send forth
Thy thunders everywhere; not with light hand,
As when thou smitest with thy lesser darts
Innocent homes; but as when mountains fell
And with their threefold ruin overwhelmed
The Giants—use such power, send forth such fires,
Avenge the banished day, where light has fled
Fill up the darkness with thy thunderbolts.
Each one is evil,—do not hesitate—
Yet if not both, I sure am base; seek me
With triple dart, through this breast send this brand:
If I would give my sons a funeral pyre
And burial, I must give myself to flames.
If nothing moves the gods, if none will send
His darts against this sinful head, let night,
Eternal night, abide and hide the crime
In everlasting shadows. If thou, Sun,
No longer shinest, I have naught to ask.

 ATREUS: Now in my work I glory, now indeed
I hold the victor's palm. I would have lost
My crime's reward unless thou thus wert grieved.
I now believe my sons were truly mine—
Now may I trust again in a chaste bed.

 THYESTES: What evil have my children done to thee?

 ATREUS: They were thy sons.

 THYESTES: The children of their sire—

 ATREUS: Undoubted sons; 'tis this that makes me glad.

 THYESTES: I call upon the gods who guard the right
To witness.

 ATREUS: Why not call upon the gods
Who guard the marriage bed?

THYESTES: Who punishes
A crime with crime?
    ATREUS: I know what makes thee mourn:
Another first accomplished the grim deed,
For this thou mournest; thou art not distressed
Because of thy dread feast, thou feelest grief
That thou hast not prepared such feast for me.
This mind was in thee: to provide like food
For thy unconscious brother, and to slay
My children with their mother's aid. One thing
Withheld thee—thou believedst they were thine.
    THYESTES: Th' avenging gods will come and punish thee;
To them my prayers commit thee.
    ATREUS: To thy sons
I give thee over for thy punishment.

Rinehart Editions